CHARLES OLSON & ROBERT CREELEY:

THE COMPLETE CORRESPONDENCE

VOLUME 7

EDITED BY

GEORGE F. BUTTERICK

BLACK SPARROW PRESS

SANTA ROSA   1987

CHARLES OLSON & ROBERT CREELEY: THE COMPLETE CORRESPONDENCE. VOLUME 7.

Charles Olson's letters to Robert Creeley Copyright © 1987 by the Estate of Charles Olson.

Robert Creeley's letters to Charles Olson Copyright © 1987 by Robert Creeley.

INTRODUCTION and NOTES Copyright © 1987 by George F. Butterick.

The excerpt of William Carlos Williams' 2 August 1951 letter quoted in the editor's notes is Copyright © 1986 by William Eric Williams and Paul H. Williams; used by permission of New Directions Publishing Corp., agents.

ACKNOWLEDGEMENTS

The originals of these letters are in the collections of the University of Connecticut Library, Storrs, and Washington University Libraries, St. Louis, and are printed here with those libraries' kind cooperation. Grateful acknowledgement must continue to be made to Donald Allen, who provided typescripts of many of Charles Olson's letters; to Timothy Murray of Washington University Libraries, who provided copies of letters as well as photographs from among Robert Creeley's papers; to Seamus Cooney, who meticulously helped to read proofs; to Julie Voss, able coordinator at Black Sparrow; and to John Martin for his continued faith in monumental projects.

This project was supported by a matching grant from the National Endowment of the Arts.

Cover photograph by Gerard Malanga.

LIBRARY OF CONGRESS CATALOGING-IN-PUBLICATION DATA
(Revised for vol. 7)

Olson, Charles, 1910–1970.
   Charles Olson & Robert Creeley : the complete correspondence.

   Limited ed. of 250 copies.
   Includes bibliographical references and indexes.
   1. Olson, Charles, 1910–1970 — Correspondence.
  2. Creeley, Robert, 1926–   — Correspondence.
  3. Poets, American — 20th century — Correspondence.
  I. Creeley, Robert, 1926–   . II. Butterick, George F.
  III. Title.
PS3529.L655Z544   811'.54   80-12222
ISBN 0-87685-400-5 (v. 1)
ISBN 0-87685-401-3 (deluxe : v. 1)
ISBN 0-87685-399-8 (pbk. : v. 1)
ISBN 0-87685-690-3 (v. 7)
ISBN 0-87685-691-1 (deluxe : v. 7)
ISBN 0-87685-689-X (pbk. : v. 7)

TABLE OF CONTENTS

Photographs follow page 160

By George F. Butterick

EDITOR

Poetry and Truth by Charles Olson (1970)

Additional Prose by Charles Olson (1974)

The Maximus Poems: Volume Three by Charles Olson, with Charles Boer (1975)

Selected Poems by Vincent Ferrini (1976)

Muthologos: The Collected Lectures and Interviews by Charles Olson (1978–79)

Charles Olson & Robert Creeley: The Complete Correspondence Volumes 1 & 2 (1980)

Charles Olson & Robert Creeley: The Complete Correspondence Volume 3 (1981)

The Postmoderns: The New American Poetry Revised, with Donald Allen (1982)

Charles Olson & Robert Creeley: The Complete Correspondence Volume 4 (1982)

Charles Olson & Robert Creeley: The Complete Correspondence Volume 5 (1983)

The Maximus Poems by Charles Olson (1983)

Charles Olson & Robert Creeley: The Complete Correspondence Volume 6 (1985)

Charles Olson & Robert Creeley: The Complete Correspondence Volume 7 (1987)

AUTHOR

The Norse (1973)

Reading Genesis by the Light of a Comet (1976)

A Guide to the Maximus Poems of Charles Olson (1978)

Rune Power (1983)

Editing the Maximus Poems (1983)

The Three-percent Stranger (1986)

JOURNAL

OLSON: The Journal of the Charles Olson Archives (1973–78)

Editor's Introduction

This seventh volume of letters finds Olson and Creeley (one is tempted to say, "our heroes," as if they were protagonists in a saga, which of course they are) where the previous volume left them—Olson at Black Mountain, like any teacher in a love-hate relationship with his place, and Creeley in southern France, the Provence of the troubadours, though there is little sense of that ambience here.

The August 8th Louis Martz letter by Olson is probably the highlight of the volume. Like many successful things, it begins with an error (like Olson's misinterpretation of Gerhardt's "gossip," or "Letter 15" of *The Maximus Poems*). No one had seen the document since its forwarding to Creeley, and Olson never mentioned it to Martz (although he did keep a carbon copy). Years later, he mentioned in class at Buffalo that he had written a "fourteen-page" letter to Martz that had never been published, so I wrote Martz, then still teaching at Yale, but he was as perplexed as I. Here it now is, a vehicle for Olson to discuss the "local" and the originary, how the "Pelasgian" or the archaic, the primitive as prime, "is not a time archetype but a permenent and present dweller in any one." We are all Pelasgians—or Neolithic or Pleistocene, however one wants to call our founding condition. It is in this context that Olson introduces his still (in his own work) unapplied principle of the archaic, of "archaism as the root from which total creation is made possible," and which will find its fulfillment in *The Maximus Poems* as well as individual poems such as " 'The chain of memory is resurrection . . .' "

The letter offers the recognition that our culture "does not go back to Athens—to Aristotle & Plato—it goes back to and through HOMER," and beyond Odysseus to the originary hero of which Maximus is an avatar. It survives, thus, as a portion of the map that would guide Olson for the rest of his life. Without such a recognition of the past, an epic such as *Paterson* "comes out thin and quaint." The letter also amplifies Olson's earlier charge (V, 51) that Williams "don't know . . . what a city *is*," by indicating that Olson means city as center of civilization and that Williams's epic lacks the necessary "rear," the requisite dimension of the extended past, of origins ("that after the ICE, there was

CITY – and with CITY man as interesting creature began"), although it is hardly an argument for urbanization in present terms. Pound's limits are also discussed, namely that he "does not interest himself at all in *place* as force," making this letter one of Olson's most significant attempts to define his own perspective vis-à-vis his immediate masters. It concludes with the swiftly added summarization of Olsonian activism: "The ACT, always, more important than the MEANS or the END, however each modify the ACT!"

This volume is also notable because it contains the first use in Olson's writings of the term "post-modern" that I am aware of, in his August 9th letter, although he will give a better sense of its implications, or his implications for it, in his August 20th letter. It is still a term in turmoil and transition, so it is too early to say whether Olson's use was prophetic or not. He does at least employ it to express dissatisfaction with the intellectual present, together with an implicit assumption there is something better beyond, not necessarily amelioration but an alternative to the Western "box." The term is a consistent part of his thinking during this period, useful to the development of his ideas, although he ceases to use it after the decade – just as he ceases to use with any regularity his term "projective," beyond the fact it had become historically associated with him, or just as Pound ceased using "vorticism" or Stein "cubism." Most importantly, it is a term of positive usage. The post-modern, in Olson's view, ends alienation: "any POST-MODERN is born with the ancient confidence that, he *does* belong."

Creeley continues to keep up with Olson, and when he offers his own understanding of Olson's thought ("space is our history," he summarizes on August 14th) it very often clarifies Olson's thinking for us, helps us to assimilate it as well, encouraging our own participation in the process. Creeley's letters can often be a relief from Olson's intensity and barrage of thoughts put down with instantaneous schematization.

During this period, Creeley himself, after an unsettled summer, has written two new stories, "The Party" and "The Grace," as well as the poems "The Sea" and that perfect lyric, "A Song." He has received word that the novel he had begun in July was deemed too "obscure" by a publisher's readers, although the rejection does not cast him adrift. He still principally thinks of himself in terms of prose, despite the fact he is preparing his first collection of poetry for publication (by Richard Wirtz Emerson's Golden Goose Press), and is still seeking to explore his "flat juxtapositional method" (as he writes September 29th), although he accepts the abandonment of his novel graciously enough, accepting the fact that it had taken him five years before he wrote a satisfactory story ("Mr. Blue"). Writing Olson gives Creeley, too, a chance to clarify his own needs; notably, when he discusses his sense of "passage," a technique that would allow "the flux to contain multiple explosions" (September 26 and 27).

We miss Creeley's description of France, the world he is immediately surrounded by; it seems a blind spot, nevertheless part of his essential nature. Only once does he mention the famous Mediterranean light. There are no accounts of evening walks, neighbors, local foods — he is clearly no Hemingway — though these will come, more or less, in future letters. Except for his brief mention of the light in the valley over to Mont Ste.-Victoire the morning of August 29th, the same landscape Cézanne captured in its refracted geometries, there is no description of the countryside until September 27th, and then very brief. It is not Creeley's way. "Must make a *means* equal to anyplace, anytime, just from the angle of, myself," will remain his lifelong goal.

Creeley provides a useful corrective to Olson's August 10th excessive reaction to William Carlos Williams, which Creeley rightly in part attributes to too much talk in the hothouse of Black Mountain, the seemingly endless galaxy of demanding and attentive minds. This will be the second time that his younger friend has so helpfully redirected Olson, the first by Creeley's refusal to get drawn into the Poundian quagmire and his advice to Olson to cool down, not send the furious letter of 19 June 1950 (I. 110-11). Olson's deeply touching, humble acquiescence — recognition, really — of the reality of Creeley's remarks, is followed by an equally expressive dash in ink over eleven pages (in the original), pouring out his vulnerabilities (and with them his strengths). He confesses (August 22nd) to his long pursuit of "beauty," but also how "maybe beauty is only the formulation of, my own inarticulateness." If that is true, he has shifted the earth to overcome his inarticulateness.

It is a great revealing letter, significant in the series and in the men's relationship, as well as an important human document, closer than any theory to the poetic soul. Could Pound, Canto 116 notwithstanding, have written a letter like it? Williams's letter, quoted in my note 64, had nipped Olson where he was most uncertain at the time — as a great starter of projects, even a starter of great projects, nevertheless a beginner (despite the positive sense to be found in his observation about Melville, "a beginner, and interested in beginnings"); someone perhaps not sufficiently disciplined, a maker of "notes" not novels (or whatever the accomplishment might be). Creeley's forthright and eloquent statement of his own feeling for Williams (August 16) summarizes the honesty that characterizes the correspondence as a whole.

The relationship between the two men and their influence on one another is never clearer than in this volume — not only in terms of general encouragement and fellowship, but in precise details, as they themselves express them in regard each other's "Mr. Blue" and "Human Universe," respectively. Creeley writes, for instance, "I damn well get to more, with you, at this distance — than I ever have with anyone else, in the same room."

The matter of influence is very much a part of the immediate exchange. There is Creeley's reaction September 19th to Vincent Ferrini's suggestion that he owes his prose to Olson, which he finds objectionable because it not only "belittles . . . that precise influence you are," but denies him, "so very coyly, the actual fact of my own existence." In the course of his objection he points out that influence is not at all the same as imitation. To Olson he states plainly: "You have been the only *possible* influence, for me; you are the only one who can give me that sense of my own work, which allows me to make it *my own work*." And Olson, while acknowledging the value Fenollosa has been for him, as for many other twentieth-century poets, answers those critics who would dismiss him out of hand as a Poundian imitator: "It burns my ass, that, so often, these idiots cry, 'Pound,' everytime they think they have a critique of my own work. Yet, fuck em. I'll not be driven off a value because of such — or, for that matter, because of EP hisself."

As might be hoped for, amid the professional and theoretical, comes the personal: Creeley and Olson on having children, Olson's account of first meeting his wife, the Creeleys' quietly-slipped fifty-dollar gift to the Olsons, Creeley's friendship with a young black American painter. We learn such interesting details as the fact that Olson considered calling his "Human Universe" essay "The Laws" (which no doubt would have earned him even more a reputation for dogmatism and authoritarianism than he would otherwise draw upon himself). There is Olson's grand proposal for a Civil War centennial project in photographs ("pitchers") and "stories" that would have given both men effectual intellectual and economic subsistence for years hence. Creeley's pragmatic spirit that has served him steadfastly throughout his career is seen in his considered advice to Olson to accept Richard Wirtz Emerson's offer to publish his collection *The Praises* even after undue and intolerable delay.

The reader also has a chance to see, as graphically as such a process can ever be seen, how a poem emerges from the original eruption of imagination: Olson's July 28th letter written high on Black Mountain conversation; his July 30th attempt to "salvage" the outpouring into poetic lines; and finally the accomplished poem itself, "A Round & A Canon," as published in *Origin* later that year. The very preliminary or still transitional condition of American poetry after the Second World War is reflected in Creeley's choices for an American issue of Gerhardt's *Fragmente*. There is no Duncan, Ginsberg, Synder, Levertov, Ashbery or O'Hara; Zukofsky, H.D., and Niedecker have not yet been rediscovered. Creeley's brief introduction, printed here, reminds the reader of the wilderness facing those poets outside of the academy and other structures of influence. Even the figure given for the number of copies printed of the first issue of *Fragmente* (5000) reveals how innocently hopeful these new writers and editors were.

"The Law" sent by Olson on October 3rd is intimately related to the "Human Universe" essay, and, like that, finds an alternative to inherited Westernism in the archaic past. The "box" of history from 500 B.C. to 1950 A.D. is firmly shut and put away, creating more area for new living. From "The Law" it can again be seen that the "post-modern" is beyond the confines of Western history from the invention of reason to the beginnings of the Atomic Age, and that it is most readily represented by what Olson will later call the "new sciences of man" (he cites biochemistry as his present instance). His depiction of how knowledge was retained and projected—"so hands, and voice, and the movements of the body were undivided from the process of retention"—directly anticipates Eric Havelock's description of the role of the poet in an oral society in *Preface to Plato* (1963), which Olson found so confirmatory in the next decade of his thought. "The Law" also includes an important discussion of history as active versus history as fact (in which past time is analyzed and described rather than reenacted), and a rousing proposal for art beyond that as "a tolerated lovely duckling," an art which is man's "special attribute," indeed that which distinguishes him from all of nature, at the same time he most deeply participates in nature, through the central role of rhythm.

The volume concludes with Creeley planning his first collection of poetry (his hopefulness somewhat suppressed, one might imagine, knowing Olson's fury with Emerson's apparent failure in his own case), unaware that he would become most active and best known as a poet, despite his accomplishments in prose; and with the Olsons at Black Mountain still expecting the birth of their first child, who had been conceived in Mexico.

It is the very difficulty and uniqueness — idiosyncrasy, if you will — of the writers' prose that allows it to be read today beyond mere historical interest, and to be read as two minds grappling — and grappling *for us* — with essential problems that never seem to go away. If it was a matter of mere style, literary style, samples of poets' prose, then we could read a page or two, or several of the letters together, as evidence of a "remarkable meeting of minds," and that would be that. But because these men are tunneling through with their minds for all of us, we want to be there until the very end, or several ends (new entrances), each time they break forth to the light.

George F. Butterick

Charles Olson & Robert Creeley
The Complete Correspondence

Volume 7

Notes to the letters begin on p. 251.

[Black Mountain, N.C.]

sat july 25 [*i.e.*, 28] 51: Rob't — you musn't mind a couple of days
gap in mails — the USP.O., as you know, has no smaller division
than ½ ounce 15¢ (my impression from the magnificent collection
of letters that spilled into our hands last night from you — 7, i
think it was! — is that the intelligent French must have smaller
weights & amounts?)

anyhow, deepest thanks, for the lot of it — for, yr own precisions
on ORIGIN, YOUR origin — all yr newses, etc: I read them, at
3AM this morning — after

what you will excuse me if i unload, 1st — a wild, and unhappy
night (well, unhappy? fuck em, not at all — that is, I am too
fucking onnocent to be guy[1] : let me get drunk with only the
greatest (let there be born a new Banquet)[2] or let me be gay in
some bed with some wild dame. Otherwise, let's — where it is
business, not be at all silly, as New Yorkers are silly, eh? Above
all, let me not mix with Neo-Classics — who are such because all of
em are, sans mit brains. Let them go by me, Performers —
Recitalists! Let the lazy, even the brilliant cats who can leap, or
stretch their striped limbs yawningly, not shit in front of me as
such do, right spang in the middle of the circus ring. Let all
simplicissimusses shut their pusses. Let us be vulgar when fineness
is dullness, brightness is a penny arcade, or, what it is when it is
not innocent, riding, a peep show. "Theatre" — let theatre be where
war peace Europe all flat walls are, pushed — aside. Let swing sway
bounce stay in the trees, or, with the children or, the balls or —
walk the dog, and curb same from, the next passerby, unless, you,
not any of them, sway swing bounce grind — do a little fucking in
public if, this, is the only answer to, art, or, anything which
proceeds from, or toward, coitus.[3] Make it clear, lads & lasses — if
you can't, make use of it — if you have to, go to the melanctha[4]
beasts, or, the coy trees. Birds, my player, are experienced — right
in front of their own eyes, they sing, morning & evening. So? can
you call em innocent? Did you ever sing from, same, alone? Bah

15

you, who, have to crawl off, where it matters, like huge animals
who cannot die, decently, in public, cannot just drop dead off a
branch. A bird, sir, is too experienced to have been born by
trauma or to awake any day out of such or to go down, as who
thinks the sun is traumatic in his descent? Be reminded, you saints
& recitalists, that this thing has a very high heart beat (Robinson
Jeffers is a 45), a high heat too, and a nervous organism so much
as any experience is that, if you try to keep it alive, when it has
fallen from its own balances, even a spoon, or the finest honey
you can find, the finest worm, won't do. It dies, without reference
to, the twisting of the neck of, the spitting, of a black goose. It
dies, as the spirit dies, right inside me, when, I am in the company
of the, gay, the so-called, the so self-taken, the performing arts! O
rain that beats down the pretty sway — o, let you, particularly,
discover the lack of roots is no lack at all as long as you can smell
the rain — can you dance a nose, can you tell me, how to make the
arms a fragrance, the eyes a dog capable of holding, a point, can
you drag — after you — as a tree can all trees with their roots after
them by — where is there a soil the equal of me? O Black-Eyed
Susan, this morning I hurry to offer you my condolences and my
apologies that, even the finest dancer, and a very good piano-
player (who knows a piano is only a zither laid out flat of its own
table) not know that your eye is bigger than theirs! And wind,
that, it is you who are the master of, sway — that you, branch of
this tree, are swing — that this child of mine who hangs there in
midair about to fall either way is such a lovely bird of a wild
will — that what it is that you do, o Gold-Hatted High-Bouncing
Lover, is, this is the root of it, you, Man, BOUNCE[5]

And only thunder does, likewise — or voice! Play, you fools who
rime too easily, play, idiot gay — and leave the birds to me, the
beasts, and the flowers. I give you art, the whole of it, for your
stage! Art, and all your gay [*broken off*]

[*verso envelope:*]
& thank Mitch,[6] please, for excellent letter; no news, him or me.
And won't be, some weeks.

[Fontrousse, Aix-en-Provence]
July 30/ 51

Dear Chas/
            You have me damn well blushing! Sit here, casting coy looks at Ann! Phew.
                        The thing : was going to say, from our own experience, do believe it very important to be *settled* when the baby comes, i.e., it is, very honestly, a shock, & can testify to same from both points of view (and/or Ann's & yr lad's).
                                    I figure, as again on past wreckage, it will take you both about 1 or 2 months to pick up. The gig is such, it deposes all other attentions, damn well like it or not.
                        SO: wd it not be cool, then, to dig in, there, at BMC, & then pick up when the kid is 3 months or so old, to take off? Remembering that was T/s age when we left for this place? (Also, check with the doctor to see at what age he or she will be able to take the necessary shots for life in the best of all possible, worlds.)
                        Anyhow : SIT. Wd say that very emphatically, & with all possible concern. Because babies, damn well : strange! So be: prepared. Ok.
                        And, as Ann insists, Con's comfort, simply the physical sense of same, so very important at such a time — that she have it as soft as is possible. That she be altogether, provided for — in the sense of, some privacy, some people around who know what the fuck a BABY is, some ease (not to make it, a nurse, etc., etc., etc., which is not the idea.)
            Anyhow : a hole/ in which to sit/ with some security. Any damn hole. Ok.

(And think you'll find, for yr own part, that it does put you off a little — not sadly, or anything like, but is NEW thing, & so : takes that attention.)

Anyhow : hope to god all goes well for you both, & that BMC can look possible for such a staking. (So much greater, finally, to be taking off for Mexico/ WITH a completeness, WITH the baby born & you both, settled on same fact.)

Not to put it : it cd not go, say, in Mexico, etc., but that the one thing be : be IN, be staked IN, for that time.

A very fine letter in from K/ (The Sneeze!) which tells me VOU will be out in two weeks, abt. To contain : 'portrait . . .' Hmmmmm/ & notes from letter to him on BLUE. Well, it damn well pleases me, & how very keen a man he is, beyond the obvious matters of falling for the occasion. When he puts it/ "How I expect your later stories . . . ," I am damn well grateful.

G/ continues to scare me. Will send off copy to Gallimard. Anyhow, wish to christ he wd write. Has me goofed, trying to figure it. And, and : cannot — which is the damn hitch.

On BLUE : figure you very cool there, & will attempt same directly. Have felt the arbitrary of same ever since you started hitting it, & wd very damn much like to have it set for ND gig. Well, will try it, & send you on what comes. (Many damn thanks for leading, there, & will damn well hold to same.)

Ok. All cool here, & coming pretty good. Want to get something settled re a house for the winter, but figure that will be set via Mr. Leach soon — & thanks again, for that. Damn hot, at the moment : baker! But nights. . . . so very great.

DL/ is Mrs Goodman.

Write soon. Wish to god we were closer. But damn well may make it to L/ at that. Ok.

All our love to you both/
    yr Homer (Band Number : 765432890.)

                                                Bob

[*On back of envelope:*] Wd you hold a copy of FRAGMENTE for
me there? This one, off to Gallimard, my last. And god knows if
I'll ever hear from G/ again.

                                    [Black Mountain, N.C.]

mon july 30   51:   lad
                        excuse, please, dropping off that letter
yesterday unsigned, but, it had to go then, or be held over, and
the way things push at me here (christ, how they create too many
things for a goer like myself — & how they want to suck my blood,
the bloodsuckers anyhow
                        but thank you: two different poems fell
out of that letter — one fairly set, called, ISSUES FR THE HAND
OF GOD, opening, I am too fucking innocent to be gay, he
roared![7] And the other, ABT ROUNDS & CANONS,[8] ending,
with what seems satisfactory

    (grabbed wrong   ⊠⊠⊠⊠⊠⊠⊠⊠⊠⊠⊠
        mss!)   ⊠⊠⊠⊠⊠⊠⊠⊠⊠⊠⊠⊠⊠⊠⊠
                        ⊠⊠⊠⊠⊠⊠⊠,

                    as, certainly, it is not you who sway
                    (Black-Eyed Susan) but it is the wind
                    who has this affection for you

                    that this child of mine hangs
                    where the arc does not yet know which

> (the swing does not) the moment
> over or back, innocent or wise
> in mid-air
> about to fall either way is such
> a lovely bird of a wild human motion.

But what I want to go over to you with, this morning, is, what is puzzling me. That is, I am tempted to rewrite the whole HU in the form — proceeding from a new title: THE LAWS.

I shld like yr response to such a title.

The point is, every damn conversation i have (and there have been too many the past three days — starting with that damnable Friday evening, which, you have the issue of one part of, the performances of this extraordinary pianist, David Tudor, who arrived Friday (he is here as Litz' accompanist, but he knocked her evening right out of her hands by playing Schoenberg's Opus 23 as the 1st no of the evening so beautifully that nothing else mattered, even Litz's fine 1st dance, Part of a Suite for a Woman, and Harrison's own several pieces for piano (very clear and delicate stuff, what i wld think are probably the equivalents of Bill Merwin or Larry Richardson's verse[9] — those most able Neo-Classicists — who are more able than the Intermitters, Lowell (who is a bore), Berryman (who has a head like brilliant embroidered drawers), Jarrell (whose brains are all he has   — peculiar how, all of these, get more like Karl Shapiro every year

The death of passion, or, the ignoring of same — the assumption, there is something else — or that Dido did not lament, that Purcell is more close than Dido to Dido![10] It gets crazy, these, practitioners (I shld like to be able to extend the word Recitalist or Performer over to cover such apparent self-initiated work. For there has come on a whole false gang — when I think how that principle you have given me such high circulation on, that, language is instrument, and any of us is, — how, even this has, suddenly, its false face in, these, Recitalists:: how quickly, they

misuse, and so, the point of it all — the relevance of same — THE
STAKE   is lost.

INSTRUMENT, BUT NO LOSS OF, THE ISSUE!

And Litz is dragged back in this direction. And it unheartens
me. Tho, I was right to write you fr Lerma, that, what she lacks
is, compositional power. Passion. What I guess you and I better be
damned careful abt in any of those who will pick up on us, that,
like workers, we know but, will they?

Which is what crowds me
on to think that what I have under hand had better be as
dogmatic as THE LAWS

Now I am not yet sure what this
means.

So far, in the rewriting, it is more like GATE & CENTER
in its tone — goes, as I imagine is just the advantage of such
dogmatism — such laws! — toward narratives: in other words, right
from the start (where I have slugged in a small incident of
Cormac, the Irish king)[11]

I don't know, Rob't, if I can do this
thing. Nor exactly how it can be done. But, as I say, everything
presses me to think it is possible now to see and set down a whole
new series of absolutes! But what makes them not so, in the sense
in which we understand the word, is, that they are neither up (Mr
Blue Plato Special) or down (Arseytotal), have nothing to do with
such polarities — have nothing to do with any polarities (except as
such are necessary poles around which, through which, force
circulates) — have to do only with irreducible minimums or bases of
movement, of *human* movement

well, goddamn it, what have we
got here, anyhow — that is, can they be organized so flatly as, say,
outline? Imagine not. But, for the purpose of seeing where I am, in
this thing, maybe they ought to be? But this is what I can't do.
And I wonder, is it because of the resistance of the material, or,
my own stupidity in the face of the problem. That is, clearly, one
thing set out already is

I The universe of discourse intermits the content, and thus
prevents form
 a. Comparison (which is symbol) and reference (which is
 classification) must go
pre-a (of II). Mime or re-enactment (transfer of force, conversion
of energy, chemistry) and relevance (the moral as non-logical
but responsibility as exclusively *human* in measurement: use
to man as man only, not as machine extending him, or as
natural universe as extension of what he also is, but, that he
also is of nature, does not allow for, either mechanism or
mysticism, by overcoming nature (equals making of
machines) or by worship of same (making of gods): man has
no permission other than to stay in there, to keep himself
alert & alive without moving either to eat nature or to fall
at her feet

II The universe of man (which is declarable, without further
debate, or useless argument, as bounded by each skin) is the
only content from which form is derivable
 a. The canard of the aggregate (society) and action (as
 activity only in one of two directions, either overcoming
 nature — will — or reforming the aggregate — revolution) must
 go
pre-a of III. Sociology is a lie, in that only action as of all the
intervals of individual experiences has any true
bearing on any other person (thus art as also
instrument, in this respect that, it is the expression of
getting-it-all-in (mime)); but, that the double here is
that art, seen so, is not aestheticism or culture (in the
usual senses) but requires what is the twin to
relevance above, that is, a recognition that rite (not as
savages initiating youngers, or, whatever, but, present
day savages running around in planes, is waste, is
dispersed, because, there are no "forms" in which
collective action is directed — but, that the cure, is not
social revolution ((which is based on a hideous
canard, of, abundance)) IS, to go back where it has
to start, the single self as sufficiently disposed toward
its own content as to create forms

goddamn it—that's the trouble—I haven't added a thing to what HU already includes! yet, somewhere, the form of it, doesn't include all that it has to include—which, I begin to think, is the *points* that narrative alone can make

                                        Which causes me to hail
you, STORY-TELLER!   C

" " " " Or as of "law" as we have it, the holy cow, let me tell all
    who are afraid of the word "slacker" and all CO's (who
    forget that, if they absent themselves, the act of absenting
    themselves is not so much, its courage is exaggerated, and
    that they better do something more with their absenting than
    organizing themselves as such, simply because the Biggest
    Bore of all, the State, throws them in the federal pen) a lost
    business abt one Tom Jefferson. It is forgotten (because he
    was a smart enough politician to get himself, later, elected
    President—from Charlottesville he organized the first city
    political machines, chiefly by way of the thugs of
    Philadelphia) that Jefferson took himself off after writing the
    Dec., did not fight in the, War of, how is it, Independence.
    That he was "sitting this one out," eh? But do you know
    what the hell he was doing *all that time*? He was revising
    the laws of the then Colony of Virginia in anticipation of the
    fact that—when the shooting was over—when all the pother
    of the "social revolution" had spent itself, that, the
    consolidation, would be, a *change* of the code—that law as
    we have it, mind you, is only an adjustment of absolutes to
    new particulars. But he knew, that such, is the harvest, is,
    the daily effects thereafter of, those who die and those who
    win, eh?

            that if we are going to moan about what war
    does—a Civil War, in these parts, fixed Jonathan Trader,[12]
    old White-Coat or Pipe-Vest & Pale-Face, on us all—we
    better go in there and figure out what each of them is, and
    does, instead of, what delivers all, including anarchists &
    c.o.'s, as well as the dead lads, over into the hands of, so
    rapidly we are being handed over, lads & lasses, to, the
    silliest one of them all, The World-State

                                    that, if this is it—

this is the Third, & Last of the American Phenomenons! — then
let's not just be Jeffersons, but, let's fix em good! let's
understand that all patterns are bad lessons except as they are
seen as patterns alone — in other words the "forms" of action
[*Typed in margin*: (why anecdotes are deadly — as bullets, eh,
lad?] — which, out of each new particular, are called new
"forms" — and of action, lads & lasses, not of what politicans
love (as well as citizens, how, comfortable it is, to)
consolidate (the dirty word, as of, anything, including, all
gains, private, or electric power!)

LET'S NOT — CONSOLIDATE!

(Intercourse the contract, intercourse — the red-headed labor leader
cried!)[13]

    You see, this business of anecdote — what abt it, why do I take
it right in flame everytime even the best pull it on me — apothegms,
or, all wis[e-]isms. Why do I find em the same as lawisms — as,
settling down on us one goddamned heel on our necks? They
declare patterns, but of another sort than law — usually, at least, of
a longer backward reference (reference, yah). What they rest
themselves on is another cow which has to be cut up for the
eating: you know the flip, of all of them, on your own nerves,
how, you are supposed to feel, o, human life, it is, very old, and,
how like it is, how it o so beautiful it is so long just like what it is
now — if you could only raise your poor eyes up from these
entangling particulars of yours and get a good look around you,
you'd understand that you are only one fly in all the flies in a fly's
eye (God, then, the great, Fly-Swatter)
                                        even when, as so usual, it
is a laugh, how, Etna threw up Empedocles' Sandal,[14] or, oi, weh,
things go up, things, go down, or
                            Christ (any of H is Smartisms)

    however they may or may not alleviate nerves & sometimes
contribute to the enabling of yrself to get the work done under
hand — who gives em (or their tellers) permission to pass them off

as relevant to the *source* of our own particulars, ourselves?

that is,

why i take em aslant, take em as corrupting (at least, are now
corrupting) is, that, the base of them is (as is true of metaphysics)
a drawn-off wisdom, drawn off from ancient practice, particulars
which caused them to come into being in the first place

that is, that is, that

little mouse, little mouse
take away this tooth of bone
and give me one of iron

is wholly intact and usable, because, it is left inside its own act, &
is not trying to put any point over on us, is, just, reminding us,
that, each of us loses his first teeth, and, when there ain't a
doorknob present, or there is, it is also, a hidden superstition here,
which, promotes, some such sympathetic calling on some other
force than our own to restore to us what we lose in even greater
force, next time

now such, is a recording of a common, which in no way
intrudes on our own particular, in fact, like all good verse,
illuminates — but without wisdomism — the common as it is
particular of our own, and, the pleasure of community (the
true base pleasure of communitas), that, somebody else has
some of the things we also have (that is, that if they also lose
teeth they also must have other intervals we have — but that
they do, does not lessen to an ounce or an inch the
unendurableness that we do

It is this hideous horizontal attempt to disperse by spreading like
manure on fields what are our emotions as commons by anecdotal
referents that sends me right through my blood bursting all over
the teller to kill im
for they rest on a humanism as discoverable in its historical
lair as all false or stiff things — all summaries, consolidations,
generalizations, all things drawn off from the particularism

which is local to the time of its existence and cannot, must not, be permitted over to cover, to try to spread out, any other time, the soil of same

                    LEAVE THE ROOTS ON, he yelled, screamed, made himself hated for, he sd it so often so often so often[15]

Laws & Anecdotes: are hereby: PROSCRIBED

But there it is: the dogmatism, WHO, can now, get himself recognized as, permissably, JUDGE? It is like the problem of — do they have ears, the jug-jugs? And I do not blame *them*. Who took their judgment away — who stopped their [inner *crossed out*] ears?

    A further huge confusion is, that, because a man has done the work he has turned his hand to well, he has the right to be heard on any & all subjects, especially, that seemingly most permissible one, what abt, human life, eh, what abt it — don't I know as much as you: look! at my painting, say, or this, my composition — my canon, this, my dance.

    BAH. It occurs, & fastens itself more & more on me, that, there is something damned off right here, too — that, here, maybe, is as root a wrong as any of the others in this humanistic un-universe we must destroy —

(1)   that it takes as much work to make accurate observations from one's own work as it takes to make the work itself

& (2)   that it comes to very few men to be able to make such comment without reference back to some other earlier formulation, which, just because it arose from different particulars, is bound to be however slightly different — and thus, any man who is too lazy or vain to put into this process the same work which goes into the other — what he makes, which, does not require comment (a painting, a

dance, a composition — or an act of writing) — has no
right — in fact, palms off — something on anybody who
listens to him

that here we are affirming an old logical fallacy, of, appeal to,
authority

that I find all these contemporaries of mine very much like the
President — or the Pope — or whoever assumes that his position or
his accomplishment *in itself* permits him to speak of, any laws
other than what lie in his own action or things —

> I say, even he who made the laws, does not
> necessarily, therefore, have the right to state
> them in discourse

I guess it comes to that, that, this whole gripe is a question of
WHO HAS THE RIGHT OF DISCOURSE

                              it sounds, put that
way, sort of simple, but, like all present planes, there are
obscenities here which, should be soon understood to be
outlawable (mob scene, was invented, because Aeschylus scared
such piss out of everybody with his masks for the Erinyes in his
first play, the Persians, and caused so many premature births right
there in the stadium that afternoon that . . .[16]
                              It all comes out of
this hammering on (of) particulars — and the hells they get me more
and more into. Gerhardt sure struck in, with, his gossip, with, his
interminable internal conversation with himself, olson, is, good for
montage, the son-of-a-bitch. Ok. I'm taking it forward,
wherever.
            And look, lad; i'm damned if i'll let you have it, that, i
am helpful to you — in what scale, who will say, how goddamned
tremendous it is to me to have you listening to these workings out
along particulars to tell me, who's on, who's in, when, is olson on,
in, when is it, making, POINT! Christ. It's terrific, to have you to
shoot at, such, as well as to wish — to want — such prose as yrs
instead of this piling, pulling unreadable stuff — can you even read

any sense into this taffy-pull I am offering you here, this day!
I

don't know. I don't know whether, all this, is getting on. THAT
IT GIVES ME THE RIGHT TO SAY WHO SHALL, WHO MAY,
and WHY!

but what strikes me, is, how, this tandem of ours! how
you take yr sentences in there so beautifully, so carefully, and,
euchering with them like the skewers in beef and fat, part without
parting the meat — how you manage the particulars so that they
throw their light!

And me: going along, dragging the whole
baggage every step, holding, not letting go — not clearing up —
anyway, not that way — so, led along to LAWS!

shit.

well, you see, so much now piles up — every day it seems
some damned new area where the laws apply is in front of me —
and i get crazy, i don't have the time & the impeccable prose, to
get it sd straight, once & for all, and away we go!

christ. i don't think this matters. that is. the thing throws up
its own results. and i am just too weak (tired, rather) to write
around the clock until, this, all this, this huniverse, has spent
itself!

Now, what i figure is, what i wrote you as the *end* of, *is*, the
poem. And so, from the rest, let me salvage, now that i have
looked at it out of the corner of, what may give you pleasure, you
& Ann, there, where, how much that you two exist is how much
to us two about to be three — do you guess?

((which last strikes me as the metric all the above is
walking itself (like the dog) about! For look:

"A bird
knows too much, or it strikes me he knows enough
to awake to a day to sing a day down

And when he falls — o
all saints and recitalists, consider
what a very high heart, a high heat

and what nerves, such
I cannot keep him alive, held
in my hand, when, winged or weakened, he falls
from his own world, his own careful context, those
balances
Even a spoon
of the finest honey, or a splint, or
tried down his throat like his father
the finest worm

won't do. He dies, his eyes
closing upward, the film first, the milky
way of his dying
(as the Two who shyly rule
off the north in the night settle, finally,
in the sea

He ceases to fly or to sing,
and with no reference whatsoever to twisting
a neck of a hen or the neck of
the spitting black goose

he dies,
as the instant dies, as I die for an instant, listening
to error[17]

Arriverderci! O

[Fontrousse, Aix-en-Provence]
July 31/ 51

Dear Chas/

Am stumped, and what it is : this BLUE/[18] the damn
thing being, have just got up from making over a draft, of same,
from yr notes. What bugs me — that yr logic is very *right*, but
that, doing literally what you had sd, I lose these several things:

1) the *use* of that para on p/ 115 ("The eyes, catch . . .") which I
   hadn't honestly supposed to be doing the bulk of work it
   clearly is, when I attempt to cut it out — what happens, so
   doing it — I get too rapid a movement, too much a loss of this
   Blue/s hit/ of his clear strike — on the narrator. The continuity,
   as the direct action, or line of action, improves, but you see :
   the strike of the midget on the man is then dropped, or
   dropped as this actual *breaking-in* on this same line of
   action.
       (You'll remember you'd figured it first as : another
   prose/ here, thru this section, & that, oddly, is what it is, &
   also what I lose if I revert to the external continuity which,
   say, is the line from the bottom of p/ 112 until this point.)

2) The 2nd para on that same page ("I could see the muscle . . .")
   is less of this problem, but nonetheless the same one — when it's
   taken out and brought in again on p/ 116 as you'd noted. See,
   anyhow, that it involves *no* awkwardness, in either case, to do
   just that — I mean, it reads smoothly, reads clearly, so written
   (& had copied out the whole biz, as it was, making a copy, as
   I'd figured, to send on to Laughlin, & was in the reading over
   of same, this loss, noted above, came so very clear to both A/
   & yr lad, tho (& get this!) I could *not* see the loss at any point
   but when I had the whole thing done, & sat down to read it
   over — & figured it altogether cool to make the switch, just
   so — up to that point of reading it as whole). But the loss, in
   either case, is very clearly, loss. And what the fuck to do?

3)   Similar headache on end biz — it is a matter of literal energy, of the narrator's, and that one fact : how much 'time' has he left, to receive any 'further impression' after being bowled over by the Blue? In short — the way I felt same, was, he's getting the word, from his wife, thru a most certain blur, anyhow. I mean, it is the tag-end, the echo of a 'reality' lost he hears it as, anyhow — and almost like a man, deadened, head shaking says, what, what, what was that . . . and cannot pull himself up to the point of any thrust beyond the one action has him on his back. So. The idea was/ to make it as the 'tag-end' of sd para/ to leave narrator, stumbling, just so, out, at the close of it.

(Her comment, disclosure, can only make it as, say, just this kind of comment, & he cannot, clearly, 'mark' it, cannot take it in, either then, or at any other time, & he mumbles it, so, because it is something hinged on *that moment*, something which 'also happened,' & so he retains it, as 'additional detail . . .' But he cd not, say, in the frame, or sense I have of him, take off on a new para/ to 'see' this further detail. It must sit there, as, say, just the tag-end, the thing he takes in, because he 'hears' it, & grabs out, at the sound.

Anyhow, to see he is, literally, leaning over at some angle of 45 degrees, from the "he's looking at you . . ." to the finish, & that I cd not, and can't see how, now, to, let him lean for a further 'time' than he is.)

Looking back at the whole works: I figure there are 2 precise *instants*: a) that eyes para/ and note, too, how the para following is this man's attempt to regain the balance, his, the literal means to position that will enable him to stagger on thru, & that it is this contest, between himself & midget which is literally begun, right here, & which causes this shifting, of his, this back & forth biz, of the prose, from here to the end; b) that of the midget's, looking/ last para. Ok. I mean, they damn well assert, it turns out, an impetus on the prose, which oddly, because it's not an everyday gig, I cannot, literally cannot, turn to other use, or set, in a manner, which is not the, same. I heard it scream, if that is not fantastic. I damn well heard it scream.

Anyhow—that's the headache. Cannot most certainly ask you to break it out, or cut out, rearrange it, literally, so you can read it, literally, as I just have—but try it on C/, i.e., read her the two ways, the two sounds, lines, of it, the one as now, and the other, with just the changes you noted, & I had damn well agreed with, reading it before this copying, etc. Well/ screwy. Damn damn screwy! All our love/

                                                            Bob

[*Typed in margin*:]
The thing is (reading over yr notes again): as soon as the midget IS there, in any sense, i.e., as soon as 'the trick' comes—he has to hit hard, must hit out, lash out, hard, at sd narrator, must declare the *full potential* of his presence, which I have, in fact, taken as his eyes.

[*Written in margin*:]
It damn well threw me—because it turns out, now, contrary to any "logic" I cd reasonably assert against the present draft (or as it stands in ORIGIN).

[*Typescript of Creeley's poem "The Sea"* (Collected Poems, *p. 30*) *bearing Olson's date* July 31st *enclosed.*]

                                                  [Black Mountain, N.C.]

tues july 31   51   LAD—yr letter just in (on, how, you too, scratched fr Swampscott—and you, pissing off, taking time fr telling me more, of the Melville Letter! (((on that no word yet fr

Kirgo))

and i likewise, this day, pissed off, from, a letter in fr Cid, quoting, this son of a prick friend of yrs, Bronk "how cute olsen is"[19]

you see, lad, i am getting this same biz, of the Pound-Williams thing   so we stay, even in our enemies, joined! — fine, ok, roll em, bro, let's do exactly what they won't (surenhell won't, by their going, go — this, it seems to me, is, what, puts em — as i happened to say, those others, previous, more and more like K S (King S

as of Bronk, it's simply matter of, his getting his head out of his own arse (his vulgarity i marked in those 1st two mss you sent me, and figured, this will be his big bass drum or, he can be a bit of a poet. So far he's boom-boom. And I have told cid, and that the shit shows himself most, in crawling all over our lad for piss poor editorial work, when, by god, you & i will look long for better

my answer to Bronk himself goes unwritten; instead, i have shipped enclosed to Cid, for, spotting, amongst Bronk's & Morse's things, there, #3

Am going back to HU now, and, shipping this, just, to join hands   — fuck even your friends! (the same Swampscott had a go on me, over, the radio stuff

but what the hell (like you say) nippers

shit on em, unless they give cause sufficient enough to provoke work (as, lad, Gerhardt, say — who, however, is, *a*cute

say to yr girl, how, con was damned smart down there, and for a total of abt 5 bucks, got herself made, to her own design, three honey dresses, which, are carrying her thru — and thanks, that, she thought of it — as well, that, my girl is doing fine — going along again as there, Lerma, very cool & happy (got over her distaste for this place that one day, and now, is bowling along

                                   in fact, the lad or
the lass inside has just taken another rise — is up again
against her chest — what i figure, is, the rise for, the drop!

damn nice business, this, of, to have Con having this
wonder bean! but how to name it (Ann) is, a problem
when, the name is O L S O N (nothing goes with such, it
is itself a false patronymic, because, son of. So, I sd, if
boy, why not, Son of Olson. And be done with it! The
result was, Obadiah, says somebody! O O . And if girl
(which, I cannot bring myself to cast my heart — it would
be ridiculous for me to interfere! — let it come, and if it
comes girl, well, by god, wouldn't that be very nice (or
as nice, in any case, what matters to me is, how good is
IT, male or female?
             Let it 1st be handsome (the odds, are not good)
             Let it also be tough (same odds)
             Let it love beauty (its one chance!
LET IT NOT DRAG ITS ASS LIKE ITS FELLOW CITS
                         (well, say, 50-50, or, isn't
                         it, such odds, abt, 51-49?)

Today it is only work which interests me. So, let me also thrust
on you, this:

ISSUES FROM THE HAND OF GOD

I am too fucking innocent to be gay, he roared. Let there be born
a new Banquet, let there be a wild bed, and you get the hell aside
    from me,
with your too easy advances, your
too easy attacks

                I'll not mix my goods with neo-classicists,
                those from the capitals, or who talk
                on the basis of the advantage of a sample survey
                of small industrial towns. Go by me, Arguers,
                even those who are a little bit right

For it is too early to be so wise, so bright
to still stay, or, to jump ahead, you, Performers,
        you!

Let my brilliant lazy cats

                    (to hell with it — it bores me today — see
you later, eh?

        the point is, after anything, who is, there, but

                            greetings,

                ROBERT CREELEY and

                    what shall we call him-her?

                    (direct question)

                Obadiah and Angela Olson

[*Typescript of "A Round & A Canon" enclosed.*]

                            [Black Mountain, N.C.]

lad (wed aug 1 51):
                    what do you say to this? THE PACKAGE
came in last night (the chap fr nuvvel, the s.s., and the theatre

note). I read all. And, without rereading — I am going to toss off to
you first impressions. OK? For, even tho I may be wrong, still,
between us, just, my thinking abt the problems over night, ought
to have some relevance. In any case, I feel very close, and figure
such, is one damned good resonance out of which to talk, eh?

the places that really send me, are these: in the novel (how do
you call it — project X), the wondrous fine moment of the evening,
the two of em, there, she, weight, and he, holding, on the
point — and going off, to make some conversation possible (that
beautiful business, no one, certainly has ever got as, you, can, do,
there — the impeccable balancing, of, the contest, the implicit,
forever, unbreakable, contest
                    ((i do *not* go with it by way of the
cigarette — taking it, here, you *had* to *invent* — or get something like
the electric bill, earlier

which brings up what, this day, I would call yr problem #1:
THAT ANY TErms of ordinary daily reality — drum-drum
reality — have to, essentially, be so placed in tension to the
terrific inside intimate tension that is yr business, yr special
business, that they must function as an *image* functions in
verse
          in other words, that, any apparent or logical or rational
item (like that cigarette, or, the tractor, or, in the s.s., the house
described in the opening paras), break off, break through the
texture, and destroy
                    god knows this sounds like a pisser, and i
dare say is: for example, the pony in ITS works completely. As
does, here, the electric bill. In other words, it is not a question
of the reality terms — it is a question of which ones where — in
what kind of a proposition

Which brings me to idea #2: there are two ways the real world
works in your hands
          (1) as here, the novel, when, the tensions between the
                two — *between two* (the two of BLUE, too) — is so high
                all such things as the dishes & the kids get off their

distance as the going "sounds"—the going murmuring
of, any kinds of life, cicadas, trucks off a way,
streetcars (of 3FT), [and automobiles *crossed out*] (no,
autos, for, this is #3, below)

when you are holding to the conjectural point hard—
getting it in, dramatizing it—as of two—as of two in the
intimate—EVERYTHING WORKS as it is around them

LOOK: my mind picks up on, you, on me, as you had it, when,
you read ISH, you told me later (as of maya & sumer stuff) that,
at the time of ISH, you didn't well see how I could take such a
position any further—in, or anywhere

NOW: (and I make these points because I damn well believe this
novel is now yr Johnson rod,[20] and that, you have yr hand
on, etc. etc)

I take it that yr problem is to move that high intensity of
the conjecture of each instant over a larger space than the
s.s. as space & time allows—right?

OK. Then I am led to say this: that the way to do is *more
of same*

And I arrive at it this way, by, the example of, these two
mss: that

leading question #1—can you well afford, *ever*, to shift from you

as "I," the very contest of reality, as you pose it, being, just such

particularism, just such intervalism as, you or I keep our hands on

only as they are delivered straight from ourself?

And goddamn it what's wrong with
just such? That is, why is not MR
BLUE *wholly* anybody's, as a result?

Now goddamn it I so goddamn well believe in you, that you can do anything, that, I am not prepared to deny you what you may have managed with Jake, and Ola, and she, before this p. 21, at which you start me. BUT, with what I have in hand, "she" stays intact, but, as the strongest force (and that I can say that immediately puzzles me, for, surely, Jake is, as always is yr "I," the conjecturer!); and Jake & Ola split (where they are both in it) into ½s — in order — it is as tho your power demanded by its own laws of physics, a 1 to 1 set of terminals

which gets me back to what I think is LAW #1: (or way #1)   — that you cannot investigate what you want to investigate unless you maintain AN INTIMATE — and of course this is palpably true, that, any such intensities as you take it are the proper place at which "life" is pushing — the only place — the edge of conjecture is,

> A MAN (you)
> in the midst of his
> preoccupations — which are HIS REALITY

and that the only *real* ones are   WHAT HE MAKES INTIMATE

If this seems to beat the obvious, it is because I am trying to stay inside the thick of it, to be of use: for I take it you cannot divide your kingdom, simply because you are king of it already!

And that already it declares itself as of two movements of the same RULE:

(1) so far as any other human being goes, it must be one whose intensity you respect as counter of yr own — that you cannot allow in courtiers, or even such flies as Hamlet's sword-carrier!
     (it was the other "he" of ITS
          so far it is "she," anywhere (tho the new s.s., raises
                    problems, only they are
                    "his'n's" not hers)

or   (2) all reality springs up—people, things, anything—when (as
     in 3FTS) you go by "he" alone—"I," his conjecture on
     anything brings it up in full life
               (that is, the cat, say, the snow, that biz, impeccable
               because the instant—the "I"—is king

                    the autos, likewise, the men moving, in the streets

That is, by contrast, the tractor (at least as I have the mss.) goes
about its business altogether not joined:
                    it hangs between the man (the men)
                    is neither the single man's problem (the
single intelligence's) nor is it, as the cat or the mouse, itself, alone
free

     Let me get at it another way. I have this impression about the
new s.s.—that, the man, in an exactly opposite bit of physics to
the bifurcating of Jake & Ola, comes out *more* than his problem,
and at the same time his wife (the helper!) becomes much less than
herself—becomes a sort of drudge, that suddenly both are sort of
seamy because neither are able to hold to their point

                    i would take it this way, that, in your
unsuccessful stories reality suddenly is a *nameless* something
                                                            (it is
as tho—and if this is a trope, excuse it—the sunken city's wall
starts letting the sea in because the tensions which keep it city in
the sea are lessened by whatever degree
                              now that lessening is, i
take it, you leaving off the sort of going which, is, your own
vision

          why you are to me so fine is that that vision is impeccably
          a vision of reality as it is, tragic—and the alleviation is not
          so much the beauty of the language (as it might be said to
          be in such a character as yours very truly—who cannot
          bear the going on, who had to will some extrication from
          it—as though it were ever stopable! the going on) but is

that beauty as it hews only to the going-on, that, it is not
divisible, it is not hierarchical, it bears on anyone as it
bears on you, and that your raison d'etre, is, honestly, that
you are being & instrument as one, and so, as instrument,
you have this job to do

so i call you king, and say, no king can be more king, he can only
be more of same, that is, he can only make clearer to others his
kingdom

which requires, the argument would go, that, you cannot
distribute as others can (dramatize) except by the very kingness of
yourself as instantly being & instrument
                                        you see, your "I" is
utterly new, is unmatched ((why it is another I in the Unsuccessful
Husband and the Honest Man — is the old Dostoevsky I::is as the
"he" of A Sort of Song::is, I take it, because you are sometimes led
to think the old habit of dramatization is worth a try
                                            I DON'T

BELIEVE IT IS WORTH YOUR TIME

what it comes to is, that you dispose of hierarchy. You damn well
know (and this is the reason anything you bear on holds and bears
in with its full force — "she," or "the other" in ITS, or, Mr B in MR
BLUE, or, the snow and the blood and the cat of 3 FTS) you
damn well know, and who knows or ever did know as well, that,
reality is equal to all, is, a constant not allowing any divisions,
and that qualitative differences are only instrumental, and thus,
excuse themselves only, as they are used

    that is, when you are gleeful that Mitch says, the last word,
    only with the last word, does anyone know anything that,
    you are up to!

    or that i say, snake, with tail, in its mouth

    this going on — this, what Con was so damned sure in putting,
    "Creeley's broken stump" (i loved it) — IS the vision, is the

reality, and is damn well STONE, no one, can budge it, for, it is, what truth there is, what tragic truth

Why love is so clear with you is, that you are not lonely, that you do not paddle in sadnesses. You cleave to anyone as you cleave to any thing—only, as it invokes you, as, it is also real, as it is a part of the going on which happens to move you

in this sense, i speak of your intimacies, that, these are your selections, and they are not selections in any soapy world, but, are, exactly what your attention is drawn to

thus, wherever anything ("she," so far, principally—but, for me, you make magical realities as well (if i may, for reasons of discourse, separate the non-intimate or at least the non-sexually-engaged, or the non-staked (in the sense of what is certainly our kingdom, the organic as we make it wholly actionable—and certainly the sexual participation is the root, the strongest declarant) such magical realities as Mr Blue as dwarf, or snow covering blood on snow, and then snow melting and, blood there again

((this has to be distinguished from image, to the degree that, as it is of magic power not in language but in the observed fact itself, it is closer to, say, passion, "I"—"she," than to the statement of same))

or those wondrous shadows of 3fts

where any of these things are strung straight from "I" as going person on the goings on, they live, because, that tension is reality and is what your conjecture on reality makes hold true

I guess all I am saying is, what I sd, MORE OF SAME, and that I am offering you back your own doctrine, that, your form is this content

Both the novel and the s.s. have your bizness—that is, they contain that fantastic going on about them (the broken stump). BUT, as of my first go with both of them, I miss the intensity which i think is necessary to such going-on so that it stays *named*—does not let seep in any of the water of the *nameless*

your point is such a close one, your interval is so exactly *the* interval, that, to offset that stasis that is the nameless (the way it suddenly *moves* the stasis is real crazy) ((and in moving the stasis, it stiffens the other, the great movement, which you so master in ITS and in BLUE, the *real* conjecture

((christ, rob't, you must be as burned as I am at you when you keep throwing up at me what I *have* done, as measure of what I am *not* doing!—but excuse, for, what the hell else can we do, eh?))

myself, I'd say, YOU MAKE A NOVEL AS YOU MOVE, without any other device than your own way— Creeley going on the going on, with all his speculative feelers out, is enough to make any of em sit up and take notice!

Let me dig the two mss, okay: let me make my points now straight on the particulars

[*Added in ink*: Let me shoot this ahead, but with this LAST WORD—who the hell can make *all reals* stand up (ferris wheels, rain, anything) as you do in MR B—so, why not any novel *real* by its own LAW!

Love   O

[Black Mountain, N.C.]

thurs aug 2   51   LAD—last night was YR NIGHT! wow. the thing was, i had mentioned, monday, bill's biz, of naming—out of GRAIN. But did not remember where, there. Well, started out, last night, trying to find it. Missed, but came up with one use of it, in his Poe job.[21] Which led me to state the biz myself—very different, i imagine: for bill has it tied to the naming of new things, sort of, only. And I figure it's too late for originality problems: the thing, now, is, to clear the naming function anywhere, old or new, as of cutting straight thru into the noun force, the magical of the noun as recurrence of the object.

So I was off, by way of Bill's relation to Poe (it has always seemed to me his best piece, there—that, & the Lincoln) and I hammered on abt Whitman as behind EP, and Melville behind who (not, of course, being able to say). Which then brought DHL as, by way of his STUDIES, practically an American writer! In any case, it was a demonstrandum:

1850	Whitman	Melville	Poe
1915	Pound (CANTOS)	WCW (GRAIN)	LAWRENCE (STUDIES)

And then BANG, I read em, MR BLUE! 1950!!

what a kick, like a mule, lad, you were on em! It was a joy. And the consequence was, for two hrs, back & over you, and me, getting it, and riding clear of the getters, having no more effect than that, they damn well knew they had been hit! (Perhaps the most fine thing of all was Shahn's wife—Bernarda Bryson's—rise to yr story! It was beautiful how, she pegged, the absolute explosion of it on the target—how she saw, exact, the bearing, home, from an *irregular* (the word was mine, &, gave me a dig, that, I shld have picked up, at that moment, after the story, on you as guerilla!) ((And Kalos, who has a thick thew of himself for like)). But others got, that, this did not disturb reality, instead, drove it, in

well, what it led to—what it does seem we fuck em with—is, the
phenomenal—and the methodological. Crazy, how, they lag, here:
how most cannot bear not to have the comfort of some fucking
sanction-system—that the holding, in there, is just what they can't
stand—and run to some mama of judgment. It bores the piss out
of me. I tried to lay em down, with as much of a barrage as I
could bring up, somewhat winded as I am, these days, after
putting it out all day on paper, it is not quite interesting to make
vocals. But there it is: Con, me, the new one, eat, & sleep, even
are supplied with lights, etc., from this chatter, eh?

What wld also have pleased you (if you didn't hate this place so)
was something I ran on to *before* my go—after supper, thru their
representative, the students presented me their wishes for the
staffing of the oscillating guest faculty of the coming year ((it is
my Chinese system, which I have pushed, through Shahn, so that,
next week, it will be presented to the Ford Fdtn, for possible
support here & at other colleges: that is, that, as Albers & I
worked it out for my coming here three years ago—once a month,
for five days, and living, the rest of the time, in the capital cities!

          for painters, they want De Kooning, & Shahn (to come at
          intervals during the year—a month, or, as I did, every
          month, for a few days)

          for dancers, Litz and Merce Cunningham   (likewise)

and for writers, there it was, it read: O   Creeley   Williams!   (")

'Course, they're a fucking spoiled bunch of sons & daughters of
bitch America. Grant you. But it don't frighten me, and I wld
rather—if it came to that—*as it actually is, mind us*—be kept in
food & pound by such than by—NO, that just ain't true—simply,
I am here, and, here, see no reason why I shouldn't seek to
improve the system, eh?
          that is, it is, UNREAL, and that's the end
of it. And I'm not at all sure I'd care to feed off it, even for a day,
if anyone offered me any alternative.

but i damn well am moved
that, these characters were the ones to reach down and haul up 93
bucks because they wanted me—i'm that simple, that, the
comparison to, what somebody else didn't offer, is, simply,
enough, eh?

Tohellwithit. It is not very interesting. And there it is: they won't
get you! Will they get me? And tell Mitch to forget James'
prefaces: tell him to come in here—if it works out—from exactly
where he ought himself to be writing his "novel": from shop
stewards, not mathiessen, from goodman—and fr a goodman who
finds out how also to read ITS, and BLUE, as well as 3 FTS—as
wellaswellaswell, NOTES FOR A PROSE   notes
                                        for

                                              a

                                                 prose

(what i did get off, was a ripping attack on, the fictive: going on
abt *the order of reality*
            (it struck me, reading BLUE, how, our argument on
            document—which you do read record, and thereby miss
            my topside meaning, anyway—is a little silly, in that, all
            that i put out in the word is, as phenomenon, what, is
            the usable given—the taken

that i, no more than you, think, that, thereafter, it isn't all
hoomin, all art, all, the keeping of it in—and that document is
only the order—the order of the content, from which, by this
addition herein called your conjecture, the other order, which we
dub form, is made

that the 1st act here—as the 1st act, there, is, surely, to get the
senses clear—is to obey, not, by fiction, to superimpose

    H O W, otherwise, do you manage—except by obedience—to
    do that which you damn well do do: to illuminate, *without*
    removal, *without* arrogating, *without* disturbance

christ, it's beautiful, in that thing, how, it moves off, and, ended, what moves on, is, that close!

[Fontrousse, Aix-en-Provence]
August 3/ 51

Dear Chas/
        Yrs in yesterday noon, & had got me out of a
goddamn slump; the thing being — we had word from Mr. Leach
that the houses noted were not, very sadly, available. Hence, we
start all over again — Hughes having never answered my final letter
on that house in Usk. Which is a mess but one hard to sit on.
Ok.
        Have just done something which may turn out very damn
foolish. To wit/ sent off a small group of poems (13) to our lad
Emerson, as a suggested chapbook. I expect it's pretty damn
hopeful — but the wt/ of such things gets to be a bug, & want,
anyhow, while I have such a bunch cd go as, unit — to try to get
them out of here. (As it does go, I toss out as many as I can ever
damn well write, in a yr : hence get very fast, nowhere.) For the
record: contents & order of same, as follows :

Still Life Or; Hart Crane (1); Le Fou; Love (1); Littleton, N.H.;
Helas; Hart Crane (2); Division; The Epic Expands; Guido;
Canzone; Love (2); The Sea

I figure you know all, of same, but for DIVISION &, is it, STILL
LIFE OR. The former : what I'd taken that line out of, "attentions
(something) cajoled by their purport or what they purport/ to
attend (something something) . . ." And still life or: an old one,
worked over, etc. CANZONE: ". . . is not even love lacking/ a
purpose or an object for/ its love . . ."

Wd be cool to have these
several off of me, but no matter; i.e., one way or the other.

All a damn boredom.

Did not damn well mean to take a by on Gerhardt poem; i.e.,
that one hit home. Not a damn kick on same. That whole string
(but for specific parts I'd noted, I figure) sat very damn cool.
(Melville poem/ same way, tho do not feel it as hard as those just
before it — C/s poem, the same, but for a matter of the intensity,
which I don't take as the bulk it is in CONCERNING
EXaggeration, et al.)

Looking back at the copies (& I have not the
DICONTINUOUS PARTS one, here[22]) : I wd feel them in this
order —

CONCERNING EXAGGERATION; GERHARDT;
DISCONTINUOUS PARTS (and a space here): MELVILLE;
APPLAUSE.

Feel you most on, in 1st. And in 2nd. But 3rd, for
my loot, cd very easily place up with 1st, with a little rework, etc.
It has the fucking THINGS, like they say! (G/ poem has the
problem of sitting against another specific intelligence, & tho its
main hits are certainly free of same — there's my own difficulty of
knowing of it, & so. Anyhow, see that I see, as well, it does not
matter.)

But I wanted to say: you'll know I have some certain
damn sounds in my ears, & to put some, of them,
here . . .

". . . He can take no risk that matters/ the risk of beauty
least of all . . ." "Where space is born man has a beach to ground
on . . ." "you who in yr thin shallops think to make the
land . . ." "You, do not you speak who know not . . ." ". . . He
put the body there as well as they did whom he killed"
"despite
New England is
despite her merchants and her morals . . ."[23]

And you can see it. I mean, see what I have here, sitting. I do take it as a matter of intensity, of the completeness & force, the straight force, of these other 'indictments . . .' And they are damn hard to beat. Ok.

Fatuous to put it so : but here it is. These several poems must come to form a 'level' for me. I do not judge against them, say, or even compare. But I remember. I mean, I have that sense, clear, of you, on. And very damn hard, on. Hence I figure that's it. And with those, & the others, I'd put in, surely, the 1st three noted earlier. These seem to me, of that same body. And certainly the rest of them too, but also of something else, a wider thing, or sweeping, perhaps, than these with their specific *singleness & intensity*. Ok.

In any event, it's yrself. I.e., the only one I cd think of, as putting a better poem to paper than, say, KINGFISHERS, wd be, precisely, yrself.

(There are some very damn wonder-ful things in CONCERNING; it is one, an item, that declares itself as a growth, i.e., the act of going over & over same makes it this. It is a damn beautiful one.) [*Added in pencil*: more I read this one, better & better. Figure it as *real* best of these last ones.]

Yrs just in [*added*: 12:00] so want another damn page:

Damn well excited! THE LAWS/ figure a straighter, much harder way of heading it. Ok!

I was damn well thinking/ reading thru this: wd this be too wild/

the blockings, even as you do it here, in this letter, literally offset against a 'personal' narrative (to mean, the simple evidences, a 'story,' or the uses of the details (as the moon/sun was), being the running off:

and the literal crystallization, THERE, ON THE PAGE.

As, to be precise: the
very fine sweet slope of, the narrative, the personal declarations: &
as these come to place, laws, then, just so : the laws, as they so
come/

     put there/ juxtapoised!

           Well, an idea. Ok.

As like this :   ". . . and as it was, the sounds came first, the
                     first of them huge, against me, the night much
                     more than a darkness, and looking, I could
                     not. The feeling was, as I felt it, and I did, the
"The law is: precision of an immense thing, immaculate
 prime, that they   against, & in, the night . . ."
 the force, exist . . ."

           Etc., etc. But you see the idea. Ok.

GOOFY little poem/ there : page 1. Both Ann & yr lad, much,
much lifted by same. Phew. (I cd never so much as
WHIMPER!)
        WOW.

Well, it is all so very fine.

           (And note this : yr instants proclaim,
and don't they?, that there is *never* one point on which a man can
rest, never a thing, so done, it defines himself? Because the
continuum, good god, the continuum — that we are not, never so,
the position even if fine, even if literally 'done' . . . because then,
the painting — does it know us?

Well, goofy. It always WAS!

"he dies   as the instant dies, as I die for an instant
listening   to error . . ."[24]

Again : WOW!

Anyhow, my fucking hand.

(Cid writes/ boy in nyc, a smith,[25] I'd put him on to, has come
thru with some prose, likewise. And that lifts the lid off, a little.
Smith : can write a damn fine prose, now & again. It is so
wonderfully crumbling! Phew. Anyhow, that was good news.

                                                                           If
we cd push him to one or two others, wd make his job a good
deal easier. Still thinking of Duncan, & thot he should be in here
too?)

      Ok. To get this off/ & soon again. Real joy.

All our love to you both/
                    Bob

[*At top, in pencil*: Later/ to wit: ½ hr.]
                                        August 3/ 51

Dear Chas/
              Cannot go, let go, of this one easily. I.e., having my
belly full (of food!), can sit down to it.
                              Very crazy that I was
reading that EXAGGERATION when, as it was, yr letter came in
thru the door : a hand!

Because/ of the piece delights me:

"how shall you find it, if you're not, in like degree allowable, are
not as it is
               at least in preparation for, an equal act?"[26]

(Which answers the biz abt: who has the right, of discourse?
Sure.)

What it is/ to see, that as you do say so damn exactly : the
universe of discourse *intermits* the content . . .

which is also why,
say, the Dr., not knowing but I believe feeling, the same, never
used quotation marks, in his prose? Well, it is of that piece.

(And
again, why Ez (& on no easy plane, say) is to my thinking, the
lesser man — granted the superficialities of these citings. But
anyhow : that Williams must have had the *feel*, of the damn
LAW — & myself, as younger, likewise : cd never feel easy using a
quotation mark, but as, very exactly, a joke!)

Put it then: that we
have forgotten just what the hell an *occasion* is! Or we have sliced
it five ways to Sunday, making use if such is use, of only that
most docile face.

(Or: turn yr face to the light. Or: this one is for
Mother!)

(Is it again, why I likewise revere Williams — that his
'authority' has never been more, nor less, than his *presence*? The
present of him, each time?)

(That there is no building, of him, as
an acquisition, a collection, a series of — dicta (which maintains
ipse dixit[27] / HAW.)

(Forgetting, forgetting that the truth IS : that is all one can say,
just so, IPSE DIXIT!)

(He did *not* forget it.)

Jesus/ that *all* he thot! " — and did you ever know of a sixty year
woman with child . ?"[28]

Well, again & again & again/ the doing, to know that much of it,
the doing, as : (the boy courier/ likewise : scout (old scout/old
sock/old sport . . .))

to have the hand on/ to have the hand in readiness as :

HERE

IT

COMES!

Phew!

      (what else?
           What the fuck else?)

Method. Just so. NO one instance, no cumulation of instance/
having a damn claim on/ the presence, the necessities, precise : of
the above.

You goof me all thru here/ the notes, the linings up (as jesus look
how you weave it, just so, faced with/ an occasion!)
                                          Jesus/ we
who have perhaps nothing to lose!
                      Wrap it up.
                            (The thing is/ you
can NOT go wrong, not so faced, not so facing it. Cannot damn
well miss, or miss more, or anything more, than what, bless us
all!, NEVER WAS.)
                  Is that a fucking guarantee or isn't it! Phew!
                          Ok/ all love to you both/
                                      Bob

                                  [Fontrousse, Aix-en-Provence]
                                        August 4, 1951

Dear Chas/
      Thinking more of it — this whole biz of Recitalists
gives me the willies. Because a) certainly the whole corpus of
poetry, of all written matter is open to use, as far back as one can
come to reach, & it's free, altogether so; and b) certainly, nothing
is of much matter more than the joining of a substance, the

deposit, with what comes to hand—& in either case, a man has an altogether free hand.

But the ones who, like those you note, make it a playing, a fingering of what is then, the corpse, what an ugly biz!

For one thing (as Ann sd): I cannot see *why* they write, because isn't it all, such a way of it, impossible effort?

(And it must be, incredible : weird fix of pride, of uselessness, of sheer dumb will—that brings them to such a damn sorry occupation.)

Well, when I do feel safe (as I do not faced with such as Berryman, etc.) is precisely when I find myself confronting a man who is, in the basic sense, distinct. Who can envy him? Or who the hell can feel, he tramples my flowers, etc. Because he is, very simply, *what he is*—& does not that leave all room possible for me?

One is in certain danger, with the others—who the fuck knows who they'll next bite (& the only hope . . . one's anti-poetic nature, as they wd have it, will save one from such uses.

Tho it clearly does not; as witness, Pound, Williams, etc. (And how, say, that Englishman in the issue of POETRY:NY had yr PRO/VERSE *did* that indescribable thing to the squirrel on some very damn odd assumption of Williams' method!)[29]

The wonder to me is, that, say, I can take yr premises, can learn so precisely from you, and just because I do, just because of it, I am able to make a verse which remains distinctly my own.

What else?
And what else, worth the time of writing or of reading?

They don't see : the 'tradition' preserves itself; the highest examples. Pound's verse, or Williams, or any of like men, needs no damn buttressing of imitation. It's the 1st example; the last—in each case peculiar to the intelligence, the body, involved in the expression.

What else?

Anyhow—damn glad to be away from such, from all that damn stench.

Wd you give me a word on this one?

A SONG[30]

I had wanted a quiet testament
and I had wanted, among other things,
a song.
            That was to be
of a like monotony.
                        (A grace

Simply. Very very quiet.
                        A murmur of some lost
thrush, though I have never seen one.

Which was you, then. Sitting
and so, at peace, so very much, now, this same quiet.

A song.

And of you, the sign now, surely, of a gross
perpetuity
                (which is not reluctant, or if it is,
it is no longer important.

A song.

Which one sings, if he sings it,
with care.

                        Not much else, these days. All
dried out—and frankly, sit back anyhow, for the moment. They're

starting to grind the wheat on the rise back of the house; whole place rumbles. Horse, on a rope, which is fastened to a stake in the center, and he drags round a stone-roller.

All the kids up there; very fine.

Anyhow, a sign, eh? Write soon.

All our love to you both/

Bob

[Fontrousse, Aix-en-Provence]
August 6/ 51

Dear Chas/

Hung for loot, just now, so will package these up & get them all off, together, when we have some. (Still bills from our arrival, & some owed to Mitch, had had to clear up this past 31 days, etc. Anyhow, straight in abt 5 days, so no matter.)

Goofy poem: & like it very much (to wit: the ROUND & CANON.) Wd be damn cool indeed, to sit same into M/ Bronk, to tickle his nose, eh? Sure. (Fucking ass-hole's words had also been sent here, by Cid, & put in a half/hr answering same, via C/.)

Anyhow: fuck them/ fuck them. It damn well does NOT matter. Ok.

Names/ you got me, & Ann promises a dissertation on same, anyhow — so. But jesus, friend, YOU have it soft; I mean, try it with C R E E L E Y, if you want a pleasant 8 hrs, etc.

Whole damn family screwed by that one: viz, my father. . . . "Oscar (!)," myself "Bobby (!)" & my sister : "Helen . . ."

It was never 'very

good.' (by how far fractured my fate (?) — whoooooooooooooooooo/
can say.)

Anyhow, Olson : shit/ that aint bad at/ all. Wilhelmenia, all
kinds of names, real COOL. (Haw . . .) (But it is anyhow, easier,
you will damn well admit, than, sd : creeley/ (ann always sd, it
had a most horrid wriggly feel! Agh . . . or, anyhow, hardly
pleasant?)

John Olson/ Thomas Olson/ Edward Olson/ Jesse Olson/ William
Olson/ James Olson/ Theodore Olson/ Franklin Olson/ Abraham
Olson (THERE'S ONE)/ George Olson/ Charles Olson (WHEE)/
David Olson/ Richard Olson/ . . . .

myself, it's that ABE/ is

GOOFY : Abe P. Olson

/ P for Plenty-Good-Pickings!

Hey/

ABE: man, get a move on: it's supp- er - TIME . . .

(a: wholesome olson!

Abe Olson/ too much!

(sounds: honest!

(Got sounds, eh? Phew!

(but . . . c r e e l e y . . . . a sneaky damn sound there . . . .)

As for a girl, that's somewhat off my beat, but/ Mary Olson/
Eleanor Olson/ Charlotte Olson (& then there was the
one . . .)

Joan Olson/ ah)

I am not good at this end of it, so will

quit.

The thing: to get one with a decent nickname, something to/
SHOUT.

(As, viz above, ABE.

The thing.

Had been reading Sterne on this same head,[31] when yrs flew in, & damned hard to get straight, here.

So,/ we will go at this soon again. Ok.

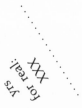

[*By Ann Creeley, verso, in pencil:*]

It's also wise to have a different middle name altogether. Viz: David MacKinnon Creeley. If he is moony he can be David, cheerful: Dave. Very large: Mac. Also all of these go well with Creeley if we can just stay off Davey. You have an easier last name by any standard. Nicknames ending with eeee go *very* well with it. by all means give him two. I like Abe myself. Give him a good long one. The nickname will come by itself after you have grown tired of calling him by his full name. All little babies are called by their full names because there is no nickname in god's world that fits a very young baby. Bob's sister called hers Alexander until he was several months old. Then when he has developed some character you can pick the one in the string you like best.

   one more thing:

It is important to have names in the family that sound completely different (the main vowel, of course) when shouted so that the right person will come. You and Con are just enough different to make it (do people shout Charles at you?) *But* if you add something like Laura to it you are lost (consider this point when naming dogs too). (Thomas was a bad bet in this respect though I counted on calling him Tombo which luckily fits) Also avoid anything that you would feel ridiculous shouting in a crowded street, example: "Kitty." And think how he or she would feel *having* to answer to it. Also if you pick two, one queer, one ordinary put the queer one second so it can be reduced to an initial in case of a conservative afterlife.

[Black Mountain, N.C.]
tues aug whatever
[7 August 1951]

my dear lad, you must, please, excuse, my falling off so badly.
but it is five days i have not been at this desk. one thing was, i
needed to kick it around. on top of that i was asked to read the
verse friday night, and it took a little time to shape up the
translation of gerhardt's poem, his letter to you & me, so that i
could preface it to my answer (which didn't go over at all! as i
take it, it didn't with you — which puzzles me, for, i am still
stubborn about it, and think it an advance). And then two days
was lost saying goodbye to the Shahns, the 5 of em — instead of
Shahn who is here now but Motherwell!

and then, like fool, last night, i got going, and couldn't stop for
five hrs! which was more than my beaten system allows! (at least,
after playing first base,. and pitching an evening, of a ball game
sunday — the first time i had played ball in — what? — fifteen years,
maybe! certainly the 1st time i had used sd body in about ten! so
yesterday & today i am just abt able to walk. Very good feeling,
tho, to be shook, up

the five hr gab had several occasions, but the principal push was
out fr the verse i sent you last, the Round & Canon, which, to my
great delight, I heard from Cid yesterday he likes and will plunk
right down there in #3 right square between the eyes of Bronk &
Morse — which sets me up, boy, that, that is there, to remind at
least that piss pot bronk to comeoffit

    also, a very moving piece by Goodman, in Kenyon, on,
    avant-garde as of now, quoting, an extraordinary remark of

Goethe's, that, "occasional verse is highest verse"[32] — coming
on me at this time it has set a lot of things in motion

                                                        as well
as Goodman's own notion of what an environment of friends
means to a poet now

no word out of Kirgo on the Melville gig, so, the weeks are
getting close, and i begin to fear i have lost the chance — for such
polemic rather serves in time, or, it better be unpolemical, perhaps

i really had a dizzy angry moment at you in the midst of the final
push on the gerhardt translation (with jalowitz), simply because
she wasn't sure how that last passage abt me should be taken — or
rather, why i started to spit to myself was, that, apparently, i
mistook the passage, and gerhardt, it now appears, in the switch
at the point of the verb GEREDET, is talking about himself, as of
his letter to us, as talking too much, trifles & all that, good for
montage — and not abt me! So, the provocation for my answer, is
somewhat stripped away! But for a moment I felt so lost without
the help of *your* translation at that point: the funny thing is, that,
Shahn, for example, took the poem as altogether too "nice," too
much an act in kind, a trade-last! My God, and me thinking i was
really beating poor Gerhardt, but hard!

Reading it, however, 1st time since Lerma, here, out loud, it seems
to me that my answer is formal, and I hope any misunderstanding
of my own has not brought him to any grief!

GOD DAMN IT — it's worse than I thought, this gap — I now find
my letter to you Thursday last sitting here, UNMAILED! Christ. I
put it in, shamefaced, and crawl away. Forgive, lad

                                            love to you both

                                                        C

[Fontrousse, Aix-en-Provence]
August 8/ 51

Dear Chas/

Yrs in on the piece from the novel, & the short story. And many damn thanks. I do figure you very right, on the short story. That is, I'd put it as a straight question: wd you figure me wrong to let it out? I.e., Cid has it, tho no word on same from him; myself, it neither stirs me nor very much annoys me. I mean, very frankly, I did it — & can't see that more cd be done, on it, & now the problem of whether or not to let it out — or to stamp on it, etc. It wd be real help, then, if you'd say (& for christ sake, don't be reluctant) whether you figure it will do more damage, than good, say, to have him use it.

The thing there — (& I put this in the content, the context, of yr notes here on *intensity*) that, finally, like they say, I cd not very much believe in, and that is the word, the reality of this discomfort. And it is, as you say, slack–off.

The one here enclosed — I don't know. I believe that the furniture should stand kicking, even in the 'dramatic' frame — & wd it not be, at that, a gain of sorts, to intrude there, to smash a little of it up. Anyhow, in this story to hand, THE PARTY, the hope is that, there'll be a kind of double action (not ironic, tho there is also that, but lower), that is, that it will be a fix wherein certain insistencies are surely drowned out, but this does not mitigate, say, their existence — they continue, tho under. And giving that flat last word, even so obvious, to the woman . . . an intention, & a hope, also, it will mark the disparities in a more than obvious sense.

Really, I hope the one now sent has a scream, somewhere back, in, way in, it. But you say: it may be that the obvious grotesqueries of the fix crowd out the other noises. Tell me, anyhow, when you can get to it.

The novel is a double headache: 1) I've never written this length, & it gets to take a new feel, a somewhat new handling. That to be: base technics, etc. I mean, there are new aspects to coherence, given a longer length. Ok. 2)

Can't see what's up till I'm done. OK.

The difficulty involved in yr own reading comes certainly from several things, or a few : a) that one of the biggest figures is, there, only in shadow, and not at all actually; or, to wit, Kenneth. He has the chapter just before this one, & stands there fairly strong. b) that the composite lean of all of these (people) *things* is not to be evidenced in one point. I mean, what Ann had delighted in, the subsequent *position* of all details, can't come clear in one chapter. In fact, all you cd dig there, given the limits of a part, from a whole, is the fix between Jake & his wife, at the end, & had I been cool — wd have detached same for you, & let it go at that.

Because, mark you, I believe altogether in displacement. I believe, say, that five people in a room depend on each other, and tho Joe can lift 150 lbs without batting an eye, in sd room, maybe it's not expected, or maybe they won't even look. Hence, a man flickers, dies down, then flares, then : at least some possibility of thinking about such a gig as this, i.e., writing a novel.

In any event, at this stage, I take it two immediate jobs: 1) to finish, & hope that I can; 2) to get as clean a hold on the problem as of *how*, as I can. It took me 5 yrs to write a short story that I was, certainly, proud of having written, & I can date it, can even damn well remember, now, the conversation, & all the subsequent jockeying, that got me to BLUE or any of those. It was, simply enough, a journal I'd kept 5 yrs back, & then reading it, 3 yrs back: my supposition — is the 'reality' put there, the things then noted, an apposite, or opposite, or what, to the then going-reality I was in on? It continues the base problem, or what motivates any of these things? How attack, reality.

In any event: time, jesus, it does take time, & now faced with a new mode, call it, I don't see any short-cuts to the learning of same.

Well, I tell you: this novel, slack or no slack, will continue the damn base premise of, form is the extension of content, & what's more, will be, again, a broken stump.[33] What the hell else cd I write.

Give me a little room, anyhow, i.e., hold
on, & will hope to show you how even the slacker, the so-seeming
slacker, parts, have, again, their place, & their place by virtue of,
the attentions, mine. Ok. (They are also *there*, I expect, but ok, I
notice them *too*.)

Because, again, this novel is not between, oddly,
the wife & husband, & that you will begin to see soon, or as soon
as I can put the whle thing in yr hand. (Only wait, dear
reader . . . !) There's something real crazy coming out of this hat,
& that, for certain.

In fact, the now slack details, or what seem
so, will be, in fact, that passage, that slough, where the damn
boat slops, then, mark you, plunges again, & is a new fucking
direction.

How can I put it/ well : like a sail slaps, loose, then
bellies again, with NEW wind. What I am trying to do here.

The thing/ that 'she' stays, yes she does stay, intact, but will not,
again, when Jake (also her rod), has himself been hit full. (Tho
this is no prize–fight — what I mean, she feels her dangers thru him,
& must wait till he has them fully, has them eating, etc.) At this
pt/ she is the rock. And him, wader. But things are moving, eh/
ok.

Well, I damn well don't know. All you say, here, hits with a
damn certain persistence. And yr right. If I figured the whole were
to be of the same cloth — wd lay it down now, to sleep. But I can't
see it, yet, as open to this same loss. Well, will keep on it, & see.

Wd you note me one thing: does the style drag unbearably? I.e.,
seems crazy thing to ask, but I have a very real fear, I'll lay my
reader to sleep — & wish to god I cd get it out of my head for
good & all.

Idon'tknow — what I fucking well need is to get out/ for a bit, to
take a walk. And don't get the chance, at the moment. All quiet,
etc. But anyhow/ let's wait & see.

All love/ and all my thanks
for these notes/ damn well fine. Take care of yrselves/

Bob

Black Mt College
Black Mt, North Carolina
August 8, 1951

My dear Louis Martz:

(And if I have yr name wrong, forgive me: I came to know
you only last night).

When I was still in the Yucatan Rolf had
pointered yr piece on Bill.[34] And last night I caught up with it.

This is to tell you what you already know, what a fine thing
it is. I need not elaborate that fact. But there are some things
which I wanted to single out which seem to me so forward you
yrself need to forward them.

And I imagine you also know what a
paradox you have on your hands: that, by doing the finest
exegesis of Bill, by stating his case so highly, you have, at the
same time, made more clear the crazy limits (I do not mean in
those idiots' sense of no culmination, or even Stevens' excellent biz
of fidgeting with new points of view and this danger[35]), but those
limits which can only be seen when one, with such love, has
understood Bill's size: the tremendous error of such a classification
as he has been led to, of such a tri-via as Paterson as a city, a
man, and a poet — how, in fact, the illusion that language has the
kind of importance he gives it is, actually, a shade off the
necessary truth now

that GRAIN must have been Bill's crisis, that
what he there says of Boone, is Bill's own real truth that Bill
himself has, somehow, not known what to do with—or has
(better) permitted to stay too "local" for his own good, perhaps. (I
should like to think about this more, but there remains some direct
connection between the "local" and a certain "exterior" use of
language, in all but GRAIN, which is the heart of this painful
thing, Bill's limit.) In any case, what I am referring to is, what he
attributes to Boone, the understanding that the problem as of an
American (as of America) is, by contrast to Ez and TS, to stay at
it H E R E, simply because the B T [added: "Beautiful Thing"][36]
lies, not in politics or in materialisms, but in the moral and
aesthetic problem *as anywhere* (that Europe won't help, despite,
her obvious advantages—then, 1925, & Valery Larbaud)[37]

What bears in right here—and what has so deeply added to
myself—is yr phrase, the permanent Pelasgian.[38] This is a very
great & forward principle you have announced. So far as I know,
it is your own. [*Added in margin for Creeley*: You will guess how
all this is ruined by discovering that all Martz was using was some
damned British monk's argument for free will versus Original Sin!]
And what I am wondering—from the way you left it, in a
phrase—what further thoughts you have on the matter. For I take
it this is the beginning of something most important. In this
way . . . but, 1st, let me just say, you pose here a proposition
which ought, finally, to undo, that false polarity, the Apollo
Dionys business.[39] [*To Creeley*: What Martz sd, was, c. "Williams
too Pelagian—a permanent class—to be taken in by the doctrine of
O.S."]

In this way: that the Pelasgian is not a time archetype but a
permanent and present dweller in any one—specifically, as of our
present context, Bill, the question is, isn't his—wasn't his "crise," in
GRAIN—how, to join himself as poet to himself as Pelasgian. For
I take it it is just that any of us as men are Pelasgian which (1)
makes a city, whatever its dirtiness, a vehicle; (2) makes a man,
whatever his distractions, a force; and (3) causes a poet to undo
himself as poet, and thus undo all three of these "separations."

It is, isn't it, as you have phrased it, a superior way to get at, now, the base of archaism as the root from which a total creation is made possible? Well. I hope I am not rushing you. If I am, I don't think it will matter. For you are more true than any critic I know writing today, just by the perceptiveness that led you so to phrase the other going positionalism to—what is, in fact, the contrary? [*Added in margin*: alas! he ain't this good!]

My own thought would lead me to say, the Judeo-Christian. But this is no longer very important (in this sense, that, that sanction-system— that hyphenate—is already undone, however much we are surrounded by a flock of mud-heads (hens, cocks, & chasubles, all of em—WRONG)

(((that is, I am fed up with this phoney correction, how shall I call it—Neo-Classicism: RWBLewis[40] seems the most alert of em, in that he sees, though he doesn't say (and this is reprehensible) that all these suddenly sharp & wise characters who are returning us to first Western critical distinctions by going clear to Aristotle's RHETOR or Plato's PHEADRUS, are actually using a hidden or overt sanction-system which neither Aristotle nor Plato knew anything about: the Christian one. So that Lewis is quite right in making it quite clear that they all have to end up in DANTE, or they are illicit. For what EZ did forty years ago—start with Dante—is the only legitimate act, so far as writing or the critique of literature goes, if you are going to back-trail to [*added*: Xtian] classicism. How clean the old man was, to back himself up to a wall, Rimini,[41] say, and say so, in so many words, this is as far as I have time to take the investigation. I rest here. (And by god these others, with all their word-nicenesses, can't budge the fact that the single Christian poet is DANTE, the single place where, aesthetic distinctions *and* the moral ones coincide organically)

In other words, if any of us are going to feel our way back along the path we are going to have to determine what, actually, was the sanction-system *behind* Socrates, A and P. And I imagine you are already aware how much truer you are in putting it, Pelasgian, than any of these overwise gentlemen are. For the poser of the whole business is, not their Dante, but S & A & P's "POET," HOMER.

(I have no way of knowing—do not even yet know your piece on Stevens[42] —I will, however—but it would be a public service, if you are knowing of Homer, to turn yr equipment on to a third part of this critical trilogy, by writing a piece on HOMER. [*Added in margin*: ho-ho!] For it is the absence of any such examination in the whole present field of writing which makes it look as though there is something in all this Neo-Eliotism (which is a little bit, also, Neo-Poundism, to the degree that Ezra spread, without his usual axe-brightness, the Cavalcanti-Dante "falseness"—I say this gingerly, knowing, that this needs extrapolation—that Ezra has never been fool enough to take himself as "Christian." ((In a piece on him, about his conversation, I quoted a thing you would enjoy, given your very clear understanding of how the Pelasgian is the contrary of, the doctrine of, Original Sin: sd the Fox, to the Possum, "It ain't that, Bro. It's o-riginal, in-nate stu-pidity!"))[43]

What yr careful distinction leads to is right into the heart of creation now—in fact, right under Bill, for, despite GRAIN, Bill has somehow been unable to unshoulder the Original Sin Boys, at least has, perhaps felt the polemic too strongly, and thus, except in GRAIN (in GRAIN probably because he is directly "historical"—was there documentary—and needed, forever, to be a documentarian in a larger space than Paterson, or even America, allows!), Bill has not got down to the base from which Homer composed

(I so regret, now, that, I stopped doing, three years ago, an examination of Melville in the context of Homer. For Melville, in his blundering way (in such other things as the Encantadas, as well as Moby-Dick) was facing out the very things that Bill needed to face out more than he has—was already *under* the American thing, however he knew, as Bill has known, that just here is a full PELASGIAN situation—even geographically. (Excuse me, if I quote Call Me Ishmael, one sentence, that, "we are the last first people."[44]

That is, the proposition you have made as of intellectual history, is the stubborn reality any creative man is confronted by right now. I go with Bill, of course, and with Boone, that this geography, this people, and these poets are granted—are blessed—with the open situation of, the Pelasgian and the "Classic" as a simultaneous possibility—that here, and only here, by the bearing of, the Beautiful Thing, as, locked in, the fact, the *American* fact—can such content as Homer had his hand to, be moved toward such form as we will make, however different it necessarily shall be from Homer (Ezra's error, which Bill saw, was, to make Canto 1 thus literary!)

What I do not see anyone saying, is, how absolutely "pelasgian" THE ODYSSEY is—and mark you, the O (and the Iliad), remain, however much the O S Boys may talk of Shakespeare or Dante, the Odyssey remains what the Alexandrians (& Pisistratus)[45] damn well fixed it as—the TEXT of CLASSICISM, the rote on which A & P as well as Cicero & Caesar were educated in logic, rhetoric and syntax.
I have interested myself enough to be able to say this, at the same time that I acknowledge my ignorance (the incompleteness of my study: Odysseus is the BEARSON[46] at the same time that he is the CUNNING HERO of a sea epic. And one could make a guess from these facts of the actual text of the poem, as well as of its morphology: that a good reason for its power in its own time and continuously since, is the fact that it is a tremendous wedding of the base archaic (or pelasgian) myth of Europe, the BEARMAN (Beowulf) story and the base archaic myth of the Tigris-Euphrates Valley, the KUR-GILGAMESH-HERAKLES tale.
((I am at the moment trying to get back from transposing the Sumerian poems to find the time to run down the backward of the BEAR business—and I offer you this guess, that, it was the Danube Valley that was its original home

though in saying this I am flying a little in the face of the very sources of my own enthusiasm in your Pelasgian discriminant. For do you know Pausanias' chapter on Arcadia,[47] with its fantastic revelations about MT LYCAON, both as literally the Pelasgian "birthplace" as well as the source place of the wolf-bear antagonism man found, then, so important to his problems? the crazy thing is, that, as I remember it, Pausanias marshals some evidences (which other ancient sources like Herodotus reinforce) that Odysseus, or, rather, his father & grandfather (the compression of his geneology is the usual mythic one — like Abraham, Isaac, Jacob) come from this very region! And you will remember that wonderful clue, about, Odysseus having to screw his oar in the earth in order to declare the place where planting may begin[48] — it is a spot north north west of Arcadia

The coming precisions in all this business will be important. But even now I think we can read the lesson — that you are *absolutely* correct in the recognition that "PELASGIAN" *is* a <u>sanction-source</u>

(that the contrary is, as you have put it, to, Original Sin

And that exactly in the seizing of the Pelasgian as we are Pelasgians — the Americans only more so than others that, from Eric the Red to the Pilgrims, a migration took place of such dimension — and to a New Found Land — that it is fair to call it the FIRST important such CHANGE since the Pelasgians found ARKADIA!

that if they were neo-lithic, if they did not, then, do what the Caucasians did at Uruk, all one is saying is, that, so far as you or I or Bill is possessed of a culture which has textural & recognizable identity, it does not go back to Athens — to Aristotle & Plato — it goes back to and through HOMER, it goes back to the Bearson, it goes back to where Pausanias, almost alone of all the historians has located it, there, in those protective mountains of the Peloponnesus

this seems to me a *crucial*
formulation—that is, no matter how much I may learn from
Sumerian cuneiform poems or from Mayan hieroglyphic passages,
such need transpositions of texture and/or nouns. And why? why
is this true, when it is not true, that the appetites of the Three
Founding Heroes in Pausanias' opening chapters need no such
transposition at all—seem precisely our meat?[49] I take it the answer
is obvious: that the cultural continuity does *not* extend, so far as
the *recognition* function asserts itself, to include the Asiatic
(whether that is Sumeria or whatever the Maya were)

I still would work with that
concept I posed of Sumeria as the Gate and the Center [*added*:
and, as of (here?), the splitting of East & West]. In other words, I
would not dare confuse PLACE— however long its arm, reaching,
as I take it, the Pelasgian arm has reached straight down to
Boone, to Bill, all the way over the Pacific to meet the Trobriand[50]
—with M A N, I would still hold to my notion there, that, so far
as the invention of a CITY goes, which means CIVILIZATION,
the Sumerians did it, not the Pelasgians—and that we must deal
with this controlling fact—that not one of us now, 1951, even Bill,
can ignore this huge ORIGIN of the ways of our daily life

(((that
PATERSON ultimately comes out thin and quaint because just
such NON-ARCHAIC facts—documentation—has not been
allowed in to Bill's own process in imagining this thing, this
river, this place

—he, in fact, has not even
allowed in, that wondrous rear—short rear—he himself was
the proud lad of accomplishment about, in GRAIN::that
GRAIN, seen this way, may be the clue to why Bill, with
GRAIN, did not take the step which GRAIN itself leads to—
led to, and not letting himself be led by his own book, Bill,
there, was in more of a crisis than the Pere Rasles piece says
anything about

((((aside: you show, again, your pertinence, in not only
bringing the attention as of Bill to G but also in
focusing the attention on the P R piece as the center)))
[*Added in margin*: This still holds! But, at this date, it
ain't so much, merely, an improvement on Koch][51]

It comes to this: that Sumeria (and the Maya) teaches us about
civilization — in other words, are the sources, now, of what is
actually culture — that after the ICE, there was CITY — and with
CITY man as interesting creature began, in the same sense that he
remains interesting now — as daily life character, fit for the Doctor's
attention!
     and that a poet, now, must be as full a culture-morphologist
as any professional, simply because the dimension of his job *is*
the restoration of culture — in the exact sense of, how daily life
is informed (as it is a collective phenomenon, & only such)

what Bill did in GRAIN was to show the sense at least to
examine the little American rear
                            but where i would question
him, even here, is that, he was not supremely careful to
extricate the *archaic* as place from place as *culture*

i will come back to that in a moment, but permit me to toss
in an important apposite, Ezra's KULCH: what K is, is an
accurate attempt to disclose the energies implicit in culture,
however much the morphology is not taken back any further
than, approximately, Athens — and actually obeys Ez's own
decision about his backwall as Rimini

         but the point is also, that, conspicuously, Ez, unlike
Bill, and despite all the throwing around of American
reference (as usual, limited to, the period of, the Republic),
does not interest himself at all in *place* as force
                            ((this has been
Ez's chief omission, and is why, he had to put it, once,
something like, "The making of how many poems equals a
home" (*Personae*, somewhere)[52]

You will already have sensed what I am getting at: that the job, now, is to avoid either of these errors (and they are hugely the errors all over the place). Let me try to get it down in a proposition:

> culture as force cannot be extricated from man as permanently also archaic, but, that it cannot be extricated is no reason why we cannot be quite clear that, by the damndest paradox of them all, the *archaic* is best got at *in space* by way of the problem *of place* and that *culture* is actually a collective and time continuum which breaks out of the narrows of place and the narrows of the organism of personality (as the archaic, exactly determined by place, confines and declares it)

Now let me take it back over what we have been going along with:

> you are wholly correct that, the Pelasgian, & exactly geographically as of Arkadia, is an American's "home," his original departing point —

> that no matter how much the Maya may be an hemispheric predecessor, his family or tribal — and thus recognizable likenesses — are there, are Pelasgian

thus, I wld say, our implicit "cannibalism" is properly documented by Pausanias (see Chapter I of the Description of Greece);[53] why the Cyclops passage of the Odyssey is so powerful in its effects on us; why Ahab is resonator of all our violences

and so Bill is wholly right to say, through Boone, that America is to be discovered by penetrating her as a moral and aesthetic proposition

that such archaism is our decisively alive CONTENT, which any of us fails to put his bare hands to at his own peril, at his

own exile, at his own ending, inevitably without a
homogeneous sanction-system, in the Dante-Christian false
one — (false, mind you, not on a value and quality judgment
whatsoever, not as adequate or inadequate vision, but as
inappropriate, unorganic, as non-Pelasgian — in fact, as it so
clearly & historically is, not at all a matter of the Greek
predecession but a matter of the Semitic and Caucasian
places — where Abraham came from

IN OTHER WORDS, W C Williams, in GRAIN, was on the truest
path an American can follow if he wishes to go back by the feel of
his own texture to his starting place. And all that Bill had to do
was to make some several natural steps back through Eric the
Red — by way of that Danish epic, say, Beowulf — and he would
have taken us — and more importantly, himself — to the very place,
Mount Lycaon, where you have now so brilliantly pointed out he
properly belongs. Bill Williams is, Pelasgian, and as such, is
opposed, eternally, to Abraham's formulation, Original Sin —
Abe's, and T.S., and all the Dantesque Neo-Classicists who are
being allowed to run so loose in the pages of all the little
magazines today

But that said, it leaves unsaid, the other error, or, perhaps fairer,
for it certainly is the other uncompleted part of what is now a
single process (that is, our advantage is, only that Bill, and Ez,
have done their work, and we can be clearer, only, by their
having existed).

    Where Bill has also harmed himself (what I want to add to
your own half-truth, the archaic-place truth) is, that, he has not
(as Ez has, so finely, but also, on the other side, so halfly!) Bill
has not (caught, I think, by this other polemic) he has not allowed
for the collective culture force as it plays on us just as much as
does our own implicit & inherited archaism
                                        (I guess I am now too
tired to make this wholly join the above. Or it may be that I am
myself only in passage about it. But I can give you the signs of the
road:

form as what can be forced out of the content above located
depends upon (1) another documentation, the one, I say, Ezra
started in KULCH—that is, I would now say, cannot be
arbitrarily stopped short of the Sumerian first act, Uruk; upon
(2) the other half—the larger half—of the Odyssey—the vision
of man as moving thing, as moving as language is moving
without reference to place or to a man's archaism alone; in
other words, (3), that Classicism as it is form as it is still the
only real noun we have to describe a complete
accomplishment of a poem, is only possible when Pelasgian
man is also able to admit that form—his forms come from
himself in his larger aspect as MAN, without local texture,
without moral source, but as source in NATURE—that culture
is, by its revelations of daily life, amoral, is, material and
political, is Nature, not moral and aesthetic as is personality

Well, thank you, for having rizz me up like this. If you care to let
me know of any of your other writings I should be most grateful
to know of them. And I shall look forward to anything of yours
which appears in print. [*Question marks added in margins on
either side.*]

With the fullest respect,

Charles Olson

PS

What—damn it—gets altogether left out, in such a go as the
above, is the only reason why I have sd it all—that language is
the issue of all these things, and that what I am really after is to
explain why Bill's language is just as divisible, alas, as is his
threepart of Paterson—as you put it—city, man, poet

that the damnable fact is that Bill—the man who, implicitly,
because he stuck to the States—*wanted* to find the
language—actually has accomplished only a divisible
and exterior language, no matter how much he sure

has taught us, where to look for, the Beautiful
   Thing

      the damn tragedy is, that, his language is not yet,
         also what a poet is finally accountable for, the
            B T as it is the ultimate POEM — what The
               Odyssey damned well is, &, for that matter,
                  in a tradition which is *not* ours, despite
                     Xtian appearances, Dante's
                                             COMEDY

[*To Creeley, 9 August 1951, begun verso preceding letter:*]
here's a real crazy biz! This bird Martz (all the over — 7 pages)
wrote a damned interesting job on WCW in PNY current — The
Road to Paterson: I read it fast, in the library, and picked him up
wrong — that is, read Pelasgian where, even as I was giving him
the enclosed go, yesterday, I began to think he had sd Pelagian!
For I couldn't believe that a man who had struck on such an
accurate contrary to O S, would just let it lie in a phrase! so here i
am, this morning, flat on my face — or he is! Anyway, I figure now
what got sd will be more interesting to you than to him, and I
shall send it to you first. And if you can waste the same 30¢ back,
maybe, after you have read it, and made whatever use, I might
send it to him.
   [*Added*: I think, here, maybe, you will want to read from
   typed (1) — 7]

now let me take advantage of the rest of this page to say what the
torn piece enclosed, says i want to say:
                                    it comes from a triangula-
tion of three things — (1) Goethe, by way of Paul Goodman's
                        article on advance-guard, in current
                        Kenyon: "Occasional Verse is the
                        highest"!!
                     (2) The NY Times, as, journalism obeying
modernism, & becoming the documentation of the day anywhere:
all the news . . .

(3) The CANTOS as, a one man's attempt to poise, all culture, to see, what modicum is, usable, out of, the welter

I am led to this notion: the post-modern world was projected by two earlier facts — (a) the voyages of the 15th & 16th Century making all the earth a known quantity (thus, geographical quantity absolute); and (b) 19th Century, the machine, leading to (1) the tripling of population and (2) the same maximal as the geographic in communication systems and the reproductive ones   — In other words, that, the QUANTITATIVE, which, as I guess you know, has been the rock I have been trying to crack, is so embedded that one should not be surprised that it has forced all old functions to behave anew

Now, as of this morning, what impresses me, is, that there is a very important connection between quantity and the function of CRITIQUE, especially the service the verse of critique can be said to serve. The CANTOS, for my money, (one minute) —   The EXPANSION of peoples, materials, and sensations that the AGE of QUANTITY involves itself in, DEMAND a heightening of that servant of clarity, the CRITICAL FUNCTION, wherever: that is, the above increases in the quantity of experience is also an increase in the sources of confusion, and so, to cut them down requires more labor than previously

　　　　　　　　　so far as verse goes, this seems to me so huge a thing that the old three — lyric, epic & dramatic — don't serve at all: that is, a novel has already shown that these descriptions are only such, that they don't isolate modes nor do they any longer cover such a function as the increase of critique in verse establishes. [*Added*: That is, as of the novel, isn't it exactly an instrument which the Age of Q invented?]

　　　　　　　　　　　why THE CANTOS is such a leader, is, that Ez, there, has tackled one thing i can't see was possible before him (before Frobenius' materials, say, or, that no man previous to EP would have been forced to translate Confucius, the Greeks, Propertius, the Provencals, Shigaku, write the Yiddish Charleston for Zukovsky,[54] and translate American

into European!) BUT, this, (the 1st true poem of critique? what
about the Commedia?), actually delimits itself to the Quantity,
Culture. That is, what does it amount to, *as relevance*, beyond the
critique & composition of, Kulch? When EP is writing abt nature
or emotions or men as friends, say, is he any different (the ant's a
centaur — or, equity, with the hills, etc.)[55] from one or the other of,
the lyric, the epic, or (a little, by way of Browning) the
"dramatic"? [*Added*: That is, even EP, has not applied the function
of critique to the archaic (which is the personal, the passionate,
the textural)]

      Now my idea is, that this comes from an inability
on his part (and who else has done as much?) to admit
QUANTITY except as, unconsciously, he had to grip it [*Added*:
the Monster], by the hair as culture — not only as above (7 pages)
the absence of the archaic, but, even beyond that, an
understanding of how *essential* critique is, all thru all

    In fact, it is easier to see this whole biz by way of the
increased awareness of the archaic as force

                      what the painters were
doing contemporary to EP was closer to anthropology and
psychoanalysis than he was [*Added in margin*: This implies that I
think we can be just as "critical" of personality as of society, eh?]
(note his choices, among painters — Brancusi, & Picabia[56] — both of
em damned interesting — more interesting, maybe, than the Picasso,
in just the respect that it was *kinesis* — in the same sense as EP's
investigation of the kinetic in language as medium are, ultimately,
more important than any of this function business i have got my
mind on, this morning)

                  ((this may be more than i can manage,
successfully, it is so new to me, but, let me try for you anyway —

  again, you see, I see a failure, somewhere here ((a failure which,
I think, underwrites the two half-worlds I was writing about
yesterday::

      let me put it this way — if I am right, that the job now, is to
      be at once archaic and culture-wise — that they are
      indivisible — then where is the principle of function from which

verse (anyway) can be written so that the balancing on a
feather which make this simultaneous act possible can be
achieved?

that is, i take it, the *means* Ez, say, gives us in the
medium of language — what i think is *kinesis* —
how come we are so involved in the kinetic problem, except
as this means is the only one to *poise* — to balance,
accurately — the very *expansions* which post-modern life have
involved us, severally, in

in other words, i think i am saying that the function of critique is
behind *everything* (and has become the crux because quantity
cannot be managed without it   ): that is, if a Sauer, by the critical
methods of science, enables me to get in place the nature of man
as a fisher-folk in the period between the ice and the invention of,
a city[57] (as Frobenius enabled Ez to at least start into the
understays of culture, anywhere — note, however, actually, what
a little distance Ez drove this, how he actually tends to fall more
toward F as only another intelligent man rather than to work F's
disclosures (as Lawrence did: it is not noticed that DH was on to F
before EP) for what new light they throw on human
consciousness)

if, due to the archeology that financing has made
possible in the past century, i can find out Sumerian poems, and
transpose same

if (what excuses Malraux's book on art,[58] the one point, that,
reproduction has made all art an available museum — has also
made the painter not only local but, violently — so quickly —
actually international! example, Picasso, raiding, *all* inventions in
design and color anywhere, in three-dimensional concepts)

well, it seems to me thorough. . . . Then, just as a paper like
the NY Times is forced into being as, each issue, the history of
that day anywhere, the record of it; just in some parallel way,
there is point to EP's old prop, that, literature, is journalism,
which stays, NEWS![59]

only, by saying just that – and to the degree that the CANTOS are
that kind of news – he has kept himself (or, better, he was so
inside the first consequences of QUANTITY) he did not manage to
address himself to the intimate or epic or dramatic materials in
any essentially different way

> he (1) attacked CULTURE in its wide expansion & by the
>   critical method so far as he could apply it
> & (2) he accomplished a kinetic of his MEANS by some
>   like process

BUT
> the job now is to figure out how to take these steps the
several further steps that – now that we can see QUANTITY as an
absolute force involving absolute change – are called for

> i hew to the notion that we cannot afford to let out of our
hand this weapon of CRITIQUE except at the peril of losing the
whole world of reality of which we are a part

> yet i know this (which brings me home to the GOETHE
quote – and all this damn funny recent verse – *all* of it, if you will
notice, directed to *actual* persons, composed, actually, *by* and *for*
OCCASION::

that all EXPANSION, all QUANTITY, as it is materials, earth-
space or whatever, numbers of persons, and such changes as the
internationalization of painting, is only actually more meat for the
grinder NOT a disturbance, ultimately, of theee et
meee!
> ONLY,
>> to get the gain and lose the dispersion,
>>> to strike
through in order to reach the more than ever bedevilled
citizenry

> to apply *kinesis* so that you poise what, so powerfully &
delicately that you make light for them

this is where I am arguing that there are, perhaps, *two* necessary changes:

(1), that, you and I *restore society in the act of communicating to each other*

& (2), that what i mark about this correspondence is something i don't for a moment think is peculiar to thee et me — that the function of critique is more than the mere one of clarities (as, say, Flaubert, &, Mme Sand), it is even showing itself in the very form of our address to each other, and what work goes along with it

I put it as of us, but, we do say to the Great Society, go fuck yrself (which Ez was not quite able to do!), and quietly create a society of our wives and friends — and without even trying to make it what DHL wanted Trigaron or some such "community" to be in Florida![60]

and yr *conjecture* as principle — & the single intelligence — what are these but our tries at exploding all by way of the function of, critique?

(I am suddenly reminded that Ortega, who has, more than anyone, perhaps, hammered home the fact of quantity, is at the same time the man who defined life — and in his Goethe essay — as preoccupation with, itself!)[61]

Well. Perhaps this all comes out a little beating the obvious. If so, just charge it to my stupidity and my weariness from too much of everything! But somewhere in it is something to do with
                    (a) a long poem
                    (b) the metric of same
                 & (c) putting it across, like they say!

[*Added*: The ACT, always, more important than the MEANS or the END, however each modify the ACT!]

All love, five thousand ways, against, the middle!

O

[Black Mountain, N.C.]

sat aug 10 51 R Cr: I damn well feel like my master, these
days, that, as he sd to Hawthorne, give me 10,000 writing youths,
and I'll make you 10,000 books. Or something.[62] I am full of
projects, and not sufficient sense of reality to be content that all I
can accomplish is what a day makes possible. I am properly
fucked up by time: can't even (by god) get back to that 8 page
letter ((no, not forgotten, lad)) of what — now, tomorrow, one
month old — and yet not off to you!
                                        Crazy place. And so far no
real loss — only, fatigue, and just this week a little too much of it
to get writing done the equal of the talking! But this has never
plagued me, so long as the talking still goes ahead. For I damn
well do talk to write (as my breed of man surely does, or so i take
it, the Old Man was correct in making, the conversation of,
intelligent men,[63] one of the mainstays of his must [*i.e.* mast]
                                                          One
thing, tho, you must allow me, because there is not a damned
second of spread in a life in a place like this: that there are things
which — practical things — details such as the several businesses
between us — like Origin, and new writers for it, etc etc — are just
what the loss of these seconds squeeze out, force aside. In this
respect, that, when I write to you, I want to give you speculations
& conjectures rather than news — for the reason that, these things,
are, I take it, substance between us in a permanent sense.
     What's on my mind today is (1) the *habit* of art and (2) the
decision of art. I am puzzled to realize that for most people art is
not natural, that nature (actuality, in the sense of *what* happens,

without reference to any "hows," even, the simplest "scientific" one of cause, on even the plane of nature or actuality) appears to them to have separable & superior claims, and that art, somehow, is divisible from it. It astonishes me considerable. I don't know that I ever had to think about it. But I am led to this: that an amateur is one for whom the habit of art is not "natural" and, because it is not, there is, therefore, a decision of art called for — a decision *for* art is required of them.

In any case, it was interesting to note Goodman stressing, for the moderns, how the "ancients" understood that the practice of art (professionalism) made a "habit" which in its turn lessoned the professional in his own business. (I am aware that I am using "habit" in these two paras differently, but, I would go on the figuring that if such a habit was natural to Sophocles it was due to no sense of separation on his part from his audience — and so, that, society, once, was not so initially prejudiced in favor of actuality as it is natural versus (by an arbitrary & false notion of "contest") actuality as it is art.

And surely the only reason for bothering with these questions at all is the palpable confusion in the public mind. That's all. I don't think you are confused simply because I don't think the problem exists for us, ever existed, eh?

(((((One biz yr scrupulous posing of Joyce led me to last night: I proposed to Jala and Con that, all psychoanalysis is like all post-Joyce novel writing — that it rests on the fallacy that, because Freud was so powerful that, necessarily, there was any reason for anyone else to derive from him!

Which leads to another: that *curiosity*, as the moderns take it, is, like so many other things, *inverted* (and not perverted, that word by which the moderns beat themselves, and, so beating themselves, it is such pleasure, go right on practicing perversions!): that curiosity used to be so understood that, if one man was interesting, it was only good reason to be interested in one self, not, to become a follower, and to create some silly new school or discipline or whatever

that the craving for newness actually destroys the old

curiosity [obviates it *crossed out*] the way they latch on to what
they take is an "original" like Freud or Joyce (or Pound or
Williams, eh, MISTER Emerson?)
                                    all over the place, these days, i
am led to quote gotama, as he was dying, who had nothing to say
to those damned flies, his disciples, except, you know what i did,
why don't you figure out what you have to do — or something
equally impatient, and clear

                              ((((Curious sensation yesterday: to
have a letter in fr Cid quoting Bill on Origin II, after having had
that long go on him sent to you two days ago![64]
                                    The breeds of
men — or is it, that, now, even that classification (classification by
nature) has ceased? I sort of think so. I can't see but what the
argument in that biz on Bill the Pelasgian — that he's half, and Ez
another — is itself evidence that the division into breeds is behind
us (as, surely, we were never aware of this phoney discursive
proposition of, art &, nature::: did I tell you the new biz, in HU
or LAWS, of the etymology of discourse? which I find the *Romans*
understood to mean "TO RUN TO & FRO"![65]
                                    (and now I can't
make up my mind whether it is a typical Roman or American
distaste for what is at root to discourse — logic, rhetoric, and
syntax (((the beast, herd, or modern stupidities in the face of,
conjecture))) — or a true characterization!)

What burns me, in Bill's letter, is, that you & I are unformed &
searching. SHIT. I have the same answer to him I first had to
you — that, if form is that, then, who the hell invented the other
proposition here implicit to Bill's argument — in fact stated by him,
that WE MUST FIND! La. FIND what?
                                    The truth is, the whole
argument is a phoney, and thus Bill misses what is in front of his
eyes, despite how sharp those eyes are (or ears, for, still, I stick to
that notion, that Bill, by *searching* for a language misses
it.
     GODDAMN IT — I wish the christ he hadn't written that letter.

It sounds so fucking *far back*: all that goddamn close going on—
apparently so discriminating—by the *local* of the instant he
writes—and yet, who has been the most valueless enthusiast of our
time but Bill? so much so, that when he did praise so
extravagantly the PV thing, I had no final pleasure in it, because,
he has praised too much.

That is, he, finally, asks too much of
himself, in this sense, that, if he is not light, as I had it there, but
the fire of, confusion (with the fineness of its combustion), then let
him, for christ sake, stop using the terms of light, the business
proper to the men of such—the men with intellects. For if Bill is
going to rest his case on the resistant going-on of his sensory
take—if he is going to be so thorough-going-ly *local* (even to the
sort of *locus*—note, by the way, who it is who has the mind to
use this root of the word!—which he is here moving from (in this
letter abt you and me)—his premise that it's time WE
FOUND

then, by god, he has to stand to the real thing, that, all
he finds, or is capable of finding, by the very premises of his own
process, is his own language

and thus the whole "argument" on
which PAT is based—even—to my mind the crucial error, to,
discussion of, the poet and the proposition, "what is, *the* language,
the American language"—is an extension which fails, is bound to
fail

it burns me, lad, i tell you: for he surely misses what is going
on, and misses it now, as he missed it then, and has so stayed
bitter, undependable, and full of several meannesses, not the least
of which is the guilt he feels that it was his goin-on, in print,
about Ez, that finally got Ez in the jug

he can't have it *both*
ways

It's so gd irritating for him to talk about FINDING, this
way: that he is voicing again a canard, a face to GRAIN which is
there, in GRAIN, and which only now do I put my finger on
(what bothered DHL in reviewing the book)

((why, for example,
he errs in his Columbus—& why he praised,—wrote the intro

for – Salt's poem on CC))[66]

that is, he's right, with Boone, for, tho
he doesn't say it – so far as I know the text of WCW to where
does he use the contrary concept to "search" – for what he is
talking abt [*Added*: as of Boone] (know it or not, he), is
RECOGNITION

this way: search is one of the phoneys of the West (can be
documented in the change of interpretation of Ulysses as
character – and I'm not sure but what I think a careful examination
of the Aeneid won't show that already, in Virgil's hand, what
Dante surely did with the image, had already happened

that is,
ask yrself if there is any *search* – any looking for something to
find – in Homer's Odyssey

the way i read it is what i find in (1)
ALL MEN ON THE 4 SEAS ARE BROTHERS, (2) in Cabeza de
Vaca (as *sure* correction of Columbus, Ponce de Leon, Bill's de
Soto, etc – add, for me, La Salle, decidedly), the 1st "Boone"; and
(3), in Apollonius of Tyana – significantly, post-Virgil, anti-Christ,
and so almost burned out of history like a witch!

that is, that the
whole modern notion of search-to-find [*Added*: "Seek, & you
shall"] (go west, etc), had its preparations in a false reading
somewhere back in that williwaw of time before Christ, in that
TIME OF LOSS between 750 BC and, since:

Odysseus, is
wandering, in on the road, the sea road, for the same damned
reasons that the heroes of the Chinese novel are[67] – not because he
chose to, not at all, and not because he's looking for anything
(except, how to get back home!), but because events or the hands
of god pushing at his back, pushing him down (rubbing his face in
it), keep him out there [*Added in margin*: Movement (as you, I,
who not, DHL) because we *want* – or *have* to – MOVE – NOT to
seek SHIT] – and keep him there, for exactly the same reasons as
the Chinese 7-footers are kept on the road so long they turn into
brigands, just to live, just to make it possible to reconstitute some
sort of life: because he has offended some laws, the same laws

once having sanction, and so, he recognizes that he is in some sense wrong, but he can't, any more than the Chinese lads can, satisfy himself the present executors of the laws (in O's case, Poseidon, and, to a degree, Menelaus) — note M's dirty fatalism, as against O's no-conclusions, against O's dependence on his own wit and strength to get him through (& Athena never does any more for him than increase both! oh yes, lends him a little extra handsomeness when he comes out of the bushes in front of Nausicaa's girls!)

(((((i sd last night, to jala & con, a propos goodman's
homosexuality, and the way he did prey on these little
youths here, ripe, as 17-18, for such tipping of, their scales!
what i sd was, that, tho i take it it was goodman's job to
decide whether or not he would take advantage of such an
open situation, i wasn't sure any of us could do anymore
now — in taking a position toward him — than to allow that
he had this responsibility and yet, that he may (or may
not!) have exercised it, has as much to do with a concept
of how men get free, as it has any sanction system — that
we have any sanction-system from which to judge

jala says, but this leads to anarchy. And I had to answer:
no, the state of society depends upon the presence of men
who can (like I think Goodman cannot) rest inside themselves
[*Added in margin*: This is a pisser to state, because it comes from
the ability to be before & after the terms of any definition — to be
post-discourse — to be back to *above* — to be as fully human as any
reality is — in its full context & actuality (which also includes the
function of definition & discourse, MISTER Williams!)] on grounds
of just such another kind of Going-on from Bill's (or Goodman's
"search," a much less interesting one than Bill's — for it struck me
then, that of all the writers of that generation and so many of
ours, only Bill and Ez have not settled for "anarchism" as a
dialectic of, "freedom": and the funny thing is, for me, that the
three I know best — Dahlberg, Rexroth, and Goodman — are,
curiously enough, professional sexual libertines!

(I could be
tempted, knowing Commies, as well as such stories as Karl

Liebknicht and Rosa Luxembourg, as well as Emma and Berkman,[68] to take this further, and say that all material & political concept of societal change ((as against, Bill's posing of, Boone, as clear that, America, is to be known by her moral & aesthetic face alone)) actually finally settled down—that is, the individual, knowing no other liberation—actually settles for sexuality)

the point would seem to be, that, only when search-and-find (that silly Western girl-boy game) is given over—when the thing is exposed for what it is—a loss of the function of
RECOGNITION
                        (form ex content, surely!) (and recognition, is attention to the moving face of reality wherever, NOT to constant moving by the observer under some bad physics that, by moving, man finds any superior angle on anything which is in front of him!) [*Added*: More, here, in my mind, than got down—more, on motion & movement, tectonics!]
                        (RECOGNITION is what knocks *place* hard on the puss, and reconstitutes it as both impossible for a man to be patriotic about—as too close to himself to enable him to penetrate *himself*—
                        (missing the fact that the psyche expresses itself *always* by objects, in a space which is, quintessentially, geographic, or at least, more essentially, topographic: thus, that the archaic *is* sensationally place in the sense of solid in time & space
                        (example, Melville finding it possible to deliver himself of the first huge images since Sophocles by putting them way the hell over there from him in Pittsfield into the Pacific)
                        the whole psychoanalytic nonsense (here is a likeness to the collectivism above seen as going in the direction of coitus—like *post*-Homeric art!) is actually, like all modernism, *asking too much* of human beings by asking the *wrong* things of them
                        (Mr Melville, in September, 1851—he had been still high in his language and his concept in August, writing the last chapters of MD at the same

time that he was correcting proof (the sort of biz Dostoevsky
alone was capable of)[69] — showed how *hellish* (and i mean the
adjective in the ancient sense, as *out of hell*) the modern failure to
see the potency and magic of place as so great that a man only
tampers with it (as even Bill tampers, and only DHL does not) at
the peril of his soul:

for what the hell did bring M to grief in
Pierre, but that he got place so close to his person that the
personal content which place has as face of the psyche blew him
up?

as all these mad & devil attempts to ask human beings to
focus on their personalities by way of the narrow particulars of
their material life, of their most obvious environment (their
parents, their home town streets, their exact sensory particulars
without the amelioration, the alleviation, the *other* particulars
which light is, which space is (which are just as much a part of
experience as is the material & the political — proof, *dreams* (as
even Freud knew, at the end, that, the physiological law of
ontogeny repeats phylogeny is also a law of the psyche,

that
you and i repeat here the total sum of the human race's experience
(Ahab and that Whale, spun though they are wholly out of the
man, and without any previous social working over as in the case
of the Oedipus story Sophocles put his hand to, *are* dependent, for
their resonance, exactly on this other kind of place that the psyche
of each of us is

((((you see why I take it that Bill's PAT fails
imaginatively as well as language-wise: why it is true
what Martz exposes, that, the division into city, man,
poet, of that sort of sleeping giant on the banks of the
river & the falls, is false — is false as in *Pierre*
Melville gets false to the human material [*Added*: or, his own
material gets unbearable — & thus unusable, to him]:

if place is not
seen as a controlling factor of the imagination — if any of us are so
foolish as to think we can lightly put our hand on the narrow
substance of ourselves

(((the function of the intellect and of "culture" as I argued it Ez is aware of both—and as I found Albers saying this, this morning.

"Everything has form and every form has meaning. The ability to select this quality is culture."

(((((—you see, another thing that is burning me about that letter is that fucking soft (and envious?) waggle-word, intelligence, as Bill there uses it

it is just damned mud-headedness, at this point of time to be insinuating (by failing to speak clearly about the difference of intellect and intelligence) that, somehow, our "intelligence"—yours and mine—is keeping us short of "form"— you, "unformed," and me—how does he have it, I'll go look: o, yeah, sort of the same, only, it's "thoughts" that I come up with! Jesus Christ. And that it is I who is searching! SHIT: come try it on, Mr Bill

that is, I'm sure Cid, when he attaches to his kind or unkind copying of Bill's letter for me the note "Real kindness here & fair judgment," is missing what Bill is up to—and how Bill's own lack of intellect is sabotaging, in this way, all our positions, of all, the central one, of, the Single Intelligence, the very thing which is based on

(1) that what's exactly in front of yr eyes, goddamnthem, is, at anytime, in anyplace, at that instant, the whole fucking business

(2) that anytime and anyplace is not *disclosable* by the terms of that time and that place at all (here be Bill's biggest error)

(3) and that the clue is not movement, not displacement in time or space (nor its false opposite, tenacious local realism) BUT IS RECOGNITION, the function of

you *find* form, have already *found* form, because you are cultural
(in Albers' sense of, the capacity to *recognize* same

maybe my
burn over Bill as nothing but one of the best of the modern is
that, like Melville in *Pierre*, he loses his own strength in his very
virtue of—what you so put it, a recent letter his sticking to
himself—

anyhow, "O brothers

smell the ground—in other words, sit on it,
without forgetting,

what you saw in yr travels!

O

[Fontrousse, Aix-en-Provence]
August 14/ 51

Dear Chas/

Had a whole sheaf of little bits, etc., but will put
them all in this, i.e., the various items:

The main thing is that
Gerhardt's back on. A letter in yesterday, & all goes pretty cool.
He's been pretty well smothered, I take it, with work, & had not
been able to get out. He now plans to make the tour in
September, coming through here, & I'll see him then.

In the
meantime, have to get on with the Am/ issue biz [*Added*: He
gives me free hand.]. So: here's what I'd like to figure, roughly, &
tell me what you think.

To begin with: Williams' DESCENT (from
ITAG, altho I note they forget it in the index . . .), the Houston
one, which I like, and which here serves by virtue of length: some

3 pages. I want that heading the works, in italics, to be followed directly by your own THE KINGFISHERS. The way it shapes up: 8pp for your work there; 6 for Blackburn, & Bronk; 5 for Sam Morse, & 4 for Emerson, or notably that one longer poem of his, THE FLIGHT INTO EGYPT.

It's rough, any way you look at it; that is, certainly the emphases are arbitrary, but mine anyhow. I want the feel of it, and not anything I can't myself read. Which leaves out a good deal, I expect.

Thinking it over, I felt it would be better to have the PRO/VERSE run, straight, against the context of European poetry, that is, not in this particular issue, since eight pages, in particular, THE K/, will maintain that ground for you anyhow. And I've asked Gerhardt if he might not plan to use it earlier, in a place that wd give it real weight.

Too, I hope you won't feel I'm riding out the poem for G/ —but here, frankly, I do want the context of your KINGFISHERS, & if you'll look at the Dr's piece, you'll see what the effect can be, so following it. I haven't a copy here (have asked G/ to send his), so cannot now say how much room that leaves you for other items; but I should think, room for at least 2 or 3 of the shorter, & I'd like to have there, too, MOVE OVER, and like items.

But say what you think, that is, you tell me; this is all open to any change. The only thing: the attempt to get it set as soon as I can, so that he can be sure of time for all translations necessary.

He asked me to write two pages on Am/ poetry; I haven't much interest, honestly, but will try to do something, when I'm out of this present lag. Anyhow, will send it on to you when I do.

He seems to have gone into a quarterly set-up; I take it costs were considerable (he printed 5000 copies, & has some 2000 moving, & of that 500 sold) & prevent the monthly issue. But he also asks permission to send poems (shorter ones, or those he hasn't immediate use for, since I take it he favors the longer) to a Swiss magazine called ESSENCE,[70] which he says is a very beautiful affair, hand-printed & so on. Which gives us another outlet over here.

Some bad news on CMI, that is, he writes the publisher has just gone into bankruptcy, & so he's forced to look for another; that failing, he'll attempt to publish it himself.

He hasn't forgotten the idea of a chapbook, and speaks of doing one first, in English, large pages, sometime early next year. To be followed by the issue in German. In any event, would be wise to keep sending him all new material, toward that end.

He quotes me a price of $175 for a pamphlet, good paper & binding, etc., 24pp, 1000 copies, so there is that hope for the HU, once you have it locked up. I am pretty dull at the moment, or cannot think, quick, where to raise same, but we can figure that when we come to it. Anyhow, it sounded very damn good.

He figures to have the second issue set by the end of this month, & the Am/ issue is set for December. He says, hopes to move into monthly issue as things get smoother.

Which gives you the main points on same. Otherwise, pretty cool. That is, I get a little more straight, & by way of same, have written Kenyon not to use that story (bitter fact of having to send back their check this noon, & how very much the gesture that seemed), and likewise Cid: A Sort of a Song.[71] That cleans me, a little. I hold to the novel because that makes it straighter for me; but in the other two instances, I couldn't finally make it, tho Cid had, certainly, the better one. Anyhow, what else? And if I start fooling around, that's the end of it for sure.

He wanted prose for this next one, but I don't have it to give. So. At that he has one poem, anyhow (Love), and perhaps that last (A Song) will do it too. I don't know, and at this juncture, am rather beyond caring. All I can do to keep my chin off the ground. (Tell me what you think of that shorter story; that, too, is out of my reach at the moment, & let it sit with [Seymour] Lawrence for old time's sake—because want it big, for Cid, or better not bother.)

But it's ok, at that. Feel surer, and tho I couldn't tell you what now happens, maybe something. What I hope, anyhow.

How is Con?
Wish to Christ, in spite of that very kind invitation, you were out
of that place; it don't sound it, to yr lad at least. Too much shuffling. Not, again, to make it: a private world—I don't know how,
etc.—but to be open, still means, to be open, & that door is shut
tight. I don't know—I hope I could dig a straight thing as quick as
anyone, world-plan or anything, but I haven't yet got it.

Anyhow,
make it straight, and/or, one to one to one, that way, and I'll
sign. Anytime.

(I forgot: G/ also asking about young Am/
painters, to do a possible gig for the cover of sd Am/ issue. What
abt Shahn? Told G/ to write him, c/o Black Mt/ & if you have
any ideas, wd be very great.)

Well, here I am. The one fact I feel
sure of. And not so damn bad at that.

So how are you. That
baby is what I'm looking for: real thing. Wait till you hear that,
eh? Crazy! (And so far beyond the boys & girls, you won't even
be able to look back.)

Ok. And all our love to you both/

Bob

[Fontrousse, Aix-en-Provence]
August 14/ 51

Dear Chas/
Many things to hand [*Added at top of page*: have put
in other letter with this/ gets all of them.], but first I want to take
up this matter of PATERSON, and this last letter of yours, just in.

It was a little hard to follow all of it, that is, just like yourself, I would very much like to know what Martz is emphasizing, or isn't emphasizing, with that word, "Pelasgian." (Am I right in taking it: the one gives us the same emphasis as your own GATE & CENTER, & the other (pelagian), the more usual formulation of the man as wanderer, or better, perhaps, homeless?) Anyhow, I don't know, and so some confusion.

In any event, it all comes back, and that's what I see as important.

1) Clearly, this statement you repeat here, "we are the last first people . . . ," remains the emphasis, remains the base premise of any understanding, now, of what is present to us. I think it sits basic to the other thing you have taught me, that space is our history; and trying, this morning, to write something of this, before your letter came, I was going back to it, and saying: it's the only history we have.

2) What concerns me now is — what is the full effect of this fact, or what effect is possible in terms of it? The continuum, the accumulation of act, seems to differ very basically in the instance of America & then Europe; and more to the point, one must, of necessity, assume different authorities.

What is our own? We know, have known for some time, that we do not actuate history by observing it. How, then, do we learn?

3) What is the premise, for coherence, but, for us, the present? And isn't this, as you have said, the clearest statement of our own roots?

Putting that at the book: several things seem actual. a) A premise for coherence that has two faces; one/ literal, that is, the matter of the first identification: man/ as city, etc., which I continue, as you, to think loss; but two/ something else, isn't it, or isn't it, that, as one reads, the actuation of these presences is not of such a logic, that the reversion is continually to the one man, that ground, and it is, again, that field, and that field only, we deal with?

I see the first as metaphor; and though I wish it were not

this one, since it hampers act rather than propels it, I am more interested with what seem deeper cohesions, the whole basis for the juxtaposition, for the relevance, which can't be defined by saying: it is; therefore . . . Why is it? That seems my own question.

Could this Martz answer me? Within the given frame? I ask, because, it turns out, and a coincidence, I'd been trying to make something here, of this book, and to find ground for a clearer evaluation of coherence, and what means are most possible as its agents. I cannot see that one can have a better example than parts of this same book; is there any other premise at work here but the very one we have both been intent on — the instant?

That seems the very actual worth, the incredible occasion. And I hate to see it muffed. I don't honestly think Pound has ever done this, what Williams does here — I do not believe he has ever stood this open, though I know that to be myself, and my own not knowing of what he does.

But it matters to me, this book, on these grounds: 1) that it is governed, its coherence, by the proposition: one thing is everything; 2) an attention is the only instrument; 3) nothing remains but what is.

They sound, I know, so very simple. But I am talking to you, and that means a lot to me. For one thing, it takes no emphasis; or no emphasis is necessary.

Your whole use of Homer must be predicated on that last ground — that something *is* present we have denied ourselves use of, even though we are its last extension.

Too, the second is infinite: seems, even, the base condition of a man's very presence.

Well, so it goes.

And I very much want to get it out in terms of this book; it seems, again, the occasion.

(Why I will not, say, go under to the predication of place; I finally think it even a prop, a kind of

furniture, which is even discarded in the actual progress. Loss, but
it is not the point? That seems some of it.

I know this intelligence
too damn well to sit there; and know even if it is damn well
arrogance, what it must come to in his mind.

A symbol, for a
man who never had one, and never will have one: a jealousy.)

Anyhow, do we need to state it any more than: your own way?
That, again, we are the last first people, space is our condition, all
we have is, what is.

There we sit, there we damn well sit, and we
make, we move, with what we have.

(It is not, surely, that I resist
the job of finding from where, or when, these governments of
energy came; but that I can never forget the commitments they
now involve.)

Leave it at that for the moment. Any man,
Williams on, any one of us—how to be *one*? Is there anything
else?

Thinking, now, of the Goethe sentence. It echoes. Or does for me,
and gets me also back. If a man has a job, is the maker of a
means to continuance—what is the condition of, or for, his most
valuable act? Occasion, which is to say, that which allows the full
weight—minus the reference of an imposed logic.

Reading back, I see I missed the quote of Martz' statement, and
now I can get it more clearly—what he is up to.

It is a neat
division, & perhaps a useful one. But I believe the emphasis must
continue: there are those to whom history is possible, and there
are those who cannot have it so—why?

And "Pelagian" is not, it
seems to me, the necessary answer. It leans, doesn't it, back again
on old ideas of shift, and movement, which have always rested in
the observation, but never in the understanding?

Why can't we
have a history? Why does our history seem so irrelevant to our
present?

(But as it can, does, on particular occasions find space in
the present.)

But we are not Germans, say? Or not Europeans? Is
it purely geography? Or history? In the sense of record?

Past is here, is all round me, right now — and I am particularly
sensitive to it, to the premises of authority, and custom, and the
weight it supposes actual.

(And what is this same thing in Asia —
where, as [Achilles] Fang told me, language stopped, for a man
writing it, in the 12th century?)

Where are we, what surrounds us, to give us substance? What, the
necessary act? But act?

Well, it is the same old thing, and I need
not go on with same, being you I'm writing. Anyhow, are those
the right questions? What I would now like to know.

It is, I see
it, on the one hand: a man as the accumulation of acts which rise
in a sort of priority, some giving way to others, a heap from
which can be taken, examples, or markers of worth, and the man
never more in the present than in the past, because he has lived — I
feel that European, or as much sense of their way as I now have;
and for us, it is not that at all — is only, what is, now, on this one
point, of whatever you call it, instant, present, or simply, now.
That is all we can have, and all I want. To be always here, and
never a thing of all times, or places, etc. I can't stand that
thought.

I wish I could save myself time; but I expect that can't be done. So
very much I want, of these things. Well, no matter.

A letter my mother had forwarded (Mrs. A/ writing to thank her,
for forwarding a present, from Dave, to Rodney on his birthday):

"My dear Mrs. Creeley,

Forgive me for being so long in sending you this thank you note for the lovely birthday present you chose for Rodney from David.

The children have enjoyed putting the puzzles together and will have a lot of fun with them when cooler weather comes.

It has been a beautiful summer here. Not too hot and plenty of rain for the gardens and crops to do well.

We miss Bob and Ann and David so much. For quite some time I was for always looking out to see if I could see one of them coming, or for Lena.

Hope you have kept well this summer. Also Helen and boys, and I expect by now she has the new baby too. If I remember correctly it was due in the month of July. I wonder if it is a girl this time. I expect you would be thrilled to death with a granddaughter.

We have not heard from Bob and Ann for about a month now. It takes so long for a letter to go.

They tell me Sandy had some hampsters. Hope he has fun with them.

Bob gave the children here some rabbits, three in fact and they had a beautiful time with them. They were all females Bob said, but one turned out to be a male and then there were 8 little baby rabbits, so cute, and then someone's dog got into the pen and killed the mother and babies, and a few nights later a dog got thro the wire and killed the last two big ones, so that was the last of them. We felt terribly about it.

If you should ever get up this way, call to see us, we would be very glad to see you again and many thanks again for the birthday cards and present.

Sincerely,

Alice A. Ainsworth"

I believe there's only one speech, very truly. Simply one. Either it is that, or it is nothing. Either one sit, in, and altogether open, or there is no good talking about it.

With Williams, I believe this substance, this way of it, very much there. I want that to get

notice, never to be lost. I don't expect that man, or this woman,
either of them, expect notice in the sense of, a caring beyond their
own.

Anyhow, what else, what the hell else is possible to us, you
or me, or anyone? Jesus, I think now, of this:

"We have bred
we have dug
we have figured up
our costs
we have bought
an old rug —
We batter at our
unsatisfactory
          brilliance —
There is no end
          to desire — "[72]

          All our love to you both/

Dear Chas/
          To add a bit. And because, last night, had been
reading these things to Ann, here, where there is no reason, now,
not to believe that it is as good, as good gets.
                              A statement: there
is no better poet than Hart Crane/ August 15, 1951.
                              Hence:
propose this — that you take one of those occasions, when you are
talking to those people, to give them force them to *hear*: an
evening in this man.
               This, if it's not again riding on you, the
possible order, & things themselves:

THE MERMEN
ISLAND QUARRY
IMPERATOR VICTUS
AND BEES OF PARADISE
LACHRYMAE CHRISTI
FOR THE MARRIAGE OF FAUSTUS AND HELEN: III

AT MELVILLE'S TOMB

with no comment, but: you are going to
hear, if you can but listen, can but, in any sense, hear, sounds as
incredible, as finely knit, caught, as any man ever wrote
them.

And sounds, put into an incredible sense. We have no other
poet of this kind; Americans do not reach this, easily, or it seems
they have other talents.

But here is one man, then. To make of
something very like a search, but one ended, to make of that,
again with the bare hands, some faith, and some simple fantastic
belief, in god knows what.

Well, I couldn't believe it. So much
has been put on Yeats, et al, these matter of the vowels, of the
consonantal shadings — and so much, too, granted Crane, of the
same mastery, one does not look to confirm it. The damn loss.
I
took it then, last night, with a pencil, reading, and as fast I could,
marking it in, there, on the page. And this morning, looking back,
see, that even at that, I had not got half of it.

Well, to look back,
etc.

[*Added*: consonantal shading]

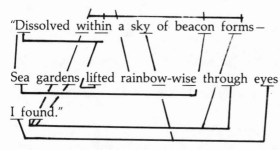

"Dissolved within a sky of beacon forms —

Sea gardens lifted rainbow-wise through eyes

I found."

(& only stop, at
that, because such
a diagram gets so
messy; it shows
nothing of the
modulations, the
shiftings within,
& thru.)

And was also thinking, who else does this:

The Cross alone has flown the wave, [*Added*: to make: Cross!]

But since the Cross sank, much that's warped and cracked . . .

How about that! I mean, that's some damn ear, to do that shuffling.
Well, again, would very much like to see if they could get it, such as are there, etc. So would you try it? Granted, an impertinence.
I can't, this morning, get over it:

. . . . We have walked the kindled skies
Inexorable and girded with your praise,

By the dove filled, and bees of Paradise.

Damit/ isn't that gentle!

But went on into marble *that does not weep*.[73]

How that hits!
How finely it damn well stamps!

How it goes there/ It is at times . . . (Is there anything finer in our poetry? Anything, more inexorable?)

And the one to Melville: that, too, seems very very wonderful.

Well, I've just sent off a sheaf, to G/ — tho it seems an impossible job, to translate.
But I don't think he knows Crane, and he should.

Well/ read them, to them, if you can, or want to.
Would be very very interested to see what they did.
All love/
Bob

[Fontrousse, Aix-en-Provence]
August 16/ 51

Dear Chas/

You put me up against a mean wall, but I believe us
of a distance, into one another, that no such thing can make a
difference. Anyhow, I do want to clear some of it, on Williams,
and my own feelings about it.

For one thing: the letter. Myself, I
took it as a compliment (and of that sort that I've only had
otherwise, from you). You see, I am unformed; and I know it —
and it has no fear for me at all. Remember, too, he says it there,
of me, and not of you. But what I want you to see — he does sense
the place, where I am. I know it so deeply in myself, I forget that
it's not, by that, apparent to others. Unformed, is the word. It's
not, here, certainly a question of disparagement, and even if it
were, it would remain true. Can I put it this simply — *he cares*, he
cares very much; and that is honest — as fine as anything I might
hope for, because I do love him for what he has written.

You
jump too fast here — I feel them pushing you, with the talk, and it
must be a pressure — not the talk itself, but the audience. That, I
come to suspect.

You say there: "then by god he has to stand to
the real thing, that, all he finds, or is capable of finding, by the
very premises of his own process, is his own language . . ."

What
more is there? I mean truly; and where does he say, he will find
"the American language"?

A man can find only his own; I see
nothing else, and see, too, in that, all the gain possible. That he

has found it.

(Goddamn it, you slap this man too hard, and too easily, and with right, certainly, but jesus, we have, don't we, our *own* humilities, somehow left us, somehow continuing, no matter what?)

I don't see it as loss, or arrogance, or meanness, any of it; and I cannot now understand, or fully, what forces you into that position. That it is basically a matter of that kind.

Where, as well, is the idea of "it's time we FOUND"? ". . . destined to FIND . . ." — that doesn't implicate 'time,' certainly. It seems we twist, both of us, on different bases of attitude — that I, frankly, am grateful for the concern, that he controls it, there, to an actual seeing (and does not make it simple compliment) — whereas you, and I do feel it injustice to you that there is the coupling, mark only the fact he can wonder. He is not us, he is not to be convinced by what we project — but as it is, altogether, the essence. I haven't made it, yet; and I can't assume an answer for you, and I won't. You have made so very clear to me, so very many times, what you are — that I will leave it just so at that. I know you; and that's the end of it.

But I insist, just as he had it — there is no end to desire. Recognition is as much a substance of his work, as it was of Boone's whole life. I cannot see these two faces as separate.

Did you remember this one, i.e., this comment from his essay on Poe, which I read again last night, thinking of what you had said : that this was his own ground.

"What he wanted was connected with no particular place; therefore it *must* be where he *was* . . ."[74]

That cleared much, for me; it destroyed, in my own mind, the conception of the place, Paterson, as being anything more than this implied use of it.

I cannot read the poem any other way, frankly. It seems to me just what that sentence implicates — or, we begin here.

But I don't want this to come, as desparate, etc. Look, for
example, if I were to insist that, because the *universe of discourse*
is necessarily a masker of actions, a false face to the whole it
prevents — that, that being so, Pound's premise of 'intelligent
conversation' belies a world, kills it as dead as any stone.

(And it
does, too, in some sense. But what a tenuous thing to hold on to,
against the face, the whole face, that appears in that passing, THE
CANTOS.)

Ok. Don't, because it is waste, I believe it, ride out on this ledge.
For example, certainly as you say, "anytime and anyplace is not
disclosable by the terms of that time or place at all . . ." — yes, just
so, and true; but Williams has premised his disclosures on what?
On the attentions, on the attentions of himself.

Isn't that the same
music, the very same sound I know of? (Recognition: somehow as
the displacement *in* the attentions, in the very entity they
somehow are, somehow there resting, to become.)

I don't know. I
feel it a backwash, honestly, of the impossible fix you have on yr
hands — of the baby coming, of the noise, of all the rush of it, and
being, myself, so very afraid of such [*Added*: that is, if I were in
yr place], not that I might be hurt, but that I will become blurred,
say, washed into trivia — damnit, I sense it. I smell it, if you
will — in the too simple belief of them there, the too easy
recognition, which, for one thing, their invitation somehow meant
to me. I can't but thank them, surely, but I must hold to myself.
Being, what else? That if I am not I, then I am, by rigor of
definition, nothing.

Albers' statement does not interest me, again
honestly. I am left, I think, somewhere back of it, or wherever,
seeing, as I must, that the implied selection is not of the thing I
recognize. I think he does not get to Klee's impact, for one thing,
in the part of ON MODERN ART, quoted in the letter Cid
printed.[75] That is where I would rather hold, and try to fight it
out. (It is different, that is, than 'select'-ing.)

But I want to get

clear, anyhow. Let's hold to it for what time it takes. I mean, take me out on this, all of it, or that last letter, on him, just now sent you before this one.

    Take care of yrself/ and tell us how Con comes. I wish we were all in China, say, some very fine mt/top, tho I wd only run back, & expect you'd have left, also running, an hr before me. Ok.
                                        All our love to you both/
                                                          Bob

[*At top of page:*]
(The thing is/ I can't see Williams as saying *unformed,* as of style, or method; to me, it has the meaning as of, the living; that one is now new, & wet, like any bird so coming out of the nest, call it.)

                                                  9:30/ thereabts.

Chas/
        I jumped it. That is, I read yr letter again, just now, & tho I'll let the first part of this one go, as of my own confusion, certainly it demands corrections.
                        1) I had gone all apart on the matter of, *search.* It is, honestly, for me so much the same word as, conjecture, that I never considered it, finally, as pertaining to a thing, say, one imagines himself after. Hopelessly naive, I know; but it is the truth. In short, you are absolutely right on that point — and it's a fantastically exact thing. I could see it, now reading, very damn clearly as put: Homer.
                                (I don't know how I have existed outside this idea, but I say it: not until now, almost this precise instant, have I literally believed that another man could be after *some* thing. I mean, I didn't take it seriously; supposing, I expect, again that it was *any* thing — or the premise of conjecture, and what is possible to it.
                                Hence, my break-up on

your making use of that phrase in Williams' letter in the way. Again, I confess it scares me, i.e., I still can't adjust to the idea of Williams' onus as being, something, I mean, some one thing.

It seems to me, that existence, or what to call it, cannot involve that attitude seriously. I test, as I can, my own perceptions; I want them to declare weights, as they may, do, find things of such possibility.

And it had seemed, does still, that Williams had this similar sense; as I know, surely, Lawrence had it.)

2) What does stick: that sentence from the Poe essay, i.e., how can one get a meaning for it, if it is not to imply, also, my own belief of, *any* thing, as the purpose? I founder on that.

3) The Albers' sentence still bothers me. I mean, I don't see it as any addition to Klee, or anything that is of use to me. But I don't know; tell me what you think about it.

Do you, then, read the poem as a simple disclosure of place, or that attempt?

Myself, I can't, or I find it continually the flux of the attentions — that they do, and very finely at times, move with the impetus of the objects which they have become involved with; and this is the finding/ I feel it, this finding, as with one's own body, as eating, the mouth is always finding, always tasting? Which is always that instant, of taste?

But I am very confused, at this point. I am, anyhow, aware, and constantly, in the act, of the two base ideas of form which confront me — the one, of the surface (as you could say to me, why not change this a little, or this, or doesn't this sentence read a little brokenly, etc.) and the other, that form which is of the presences involved, my own included — that thing I suppose we call point, or meaning, or content (glibly), and that which is content (deeply) and waits so very calmly for the declaring of all its presence — never anticipating, never giving itself weight until it all be there.

But the real thing is your point here on search — & Williams or no Williams, it's what concerns me.

(Though isn't there an impossible irony latent in the fact that Willams would not go west, or anywhere — did hold so very rigidly to the implications of that sentence from the Poe essay?)

(Or where did this material come from, what made the poems, I now begin to damn well wonder — that are so beautifully free of, search, so many of them.)

(Desire/ that isn't search. The will to recognition? Something very close to that, it must seem.)

But the point: a loss of the function of recognition. It seems that the senses, so intent on their burden, call it, of a possible object, over-ride, and so lose, that which certainly must otherwise have offered itself — without more force than they did meet, or less.

It is a fantastic world. "Recognition, is attention to the moving face of reality anywhere" —

(girls go by, singing: 9:45 — a full moon/ what else.)

that is, that there's always that lunge, the body so bearing, that way, that angle of attention: / .

Isn't that all of it, all there is, recognition? (Even: "eyes I dare not meet in death's dream kingdom . . ."[76] / even that inverse of it.)

And what, and it's odd, now recalls to me, all of Crane: all of it. One moves, on possibility?

"I dreamed that all men dropped their names, and sang . . ."[77]

It is very deep. ("And the North Pole said to the South Pole: 'Heteroclite is man and there is surely room for a great deal of difference.' ")[78]

Which he hadn't meant to say.

Which no one *means* to say; no one.

(Is there any place, but me, and yet there is, and that I know there is: my possibilities, and why I maintain it: conjecture.)

I am very off, but float, anyhow. A wonderful wonderful night. ("On such a night . . ."[79] Well, something.) Anyhow, I can't ask you to overlook the first jump, but see I get it in spite of myself. Ok.

Again (and again, & again) all our love to you both/

Bob

Later/

A note, I'd been meaning to get to: what it is/ that a friend wrote me, of the stories in ORIGIN, that he took them as almost classic examples of the existential position.

Now that, beyond I think it's essentially ass-end-to, is fairly useful. I mean, haven't they got, at that, the hind end of somewhat the same thing as we try for?

Being, they, only, make of it: a fatus, a doom. Whereas, clean it off, put it back to the other emotions, granting a despair, naive or profound, is not man's sum, and you have the initial position of,

let's look around.

It interested me, because I had not, frankly, been very interested in them — but for a few things, like, and briefly, Camus' THE STRANGER where certain weights are used because they are there, not because he would use them.

(See how that turns to loss, this direction, in Sartre, & Camus' own THE PLAGUE.)

So it comes out, at that, a classic joke: being, man directing will at things, purely, does confront, just so, the existential position.

Whereas, cool off, i.e., open up, & not tack the only will-ful comment you can upon them (to wit: they won't play it

our way . . .), & you have something else, quite to the contrary,
back in business.

(But loss, again: that this is a danger to the
whole potential of, recognition; since it anticipates that the sum of
recognition, is, despair, etc., etc., etc.

Which is not certainly, the
case. It wasn't with Boone, etc., and surely, surely, he is likewise,
an existentialist!

Why, it must be, the American (altho I'm told,
by G/, that Heidigger (or how you spell his name) finds his most
exact exponents in the US) cannot get too excited, because, even
tho muffled & beaten down, he can only come up with: *all there
is, is* . . . everytime.)

[*Verso envelope*:]
                    Aug. 17/ 3:00 PM
                    Damn! Damn!
                    Damn!
My bicycle *being* unequal to Mrs. Crosby's Stutz —
I missed her by some 5 minutes — off . . . to Spain.
(in Aix)

                                        [Black Mountain, N.C.]

Monday August 20, 1951 (is it?)

LAD — i beg yr forgiveness. abt ten days ago, the whole thing got
too much, that is, too many things, and my tone suddenly left me,
i just went dead (you know that sensation, in which all yr
appetites are still up but the will to do anything with them dies)

the hitch was, i couldn't get out of some commitments, especially
those i had myself got into: two publications, two books, (1), a
handsome APOLLONIUS book i shall have to send you in about a
week or ten days (a limited edition just for here of 50 copies, 20 in
boards, 30 in paper—designed by this man, who came here, out of
nowhere, 42, ex-sailor, ex-commercial designer (San Francisco),
and who walked in to this desk at the moment I had blocked out
the mss, asking, for it![80] So I gave it to him, and this week have
to finish the writing (probably a wrong thing to do, to have a
thing already being type-set while you are yrself still writing! but
this once, for the throw of it, eh?)

                              & (2), a decision to go ahead
and issue LETTER FOR MELVILLE, 1951, right now, right here, as
a piece of verse pamphleteering (having had no word at all from
Kirgo)—to get it there, Pittsfield, for "Labor Day"! and
elsewhere—an issue of 100 copies, which I shall also get a couple
off to you, as soon as
                      (the kids financed the Melville ahead of
time—which moves me—and shall pay themselves back out of the
proceeds from the Apollonius, leaving me the whole Melville to
sell as I can—a damned nice business, what?)

but it's all too much, at the moment, and I shall be not much
good until this place is closed (two weeks)

it is why yr long letter of last night was such a lift, and brought
me up, sharp—all yr news of doings, plus yr biz on Bill, and
especially, yr push on Crane: my intention is to do just what you
suggest, there, this very night! Crazy, the way you rolled in on
me, for I had gone up to the office, looking for some verse of
Skelton and Herbert! and had not been able to find what I wanted
(H's sacrifice, and S's roundelay on Christ) to hit these people on,
Christ as subject, instead of, all the present shit of same—how,
once, such was possible but how, today, it ain't. And I pick you
out of the box and BANG, there you are, on the Cross, and the
Wave of Crane
                    and of course you will know, knowing what I
myself did with him in the MELVILLE poem, how, my own

weather, just now, is, likewise:

> the diced bones — now his too, he
> who is also of the one society
> who likewise lifted altars
> too high (a typewriter
> in a tree) and spilled himself
> into the honey-head, died
> the blond [a white *crossed out*] ant
> so pleasantly
> > as though he did not want to woo
> > to chance a Bronx grave, preferred
> > to choose his own wild headland

and that society, by the way, i did, in rewriting, include Mitch in
thus:

> What they'll forget — they'll smother you — is
> there is only one society, there is no other than
> how many we do not know, where
> and why they read a book, and that
> the reading of a book can save a life, they
> do not come to banquets, and Nathaniel Hawthorne . . .

So I shall give them, your lecture! And it comes right, to hand,
lad, and I am most grateful:
                              with less clarity than you, & also
with less tenacity, i also have the sense that crane & bill are more
naturally of my predecession than some others — in fact, before
them, solely, for me, melville (was gabbing with Motherwell, the
other night — he succeeded Shahn, for August — & was bewildered,
to find him, making so much of Poe as, the usual business of,
Baudelaire's, the FIRST of l'art moderne! before whom nobody

but — to my peril — i take the demand of the instant to be a bearing
in, and on, of more than the single I — the single intelligence is, is
it not, exactly — exactly by that formalization which you have
already made your own "I" — a tremendous act of selection

                                                          and as
such has to be as much the gratuity of a Melville (or a Pound, for
that matter) as it is the tenacity of bill, or crane
                                    BOTH, AND
                                                          not
either, or
              and the AND now the overwhelming place where the
verticals jam up, where the real weight gets in
                                              that is, any
positionalism (even that of the tenacious self) is behind, in the
sense that, the INSTANT is such a pouring that the tenacity is in
how the SYNTAX is so set, by the noun and the verb that the old
assumption (discourse in art) that a sentence is a complete thought
(which is a sort of single assertion of the self) is done not by
completing itself (not by being spelled out but by being so
directed, so *pointered* by the severity that the physics of its force
goes on while you or I take up the INSTANTER perception which
follows from its origination, and from its declared directionals — we
move on, instantly, to what pours in, and thus, the density, the
massive, the thickness which is THE SINGLE INTELLIGENCE

this must sound terrible abstract, but is not so felt, and it may be
because I am analyzing a huge man I came up[on] yesterday
whom you MUST give yrself the chance to hear, now that you are
in France — where he is
    I, at the moment, go this far, as to say, he is the 1st composer
    since Bach — for me (granting, of course, my peculiar ignorance,
    or arrogance, about music as an art!

PIERRE BOULEZ — only two things of his exist here (the 2nd
Sonata, which I heard yesterday impeccably played (piano) by
David Tudor; and a recording in NY)[81]
    but for god's sake, go get him, when you are in Paris — he is
    25, and I shall try to find out his address for you — Christ,
    does he come *straight* from himself, compose as a man, with
    none of the shit of "music," or experiment
                                    put Gerhardt on to
him, too

(and if Shahn dont bite on G's cover, for the Am issue, I have another lad sitting here for us: Cy Twombly

(again, 22, 25, and huge with himself already – beautiful ((you may remember his old man as ex-Big Leaguer, and now coach at Washington & Lee))[82]

((I am going to throw Twombly first, on a cover for the REVIEW i shall have these characters get out, of their own work, shortly))

I figure it this way: there is no harm at all in Shahn doing the G – just because he is the best of the Ams because he is *calligraphic*

but, when it comes to feeling what is really up, none of these elders compare to your bunch – not at all

for my money, YOU, and BOULEZ, are so far the single ones

as of the AM *fragmente*, what you propose makes all sense to me: THE KINGFS is as solid as i might wish to be, and yr context, is beautiful (to Bill); hope you have MOVE O (yes, of course – and i not yet have seen that golden goose! isn't he the BIGGEST PRICK IN THE WORLD?)

but do put yrself on the verse in there, say, making the three of us, a tryptich – for, as you damn well know, i'm with bill on what this creeley is (and tho you are editor, let's keep the proportions – that is, whatever Blackburn, Bronk, Morse, Emerson are, they are not . . .

I'll write to Ben direct, getting him started (and to send direct to you, I guess, eh?

It's damned good news ((I figure between you – you & G – you have any of my stuff you might want to hook on – smaller things, as you say ((the smallest is, that gig, IMAGI:

THESE DAYS

whatever you have to say, leave
the roots on, let em
dangle

And the dirt

                   just to make clear
                   where they come from

wasn't it?

         Con is terrific. And all's well (a bad 48 hrs last week,
when, due to this cough, which has hung on since the last month
Lerma, the doctor ordered a chest Xray, and hinted, maybe tb! but
Sat. she got a clean bill!) Only problem, is, what to do, where to
go — agree with your sudden exaction GET THE HELL OUT OF
BMC
         ((((has my tone been that bad!))))
                         BUT, man, money? and
movement, a month previous?
                     I'm damned to know what to do.
Figure to ride right up to the end here, and then

                       (((this
fuck[*remainder of letter written in ink*:]ing machine — sticking plus,
yesterday, 3rd Sunday of baseball (in 17 yrs!), playing 1st, the
most knit bastard here hit me, & I'm afraid I got a busted rib, god
damn it — had a bad night with it, & today
                     Must take the rib &
the machine into B/Mt for, repairs

Agree — the place for me, or any man is where — he can stay open
Sure. But am just puzzled by, how, & money too!
                         Well, it'll work
out. Will let you know what breaks
                 (& Mitch: so far, no action —

the regular instructor, M C Richards, has not yet decided, whether she'll stay, or go — nor have I!

Am figuring, for one thing, to try to wrap the HU up for Cid's #3, between Sept 1-15th, if he can give me that time — he's locking up, Sept 1 (will have, I guess, fr me, only the poem, Round & Canon, if I can't get HU ready)

The idea of G shooting stuff to Swiss ESSENCE also makes sense — tell him, I'm for it
((as of new material, to G — have not done that, but will, now that he's on, again: if any sudden demand, you have copies of most (tho I am still looking to chance to rewrite, such as, & along lines, you have suggested: the *Concerning Exag*, which you take as best, may be, you might get off to him, if you have a better machine than mine is — at the moment!) *obliged*
(((And what is the shorter story — with Lawrence? Am bewildered, anyhow, that some mail may have gone astray

And LAD, like you, that you stuck that check up their ARSES! Jesus, you got guts

BY CRANE, THANK CREELEY! have just read AGAIN what you propose — there — to prepare myself, for TONIGHT. And how true it is, his, sounds *AND* his LINE — how, in *PV*, I might have made MORE of him (but that I *have* him *there*, delights me —

What still bothers me, is, the *lifting* — the allowing, the phrase, to *rise* — instead (exactly *instead*) of what I was getting at (above) of *pointering* & then, instantly, *because there is so much*, pushing on
— *composition*, now, has to (to pile up, to have,
percussion in
the vertical, has to
fight the allure, has NOT to
FIND

and it is some SCHMERZ, *because he hasn't found,* which leaves
these lesions

    —or, better, which does not make the packing hard
& firm enough to remove all question of HOLES

      —that is, I also
take it his animation of the inanimate—like the sill's one
unyielding smile, say—comes from this WISH[83]

      —you see, if a
man does not stay OPEN, in exactly the sense of OPEN TO ALL,
& ANYTHING—not just to what is sensory (which has a funny
way of getting spiritual—almost from too much *asking*—(from too
much hardness!)—he'll find the NOT-FINDING so hard to bear
he'll start to RIDE—and jesus, that means, he'll put his elbows on
something *outside* himself (the deception is, a *modern* one, this
way:

  the *modern* (and we have to push this biz, of the SINGLE I,
to undo the modern) does—admit it or not—feel he does *not*
belong to what—just, quick, call it, the universe

      my assumption is
any POST-MODERN is born with the ancient confidence that, he
does belong.

  So, there is nothing, to be *found.* There is only (as
Schoenberg had it, his Harmony, search[84]) tho, I should wish to
kill that word, too—there is only examination. And I hew to ED's
proposition, one perception *instantly,* another—as, the *INSTANT*
is, that fast, *another* : why, too, I take it, the *flaws,* when they
exist, are COMPOSITIONAL

  Yr "Conjecture" is *examiner,* no? Quite clearly *NOT* search.
BUT, there it is—that the marble does *not* weep—that (that
negative) animate properly—AND HOW!

  And that you send me Alice A. Ainsworth is what, of course,
is—for me—the *real* (& without reference to bill, or, crane, but to
you, to me:

    I simply say, she's *on,* because—well, in a way they
are not

    (that is, don't be bothered if I seem all the way to hell and gone away from what you are so impeccably reminding me of: AAA, she, is my gal now, Lerma or BMC, always: and the reason? well, where does her language come from? (neither fr God or fr America

BOTH *AND* what poets better remember if they are not to smell of, poetry—as music smells as paint smells when it is not this severely limited as AAA when she says, with not a syllable of rise, raise—she says, that was the last of them (a wipe-out). We felt terribly about it. STOP. The law of discourse is to say what you got to say & STOP.[85] Jesus, does she.

BUT THERE IT IS AGAIN—Christ—*who* wrote—"We have bred
                    Bill?   dug
                                        . . .

By God, it's *Beautiful*   no end,
                                     to desire."

                    Well today, *lad* & *what*, for putting me on!
                    Love fr us both to you both & the boys
                                           Charles

                                    [Black Mountain, N.C.]
                                         Monday night
                                      [20 August 1951]

Rob't—

I have just come back from a very bad job around & abt yr Crane things—to READ yr letters, just in, on Bill. And I am done in, spent, & damn brought up sharp by you. That is, I think you are right, I am *off*—put off by this place. Have felt it, as enclosed (which I'll let go, to give you, some feel of, the whereabouts (though it may be more of same)   Don't know.

Will go out now to do two things   (1) get this off to you, & (2) cancel the Apollonius—I am too convinced, by walking over you, that I am in no condition to write it.

I am deeply sorry. That is, I have the feeling I was on to something, in all that business 10 days ago. But, surely, if it invaded you like that, then, something got left out—I must have been pushing Bill around a counter in some game of my own, & both ways, it's no good, no good, and what I get of it tonight (not figuring myself as too sharp). I am just god damn winded, god damned broken in the place. Please let's come to it again when I am sane. You see, a poem like that one—of his—is nothing anything I said could cause me to close myself to. And so, the whole biz is, something else, somewhere else, is over here, where I am—PLEASE, above all, just keep em coming at me. I'll just quiet down, as of now.

Yr lad, and exactly lad,

C

[Black Mountain, N.C.]

Wed Aug 23 [i.e. 22, 1951]

I stay distressed, & puzzled over the effect of the WCW biz on you. It won't clear up, I know, in any one go. But let me say what's on my mind—or take a crack at it.

Or maybe it's me that's now hopped up—or was, from the start. For this sort of concentration that you speak of, as well as that—surely—Bill *is*) has always been a kind of terror for me. Yet I don't know: I love him (and I believe he has me, the once, at least, we were together for an evening) easily, naturally—as though we just got each other, straight, no trouble, no fuss, just caught, were hooked, without any personality matters — were *organically* recognizable, to one another.

I was writing, not at you, but to you, about this thing, as it was on my mind — that's why I was so suddenly brought up, to see how you had felt the thing — taken it — as something more — that you felt I had in any way put *you* — as you had it — against a mean wall.

I don't know how that came about — surely, there was no hidden cargo in it — it was all there, straight out, because I was just emptying my mind on the subject as, suddenly, it had once again & anew presented itself to me.

I have just now (& strange that, one of these, should last night, put in my hand Bill's Dream of Love!)[86] read it. And it seems so altogether all right, so exact, so lovely — such a beautiful thing — such true language — all of it — as good as ever, he, more so, actually, the way the tragedy of it stays *inside*

Christ! I envy you, him, to work there where you do. For that is it all, isn't it, all that has ever bothered me, that I come at it an altogether other way — can't for the life of me, bear on but have always to bear in, to bring to bear from some other dimension than, the real, or whatever.

It makes for a hell of an unsatisfactory life, the *discrepancy*. For it is that, so far as I feel it, inside me, a, discrepancy — & the fiercest sort of separation. I can talk all I want about image, & where it comes from, or "culture" as a dimension from which I bear — and *must*, for, if I am I, as you say, by rigorous logic (which, I'd guess, I am by nature, rather, & by whatever *shaping*, correct or incorrect, I give same) then, there is nothing to it but to make the best of it, to make it be what — however much I may try to lessen the discrepancy — it is. I don't know any other way, & I believe, so far as it is capable for an Irishman (with a boggish sort of soul, perhaps, as Dahlberg would have it — Bill's AJ)[87] to believe anything — that is quietly, without believing by an act of aggression!

God damn it. Maybe this is a hell of a time for me to venture into any of this. For I am otherwise unhappy. But then — I never did believe one can pick & choose. Here it is. And I give it to you, for what it's worth.

It comes to such a business as the red selvage, say. For me, that comes in *this side* of the business — or even the brilliance of the climax, the battle, to Dixie. (*reduces* the real)

Say I stay a romantic, instead of, such a realist. I'm not at all sure there isn't a hidden premise of human consciousness here (take the play on the Achilles quote, to Priam, also)[88] that I don't go with it —

I damned well don't know, but, it is my hunch (and I play it) ((granting, as always, the peril — & which same peril scares — has always scared the piss out of me, because, despite my protests, I do believe there is truth!)) that the real is much more multiple (and that this is where the confusion & the conjecture really comes in) that we — or our fathers, say, have been accustomed to allow

                    SHIT with IT. The point is, I wanted to say, maybe you would use *Preface* as one of the shorter ones with *Move Over*? Or is the Buchenwald reference too close? (It kept me from sending G the little book until *after* he had seen a lot of my other stuff. Think abt it, anyway, will you? For, the *parenthesis* business, there,[89] comes back to me again, now (came back to me thinking, of, Bill & Eric,[90] or, Ez & Rimini — & how the only parenthesis I know are open which does not close, is, each our own birth

          (1910 — or whatever — so ——

                    no para

You see, maybe my kind, are always fucking generalizers, however the appearance — that is, Ez, or Melville, or — the only man who, properly, taught me, I wanted to write, & what it was, William Shakespeare (Homer is a part of this, surely, but he came later, & if I have learned anything from him, it hasn't shown yet

— look at that — even there, the other dimension, the fatuity of it! The assumption of, simple like, to *belong*! Cool, real cool! SHIT. As though it made any difference.

But it *does*, when you come right down to how it feels to be

inside—what I feel like—about anything: done. I don't know what
the Christ you meant by "we do have our humilities, any of us."
And how!—or do you think I buy that fucking tone of mine (that
tone which buggers me as much as I damn well know it drives
everyone off me—everyone, goddamn it, however they may even
praise—except you, damn you, you have always given me the
sense you were willing—did—RIDE, without interference of, me—
that, as you have it, there, that notice of Y & X, the line on the
language is *more* than a wagon!

I don't buy that tone easily. I'd be
rid of it, if I knew how. Sometimes I take it I am not born, the
real seems so real to somebody else—and all I know, have ever
known, is *not* the real but is Beauty—whatever the fuck that is.

It was you who made it, "Lawrence, or Notes on the real"—
and jesus, how proud a subtitle it is, how proud I was, that you
could take it (that *you*, just exactly *you*) should find it possible to
see anything I had to say had to do with the REAL!

(it was just
abt the handsomest gift I ever got)

It's what fucks me up, how little, I feel in touch with, the
REAL. And why—when I go off—it is always *TASTE* that I'm left
with (like some goddamned interior decorator, with that swing, in
his, *gait*, eh?)

When I go horizontal—literally fall, lacking, the standing-
up——

If I could once more write as vertical as I take it Boulez has,
in, that 2nd Sonata—as, indeed, I take it I did In Cold Hell—
which, by god, if I don't write that poem, I'll inscribe (when
somebody else but that prick Emerson prints it) "to Pierre Boulez,
for, his 2nd Sonata"

Look, Rob't, *none* of this is any more than what it has always
been, to you—spilling, all, I got on my mind—and *innocently*,
real, innocently—no tricks, nothing of (what breaks my heart, the
way Bill puts it, that "all the writers, & the neighborhood shits,
have never wanted anything more than to make use of him"—god,
god, that he does honestly not know—*innocently*—how, who of
us, can, get outside the (how do they have it?), the, egocentric
predicament?

The point is, I'm stuck with my given — & the lousy job I have so far done with same (and that "lousy" is meant, & isn't asking for anything, for no fucking reassurance — which none of us can give each other *enough* of, any way, any time

And I don't know (I don't consciously ever) that I stick my finger in another man's dish. Just don't believe in it.

What I was writing to you then (as I am now) is what's on my mind — and I remain in terror how much any thing I say is *off the point!* For I feel so, forever feel so, except, for the day, when, I am kidded I have, in some act, got at, some little look of, beauty. It's the only thing I damn well know. I don't even, you see, really know what life is, except, this — how, it does get, somewhere, that sort of charge: only beauty.

And I am quick to admit — ahead of time feel the pinch — that, there's something wrong here.

It completely buggers me — always has. I honestly don't know *how to act,* toward any one, or any thing, except, to *shoot* myself — the only law I know is, that, energy, provokes, what I am interested in — what I *have* to *do.* And it has forever got me into nothing but confusion, & disappointment: bewilderment, as to what happens, what the *response* is, of persons, or things, how, suddenly, usually, they are scared — wrongly charged — or repelled.

I put it — always — in terms of *justice:* though, in the last two years, I have had to knuckle under here (maybe the beginning of birth, to the real, for a character of my ilk), to admit, there ain't none — but, admitting it, has not yet enabled me to stop acting as though it (justice) existed. (The result, of course, is the very arbitrariness, which keeps the real running away from me, right in front of my eyes.)

So, such *realism,* as Bill's, has always put me off (as the same in existenz, or wit, or woman, or Apollinaire, or time, or even Rimbaud, except, when, suddenly, I feel all the way inside, & then (& when that, is, in some unmanageable innocent business, which when it happens, I am free from, consequence)

You see, you make it possible for me to feel *on* — like that — & for that, well, it's beautiful

(maybe beauty is only the formulation
of, my own inarticulateness
                    —which last, surely, is my most
marked characteristic
    (that's why I love, I guess, in this play of Bill's, the *real* truth,
of these women that, it is his *talk* which gets them *on!!*)
                                                        hell, I
was using Bill—am using him—just to find out better how to use
myself—isn't it just as simple as that? and what's wrong with that?
how, otherwise, does a man's work make itself felt? why,
otherwise, does it exist, for anyone outside himself?
        I can't worship him, or it. I can't make him a
surrogate for something else—there is too much of this turning
men or women, or their things, into fathers or mothers or sisters
or brothers. I can only feel his work (as his work is different from
himself as he might have been intimate to me, or I to him, or
anyone is intimate to me, & I to them) as an object—out there—&
more or less *animate* (in, again, the sense of the *life* of the thing,
granting, as I have, above, that what is most animate to me is
beauty as it is *truth* (((however much I may sound like John
Keats!)))
        The trouble is, I don't know when one ceases to be *unformed*
(again, the peril, the damned business, in saying that, that, my
mind knows, it surely is a sign—given our present premises—that
I, myself, stay, *unformed*! Which is a risk (the risk of innocence,
least of all!) I have, now, age 40, no alternative but to take! (I am
thinking, knowing, what knocks, in the cellar, of a passage in
Herodotus which has stirred me, keeps stirring me, of Herakles, in
the arms of, some goddess—& how silly, & little, & what a
goddamned little baby the Strong Man comes out!)[91]
        I am not at all confident, except, by moments. And the
real—so far as I know it—is *only* such moments. That's the
trouble—that's, the *selection*, I am always talking about: the
selection of, out of *the* multiples, as well as the multiples I,
actually, think we are (I am I, not because I think I am a single
creature, but as I am—or as a moment is—single)
        And I take the *preparation*—the preparation for the
recognition (the recognition of the instant)—to be *necessarily*,

exhaustive (that personality, or passion, or mind, is, only a few of
the *several* preparations the human capacity is capable of

So that *place* sits, *amongst* these several. And no more. But,
to invert you, certainly no less, no less than a saffron, or a red
bird, female, in this small tree, with a tarred broom caught in its
crotch, than a sudden woman on a street, or one in bed, than a
broken arm, than a real image, than Bill, of an evening, talking
about plays —

that is, I take it, a *difference* is, that I am an
American and not, a Hindu —

& that, however that Hindu & I
might get along better than I'd get along with Bill, still, Bill & I
have a topography *different* from Virgil &, Dante, eh?

walk a
different hill, *even*

however much more, I might take it, it would
more resemble Herakles', & that woman — or, how those people
feared bears & wolves around Mt Lycaon[92]

SHIT — there I go, off,
to my own habitats!

That's all that all this — or any of that, that
bothered you — is about: my attempt at an old answer, who am I
& where do I belong

Love,

C

PS
And to keep abreast! (1) the baby things came today — the
loveliest of surprises, and though I shall want to dip the little
sweater into a bath of red dye, & Ann mustn't mind, you two
have given us, as wonderfully as it should be, the *first* things (oh,
a pair of *pink* socks! ((also to be dyed, came from Mme
Goldowski!)))

& (2) I *was* right, there was a broken
chain, in the correspondence — came yesterday. the long letters of
around Aug 4th, & later, including, the *story*, which, I am holding
to read the moment this blackness, which has been on me, is

broken —

I hope writing this letter to you may break it!

Love fr us both,
Charles

[Fontrousse, Aix-en-Provence]
[25] August [1951] / Saturday

Dear Chas/

Yrs in, and finds me all but dead with a cold — I thought I had the mumps for sure, but turns out otherwise. Anyhow, am picking myself, just about, off the floor to answer.

Have been circling round Williams all this past week; the thing, that you are so very right on the biz of enthusiasm, & the cost that must imply. And writing, a short thing for G/ (a copy of which will get on to you this coming week), can say, of Ez: "We have experienced the phenomenon of a man *committed to particulars* and that *must* be made known." But cannot say it, oddly, of Williams — not surely. And why? What is eating me now.

Cid asked me to do a job on Paterson (for #4) and don't like it too much at this point, sd job, but want to try it anyhow — for my own uses, at this juncture.

(But there is, always was, a lot of rightly called dross; but to somehow walk so one doesn't trample the daisies, or some damn thing. It's work.)

That story: was a short one, THE PARTY — & card in from Lawrence, saying he doesn't like it, etc. Myself, I don't know —

Ann sd she sent it to you slow mail, so that will explain the delay
there. Not much; I don't know. I don't want to put anything to
Cid but what I do like altogether. (I had to give him some lee-way
with that SORT OF A SONG because he had planned on it, or
prose, for that space — but he says: won't use it, if he can get out
of it. (Which would be, yr HU — & for god's sake, do get it done,
eh? As the alternative might come to that story, which I don't
want to see there. Ok.))

It's been an oddly dead summer, in spite of that 2nd issue. I wish
that summarizing, so, wd complete it, but suspect there are several
weeks to be got through, no matter what.

                                         A flatter one I have a
hell of a hard time remembering — or put it against 1 year ago,
today. That was something!

But to pick up anyhow — hoping that sd process is the final one of
this life, to keep moving, in spite of the etc/s.

A footnote to Mrs/ A/s letter: that my sister, calling Bill Gordon
(the house-owner) in Cambridge (he lives well, plays around, etc.,
has an odd wife & two small children), was answered by Evelyn
A/ — why she is there, I wonder about.

                                         Anyhow — they do make
it. Or she is one of the greatest. I could always put it to her,
anything, as of myself, i.e., could talk. The little girl, E/ : age
about 14 (?), almost. Fat, takes very good care of herself. I
imagine G/ overstepped the grand manner this time. Ok.

Well — dead, I have been waiting to hear what Morrow's says to
the 1st part of the novel. All week, & no word from the woman
there, who was to have written me directly she got back (Aug/
13th). A nuisance. And sometime, could you send back that odd
chapter? No copy here, & cannot tell what to do about any of it,
frankly. I feel so very out of it, any of it — blahing. I sound like —
but damn tired of it, at the moment.

The waste, continual, of having these tag ends out, to be tugged
at, again: common character — you sd. That was straight.

And it came to: sitting to read, always sitting I am, Ez' gig on
Guido,[93] and how he lined it there—the parts.

Respect, an infinite

respect, for that sense of care. (. . . the house was put to the
earth . . .)[94]
>   So.

The Cantos too. Had been trying to make them, of a piece—and
stand, this moment, at the beginning of the last. The Pisan
Cantos, they said.

(The last? What do you think? Doesn't sound like it to me.)

Emersons/ all such: nothing, nothing, nothing. A letter in from
some man in California rejecting a poem I must have sent him
close to 2 yrs ago.
>   Or Ez sd: There is a TIME in these things . . .

All of us do not inhabit the same time, he also continued . . .[95]

Well, to be holding. I think circa Winter 1951 will hope for one or
two things I can put my name on. I hope, anyhow, hope.

This hadn't got to you/ :   A SONG   (?)

I had wanted a quiet testament
and I had wanted, among other things,
a song.
>   That was to be
of a like monotony.
>   (A grace

Simply. Very very quiet.
>   A murmur of some lost
thrush, though I have never seen one.

Which was you, then. Sitting
and so, at peace, so very much, now, this same quiet.

A song.

And of you,. the sign now, surely, of a gross
perpetuity
          (which is not reluctant, or if it is
it is no longer important.

A song.

Which one sings, if he sings it,
with care.

          (Somewhere back there. One item, that is, with the
other LOVE, 'Tell me something I don't know,' that seems ok, in
some sense.
               But prose. That has me bugged. That novel holds all
of it, still, or all that I can get to, it seems.

But no damn matter/ surely no damn matter. I have a great deal
to be sitting on. So/ to sit. For the time being, & keep awake,
somehow.

Crazy letter. And very very grateful. Cold should be gone by
Monday, or hope so, & will get one off to you, again, then. And
take it all in.
               (Crane holds. Fantastic juxtaposition of his
innocence (certainly that metric?) & then, the hits. Well, another.
But always yr care—no good swallowing all, without looking.)

Hot as hell/ looking up at this ceiling (how many damn miles) :
where the hell am I. You say.
                         All our love to you both/
                                        [Bob]

[*Verso envelope:*]
                    a broken RIB?
                    What do these

          people WANT,
                    eh?
          Wow . . .
(Enclosed please find one thumb.)

―――――――――――――

                                    [Fontrousse, Aix-en-Provence]
                                         August 27/ 51

Dear Chas/
          So very very grateful to you for this last letter —
meant, it must have meant, a good deal more than you had reason
to suspect.
          What happened — that it came in with the enclosed
letter (from Morrow's) which I'll put in here (a copy) plus my
answer to them. I mean, it's yr answer made it possible for me to
tell them. And because I had got so damn hung with the whole
biz, the novel & the possibility that they might have taken it — you
clear it all out for me, sweep it clean, & make it simpler, very
much simpler, to pick myself up.

                              The real. Surely, infinite
gradations? Surely each man able, even obliged, to assert his own,
and somehow of that complex, all the many things hanging: a
common world.
                    Which, being so, has only its life in that flux of
attention so given it.

I know, as it is, much less than you do, much less of all of this. I
think you were precisely the one who made clear to me — one's
speech, the issue of one's speech, is all one has to give, and damn
well to be given without question.
                         I wd put it open: that I am

alive really in this one act, to write. That there, like it or not, is what's possible to me, what can effect myself.

Otherwise : so very damn under it all, so goddamn smothered, I cannot be, say, anything but one extension, or limb, or a multiple — which I apprehend, or get peace from, only thru statement, only thru my own passage to myself.

Wd you do me one big favor — i.e., have asked them (as noted) to send the ms/ to you there. Wd you run thru it, I mean, read it when you can, & make (directly on the copy) any comment that seems to you relevant.

(And will get you loot, then, to ship it back to me here.)

I can't honestly find the push, now, to finish it, but I want to know, clearly, what happened there. I want, then, to try it another way, this winter, say, or just soon, and want to get whatever was clear, there, out, & available for the next time.

It may be, or may turn out — to try to finish same, reworking the lapses. But I think I wd now make it cooler, to throw myself out, as deeply as possible, & clear of any world of 'memory' of which that is, I think, too deeply a part.

That is, again, to set out clean, straight, from the premise of, I am — & to let encrustments, involvements, then declare themselves.

Frightening thing. All the past months I've felt I'd lost all of it, and setting down to something, lifted only phrases, or sounds I know by heart.

Dull damn summer. Waste, all of it, & to be chucked out, now, for same.

But say what you think, i.e., hit it there, on the copy, and I can then get clear. (I owe you so very much; all, or any of this sometime clarity, just yrs.)

Well, we *do* hold, both of us, in our own way. What the hell else can matter?

Just one thing/ just that: that you/me will, are, there. Will be there. Ok.

Ann says: take care on dying the sweater, i.e., have to boil it real long & hard to make sure it won't run every time the baby gets it wet.

(Well, these are tenuous matters. Ok.) The blanket was, 2nd [*Added by Ann Creeley*: (Thomas's)] hand/ but warm, but warm. Ok. [*Ann Creeley*: Why don't you dye that red too. Babies get attached to their blankets and won't go to sleep without them and he will look mighty silly aged six clutching a pink fringe.]

Crazy.

(Like this/ so many times have gone back to yr writing, notes, on BLUE, on the gig for Guggenheim, on all the stuff. Gets me clear and no one else ever cd put it in like you do.

So what I damn well must have — yr eye on this novel. Am 25, pretty cool health, & means to exist. Am damn well going to write a pisser, one pisser of, a novel, so got to get on it? Sure.

And sooner I get yr eye on the shit, to cut same, sooner will be on to it/ as what it's got to be.)

Whistling in a christly dark place, but what else would they expect. Ok.

Write soon/ and all our love to you both,

Bob

That we are at this distance, from one another, only rub. But letters — they do damn well come.

Love/ love. Ok.

August 23, 1951

Dear Mr. Creeley:

I am sorry it has taken me so long to write you but I came
home from a glorious vacation to a desk piled high and sweltering
summer weather. At last I have time to breath[e] and look around.

I read the first part of your manuscript, and two other editors
read it as well. I am going to be perfectly frank with you because
I am sure that is what you want.

First, the good things as we see them: you can be wonderful
on mood, on atmosphere, with the small descriptive phrase, the
telling sentence; on the mood of your characters and the feel of
the place.

But, as the beginning of a novel, we find the obscurity
discouraging. As one report says: "I suspect there were several
other events happening . . ." And most readers will not be satisfied
with a suspicion; especially in a novel that is going to go on for
quite a time.

You have a definite, individual style (inclined to get a little
self-conscious), and you, yourself, seem to know what you want
to say. Perhaps the fault is in us that we can't see it in a book.
That first story (U[nsuccessful] H[usband]) of yours that I read,
and that interested me so, said a great many things very clearly,
however.

Well, that's the story as we see it. I will hold the manuscript
here for further instructions. Many thanks to you for letting us see
your work, and being so very nice about everything.

With the very best wishes,
Sincerely,
Adele Dogan

over)

August 27, 1951

Dear Miss Dogan,

Very, very sorry to learn that the manuscript does not interest you; certainly a disappointment, although I do appreciate the difficulties you've been kind enough to note for me.

I dislike, very much, having to bother you further, but can you please bear with me for just a bit longer? That is, I have no immediate way to pay for the mailing of the manuscript either back to me here, or to anyone there in the States. What would be particularly helpful—if you could send it, 1st class, to CHARLES OLSON, BLACK MOUNTAIN COLLEGE, BLACK MOUNTAIN, N.C. And I'll ask him to send you the cost of the postage as soon as he has received the ms/ and can tell what to send.

Again, thanks for your honesty. It is, frankly, a frightening world : publishing. I wish that I were somewhat nearer, so that I might ask you these questions, call them, in person. I have so very little knowledge of the procedure, and only wish that one might write free of any pressure, or obligation to a public he can hardly trust.

Well, be equally honest, that is, if you will want to see the finished draft, I'd be glad to send it on, once done. But you'll know the bother involved for us both, in any such sending, so don't ask, then, if there isn't any hope. I've always written, stupidly or not, for my own uses; and that makes me keep at these things anyhow. It's my only grip on the world I do have, and suppose that others have rights, also, to worlds of their own intent. Well, again, thanks. The compliments were very much enjoyed; and the admonitions will be taken to heart.

(One screams into nothing—flesh or whatever one calls it, there has to be substance, and I cannot see it as construction, or that one has any right to warp anything, but to that exactness of his own living; and that isn't warping.)

All my best to you, and very good to hear that you had such a fine vacation.

Yours sincerely,
Robt (Fuck you All) Creeley

[*Verso envelope:*]
Goddamn LIKE when I sent birds to shows (R.R. Express) and get
them back — sick — not getting any DAMN CARE. viz inside

[*Note by Ann Creeley:*] Hold the dy[e]ing till the socks arrive — 10
days.

———————

[Fontrousse, Aix-en-Provence]
August 28 [*i.e.* 29, 1951]/ morning

M/ Goodman on C/ Olson: A PLEASURE [*Added:* sd : Gertrude
Stein!]

"Olson's thing in PNY is very good. It has a hardness, a direct-
looking quality I don't find in his stuff on prose (I figure he aims
that, mainly, at the DHL piece, & will make comment re same, at
end). Here he knows the materials, from working with them and
not just from looking at them. Like a carpenter who *knows* wood
and what you can do with it. This is looking at the stuff itself,
with no sliding off into ideas as he does I think with things like
the notes on Lawrence. What he says about poetry has much more
use for me in thinking about prose than his stuff on prose, or than
most things written about prose. Pretty damn near anything I've
read, at all, on how it's done, how it happens — or, more, where it
comes from . . . Just been reading it again: it's terrific, terrific.
Damn sorry we didn't get a chance to talk about it. This stuff like:
get on with it, keep moving, keep in, speed, the nerves, their
speed, the perceptions, theirs . . . keep it moving as fast as you
can. (That adds something to what you told me about keeping it
pitched high, in that first part of mine I showed you.)

"On p. 15 he has this paragraph beginning: It is by their syllables that words juxtapose in beauty by these particles of sound . . . This ties up very closely with what I've been thinking about Italian.

"And . . . the ear has the mind's speed . . .

"The stuff on pp. 16 and 17, head ear syllable, heart   breath   line

"the Play of the mind (what we are after) That's what it means, this thing you're on, the not setting it up in advance but letting it come. Too many people don't want this PLAY, they're afraid of it, they don't know where it might go. So they make a roll for the player-piano and sell it for the real thing. PLAY with the syllables, Olson says, for poetry. But you can go further, PLAY with the objects, the things impinging (outside) and the other objects, the people, Played back and forth and against each other. Until they explode and start throwing light (illumination).

"And that business: the heart gone lazy and the line gone dead with similes, adjectives. Descriptive functions with their drain on energy (which tells me what I lose when I start explaining, as you pointed it out). *Any* slackness takes off attention . . . (that too tells me something, altho I think in prose, in a novel anyway, you can't avoid slackness . . . it would be too highly charged, exploding too soon, before the full energy was created. I guess this has to do with pacing.) [*Note by Creeley in margin*: only slip]

". . . the going energy of the content toward its form (Right in, smack, he's hit it). Objects handled in such a way that a series of tensions are made to *hold*, and to hold exactly within the content and the context of the poem which has forced itself, thru the poet and them, into being. (COHESION, huh?)

"All the critics have been talking about the importance of *speech* in the writing but none of them has known why. Olson: Because the breath allows *all* speech-force of language back in (again, how it works, from the end of the man working with the materials)

". . . each of these elements of a poem can be allowed to have the play of their separate energies and can be allowed, once the poem is well composed, to keep, as those other objects do, their proper confusions (their proper confusions: WOW) That last tells me as much about the range and capacities of the novel, about WHAT it is as anything I've ever seen or heard. If it's anything, that's what it is: a FIELD. What else are you trying to do in a novel but allow the elements, the objects, the people, everything, their proper confusions. ALLOW, and not *set them up in a neat diagram.* Confusions. Jesus, that's what it is, and the PLAY of them to get the tensions that crystallize them.

"What he's got in the first part of part II, about *objectism* says everything he was trying to say in that essay you showed me, the one he sent from Mexico: this is the answer to the wrong kind of humanism, and here stated in His Own Specifics, in a language he knows. [*Added in margin*: If the emphasis is only CONTRA-humanism, this is true—but make it—metaphor as symbol, etc—something else again!] 'What seems to me a more valid formulation for present use is *objectism*, a word to be taken to stand for the kind of relation of man to experience which a poet might state as the necessity of a line or a work to be as wood is, to be as clean as wood is as it issues from the hand of nature, to be as shaped as wood can be when a man has had his hand to it. . . . getting rid of the lyrical interference of the individual as ego, . . . that peculiar presumption by which western man has interposed himself between what he is as creature of nature (with certain instructions to carry out) and those other creatures of nature which we may, with no derogation, call objects. For a man is himself an object . . .' etc. (He's said it, that's it, in his own terms and without generalization and the dragging in of references he's not at home in).

"And on Eliot. that 'his root is the mind alone, and a scholastic mind at that . . . —and that, in his listenings he has stayed there where the ear and the mind are, has only gone from his fine ear outward rather than, as I say a projective poet will, down thru the workings of his own throat to that place where breath comes from, where breath has its beginnings, where drama has to come from, where, the coincidence is, all act springs.' (From the word *down* on in, this thing *rings*, you can hear his voice.

"I THANK YOU"

[*Added*: (all . . . : his)]

Jesus, I wonder if it's possible for any man, in this case yrself, to realize what he can do. A hell of a way to put it, but I don't figure it 'imaginative' to say, certainly, that there must be any number of men, like Mitch, able & willing to pick up the sense of such a thing as PRO/ VERSE. It takes time; a matter of distribution — but can see, surely, that they do make it — and that in giving them that substance, to put such in their hands, you do them a damn actual service — & a service it wd be impossible to ignore.

I damn well want to lean on this biz of distribution. I.e., I had hoped, then, when it was going on, E/ wd suggest the inclusion of that piece as a appendix, or kind of preface to the poems. Or that you had. To keep it going — being that a magazine like PNY does slip out of circulation too simply, & have to keep this thing IN circulation by other means. Suggest, at least next yr, that we attempt its issue as a separate pamphlet — with added material if it seems wise, or simply for itself.

The comment on HU may seem rough; the main thing, that he did balk a little at some of the emphases, i.e., I think those parts where I had felt, too, that the thing was spreading a little, etc. I disagree with him on the Lawrence notes; a matter of attention, I suspect, but they are valuable, very valuable, if only for the formulation at the beginning, i.e., 2nd para where you state the evolvement of contest/ to change. But I hardly leave it at that.

Jesus, I don't know how to put it — of the many, & there are many, that much certain, you give an actual substance, a thing which one can USE. You do it in the poems; you did it on the Melville; and you certainly did it with the PRO/ VERSE. You

carry it on in GATE & CENTER & related gigs—myself, I take
you as on the lip of, the big thing (for lack of better title) or
exactly, the digging into the DESCRIPTIVE function which I begin
to see as the self-same Cross on which they nailed our gentle jesus,
etc.

I see you stripping that one back, for, let's say it quietly,
anyone who has eyes in his head, & something of a brain, back of
them.

And you will, again, do a service to prose (such as Mitch here
emphasizes) that this PNY piece does.

We are working toward,
god be praised, a sense of both of these acts which allows them
BOTH room in language—which sees, finally, the problem as
related to BOTH.

(Ez never got this one altogether, it seems to
me; and did go soft, saying it was a matter of energy (in one
place) and that prose came from an instinct of negation (in
another).[96] Goodnight Ez, & do not feel you have to make
breakfast . . .

Because, it is, again, this christly DESCRIPTION
(symbol/ recall/ record) which has fucked prose for, god knows
how long. And Ez was real close to it (for ONCE) when he sd, of
Joyce: NO ideas after the 1st 100 or so pp of Ulysses—or once he
sees, WHY, we can all get some sleep.)[97]

Did no one ever dig: that
Melville is different IN KIND (but as a wheezy christer biz) from
Joyce et al, IN KIND—& that that difference relates DIRECTLY to
a concept of the use of ENERGY in the novel-form, a means TO
ENERGY???

They only say (wha ha ha . . .) : it is not 'quite like'
the 'usual' novel . . . (wha ha ha . . .)

Damn damn damn. Who
wd NOT see/ he had junked, once & for all, that self-same
method that Joyce, one must think of same as, tired, picked up
that time later. (Flaubert/ James/ & so on: DESCRIPTION. And
good or bad—neat or sloppy—IT JUST AIN'T IT.)

                              Yrs/ per the miasma/ a cloud
All Hail/ etc.

                                                       Bob

                                               Monday aft/

Dear Chas/
              Ann off with the last, & can get, now, to the rest of
it.
     The main thing: to keep going. Jesus, a merrygoround, or
whatever, but to same: one is committed.
                              (The way the kids will
eat in, of any instant, something setting them off, & one never
ready, but HOWL. Ok, I mean, there is that sense, & reminder.)

The real/ or this sense of it : to be that instant (any) when a thing
(anything) coincides its presence (all aspects of that presence) with
one's own.
                    The rest/ waiting, & usual. Shade, or shadow, or
simply: ya/ selva oscura, & you know all of it.

One gets off, now & again, is able to get out of it, but hardly,
that is, hardly any way that remits the pressure.
                                        Lacking the thing
in myself (& I can't read my own work, good or bad, with any
pleasure that can hold, frankly) : yrs. That's something. I mean, I
could like it only for that, what is there for yr lad, as it does, and
can, stand clean & clear, of both of us.
                              It can't be, intention. I wd
never know what you intended; or cdn't. Have always to make it:
what's there. Hence, if I do ride, am able to, make sure that it is
just what the poem makes, & no will to same, or hope, or any
other thing, on my part. I can defend, if it comes to that, any
instance of my taste; and that defence is certainly as available for
any instance of yr own work, as it wd be for anything else I like.

You give me the same; i.e., it was the same (& is) with the prose,

& the poems. Never cd, or will I expect, be able, in any sense, to thank you for what, exactly, was possible between us this past yr. Namely, BLUE — same with 3 Fate Tales — & the impetus certainly you gave me on that 1st critique of ITS. That has held me up, now, for over a yr, & that is as much as one man cd ever give another : what can hold him up.

But that cramps it, that is, forgets all the instances, that continuum. What is it anyone hopes for, in this work, but that somehow, will be present *one other* on whose insight he can put some wt/? SOME wt/ — SOME of that responsibility he can, finally, only see as his own.
                        You can't, I know, block it out, or anticipate. Some of this — the fact that yr work which hangs to me most closely has been just that which I cd never have anticipated, never have plotted in terms of what I did know of yr attentions; that loses the sense of it a little — I mean, only, that a poem like THE KINGFISHERS makes clear to me an *instant* (it is an *instant*) that you have held, or had, just as, yrself.
                        But always I feel the incredible cleanness of yr reading; one reader, put it just like that, ONE READER who is capable of attention, and attention that even can show up those places where my own has slipped.

                                                        The real/ jesus : it's a hard question, & one wants to slide off, somehow; and cannot. Saying, here I am, etc., there it is, the wt/, and what's to be moved somehow. Being: I must, I must keep moving. I am committed.
                        To take it as 'history' : I suppose there is very very little. Or only some 10 things, quick, that have what holds in them. The rest/ either waiting, or loss.
                                                It's my belief: one apprehension, one perception, one gripping of anything, anything, NOT dependent on one's own consciousness, of it, is as real as anything can be.
                        One damn chance stroke/ so. That the kid cries now/ that I suppose I didn't want him to. That against myself,

what I intend to do, there is the wash, & that it is,
articulate.

And myself/ real: as I hold, can hold, to my
perceptions. That straining, certainly, if, say, you toss a stick in
the river, and watch it go off, out of yr sight. Being real, beyond
you, & to whatever distance it can get. To let it go.

Which is eulogizing of a sort. Tom really wailing at this point, so
have to get up to him. Back soon, & you too/ i.e., write when
you can. Hate to shove that novel at you, now, but I'll be damn
honest: I have to, & there's no one but yrself.

All our love to you both/ Bob

Ann just back/ I was standing there, holding sd Thomas, etc., etc.
A bad day for everyone, like they say — at which point I begin to
laugh hysterically.

But art, etc., etc. La vie art, etc.

At least to dissuade those who consider this, at best, a kind of
hobby/

"There's not a damn thing else." (August 27, 1951)

("Turn back, etc.")

On sd novel : hard to note which way I figure it to be leaning,
without betraying that fact, I don't honestly know.

Roughly, as I
figure some kind of rough frame is possible, if only to work
against same, or discard : the obvious gig is that Jake & wife do
go on, that tension, & break, as exterior occasion, call it, makes
such possible. Other characters/ partly variation. Almost wholly
variation — to be honest. I.e., Wilson/ playback, or even inversion,
of aspects of Jake; likewise Henry — passage between them.
Woman: recurrent/ Else/ Jo/ wife.

We know them, etc.

What bugs me : is enough moving there (cleanly) to get a reader that far without going dead, himself, on me, myself.

Well, you look—when it gets in. Ann figures it to hold pretty good, even very well—according to her. But much as I wd like, say, to assure that reaction on yr part, I suppose (haw) I cannot? Anyhow. It is to play, if at all, all ends against the middle.

(No, madam, it is NOT obscure . . .)

How do they get that shit/ ob-scure . . . What do they, for the main thing, think they're saying with those words?
                                    (I knew it/ I knew it : I felt this damn one coming, when, when: no word when she got back there. Smelled that one way off. And sure was right for once.)

That was what got me/ that is: her saying, 'not in a book . . .' What IS that/ shit . . .

No, can't put that, in a book. No, that can't go in this book. No, that isn't for a book, son. No, books don't have that sort of thing in them. No, we don't have that kind of thing in our books. No . . .

(No.)

Crazy to read you on DREAM OF LOVE—because wd begin to say/ IS as good as it gets/ and GOOD ; very damn GOOD.
                                    Put such against the stories (LIFE ALONG THE PASSAIC RIVER,[98] for one item, & what I know)—some gain.
                                    And crazy thing, or what delights me : poem he quotes there, i.e., 'we have bought an old rug/ there is no end, to desire . . .' etc.,[99] is so goddamn much greater than it is IN TOTO!

I mean, I turned to sd poem (Perpetuum Mobile: The City) & does

it drag, some of it/
                    but how very *clean*, just here, & just what he
does say, of it.

                    I think it clears a lot, that bk/ a damn lot. Clears
air/ makes a clean thing.

Voice/ so damn strong all thru there/ so damn straight.

But wd say, too, jesus : reading yesterday, here, Cantos/ clean
fine day/ sun & pigeons, & all that stretch of the valley over to
St[e]. Victoire. You know, this damn LIGHT here/ is Ez'. You can
get it real strong.
                    Anyhow/ 'think not that you wd/ gain if their
least caress
were faded from my mind . . .'
                        'I like a certain number of shades
in my (MY) landscape. . . .'[100] (WOW.)
                            (That's a wild one/ & feel
stronger, yr ABC's/ for those birds,[101] — this spreads it, tho I had
it anyhow; the fact.)
                    One thing/ tho: he says: *amity* with the
hills/ — & all my copies of Origin (all I ever [got] was 2, but more
coming) gone, you sd: equity/ I mean, I remember you had it
there, so.
                'the sage
delighteth in water
        the humane man has amity with the hills'[102]
                            (Wish to christ I
cd track thru this with you closer/ gk/ throws me : the sounds &
meaning. Can make out most of the rest, etc. But, one thing :
aram vult nemus — means, something/ the groves demand altars/
i.e., woods need rites? (Achilles Fang/ hitting same, was something
like that (he sd) & cd not settle on, from what Ez had taken it?
Do you know?)[103]
                    But shit/ IT READS. What I can't make, of
those say, it doesn't. You can read this as fast, as surely, as you,

any man, can make same, at that speed of, his own head/ — there
are NO 'separations.' What kills me, frankly — just this flow/ &
shift. There's nothing like it I know of.

The fact is/ CRAZY just
how they DO READ. What knocks me out.

Other items/ I don't see that PREFACE can't go with the bunch
there. What I'll do — ask him straight, i.e., say that I want it there,
& ask him if sd reference wd constitute a difficulty. (In the
meantime, have you got any way, there, to get me a copy of
KINGFISHERS? Can't get a copy out of him; or haven't yet, & so
question as to how many pp/ it will run in G/s format. What you
can do, to save mailing, etc. — count lines in one of G/s
translations (think it runs to some 27 or some lines per) & then in
THE K/ & figure, roughly, how many pp/ will go to that. Then
can figure, on the others, with more surety.)

One thing: if, on
reading THE PARTY, you think it any gain over SORT OF A
SONG, wd you ship that copy to Cid, with note saying I asked
you to, as possible substitute for the latter. I am nervous as hell
abt that story/ both of them, for that matter. Wd be very grateful
for yr notes on this last one; just all to pieces on this biz, at the
moment.

(I have that very sick feeling, yr holding a damn story,
twere better, like they say, I had not sent.)

Anyhow, anyhow. You drive for a bit, eh? Ok.

One last volley/ at Miss Dogan, & then no more; I will give it up.
But. I do not see. I don't see any of it/

or was going to say, I
don't see how I cd be so 'wonderful' at what she so glibly states, &
so discouraging re : obscurity.

I don't get that, in fact, I don't get
any of it. And never have/ any of the damn twaddle collected
from so many christly editors it wd make you vomit to think I'd
damn well tried them in the first place.

Amen.

Or simply: the walls pull in. Sure. So, to hell with it. I suppose
it's insufferable arrogance to even bother them at all; but they ARE
publishers? They DID 'solicit' me? Fuck it/ I mean it's all their
damn way, & they know it/ so: to hell with them.

Damn damn damn.

                    Anyhow. To wait till you've seen it/ I'll do
my damndest to keep cool. Ok.
                    (And don't let me make you
nervous, he said, don't let me interrupt.
                              Fuck it/ goddamn JOKE.)

Someday, when we're both in NYC/ let's go SEE that woman/ eh?
A bargain.
          Yrs/ in chrIST!
                    Bob

NOTE ON AMERICAN POETRY: 1951

It is difficult — it's impossible to offer any comprehensive
representation of *everything* that's now being written in the States.
Pound's *law* (". . . any tendency to abstract general statement is a
greased slide . . .")[104] advises me to state, and clearly, that I do not
know all there is to know about the subject. My credentials are
my own practice, and an attention to that poetry I've found
available in the periodicals and books of said country; but that
can hardly assure completeness.
    The question is otherwise. The present reader wants to know
something about American poetry; he wants *some* indication of
what, now, is going on. He will know, as I do, that he can't tackle
it all in one lump. He has the poetry of his own country to
occupy him, and his attention to that of another must imply a
search for what can be of *use* to his own.
    There is a criteria which be a help to him: 1) the *speed* with
which one perception issues from another (Olson's formulation)[105]
[*Added in margin*: I figure that as *yr* formulation — i.e., implicit

perhaps in some of Ez' comment, but stated?]; and 2) the *concision* of presentation of all such perceptions (Pound's).[106] This will cut out the deadwood in any poetry, in any country. And in this instance, it will give the reader a gauge by which to judge the present state of American poetry.

Certainly, I may have been unfair to any number of people. Which is to say—there are any number of other poets whose work could have been used here. *But not on the basis of the above criteria.* The five men whose work is given are, insofar as I have knowledge of the matter, those of my contemporaries who try for a major clarity, who intend, first, to *present* the issue of their thought and emotion—and then, if at all, to be 'poetical.'

There is now, in the US, an attempt to return to some notion of 'form' which I had thought to have died out with the Georgians. It consists, briefly, in a *simplified* stringing of loose thought in loose metric. No man forgets what rhyme *can* do; but if the filling of lines with extremely porous matter can get us anywhere, then I very humbly ask for proof.

There is, as well, the old idea that *vers libre* can admit anything—no idea too vacuous, no emotion too general. It was this same idea which (by Pound's statement) brought Pound to the writing of *Mauberley;* the dilution of a master's practice seems inevitable if all one attempts is to be a disciple.

Diction also suffers, that is (again Pound's point), somewhere back there in time ("Dublin 1888") poetry was thought to be "lofty thoughts expressed in beeeeyewteeeeful an' FLOWERY language . . ."[107] It is *not,* but the supposition continues, and language, strung to the tune of any maudlin sentiment, must inevitably arrive at a certain slackness.

To the contrary—an incredible debt to Pound. Any man who writes verse in the States (or in any other country where Pound is, in any sense, known) must acknowledge it. We have experienced the phenomenon of a man *committed to particulars,* and that *must* be made known. The reader is asked to try the criticism, if he has the means, as well as the verse; it is of no matter that some of the 'subjects' here and there are behind us. Harold Munro[108] is dead, and so too, perhaps, his work. But the character of the mind which confronted that work, which attempted to give us some sense of what it was, we can hope is not — *it remains our only civilization.*

Very well then, to be glib. It is the usual way. And American poetry is as sprawling, as inchoate in its bulk, as that of any other country. But there is, contained in it, the work of some six or seven men who remain free of generalities, of occupation with the fancy, the fad, or the more simple expressions of the bankrupt mind.

I advise the reader to add William Carlos Williams — IN THE AMERICAN GRAIN; a good selection of the poems (from the first COLLECTED POEMS and also from the LATER); and PATERSON (his long work). I ask him to try both Stevens and Moore, but suggest that he will find more of interest in Hart Crane, despite the difficulties of language. Eliot, I suspect he knows, and certain others who have received some recognition in his own country.

Of the younger — he has only my own guess, based on the criteria given. He cannot, anymore than I can, keep up with it all. But he can be aware that there continues, in current American verse, some sense of that integrity which both Pound and Williams have gained for it; at least the present selection is an attempt to make him aware. In the verse of *any* country he should demand that *that* quality be present.

[*Added in pencil*: (Had copied this out, plus note, before yrs came in — so will enclose it with present letter.)]

O/ the problem is considerable, i.e., I'm obliged to face into this selection as, frankly, a reader of poetry, & not a writer. I have my specific commitments to you, for one thing, both as reader & writer; and on the other hand, I have some of that same tie to the others who will be used, but only as a reader. I.e., they have nothing to teach me (but for, possibly, Blackburn). In any event, I want to make a frame, a *reference*, for the selection — not an apology, but a clear statement of what is the extension of the intelligence implicit in the selection. Too, to indicate some of the range, some of the loss, some of the main gains (as, precisely, Pound). And to keep the whole thing moving pretty hard; or as hard as I can. I want to maintain the reason for my interest in each man printed; and not get off, too deeply, into especial problems of my own work. In any event, hope that the above makes some of it, without getting mushy. Say what you think. Plenty of time, etc., if this doesn't seem it.

Bob

[Black Mountain, N.C.
ca. 31 August 1951]

Bob
    (the enclosed,[109] will give you one of the two reasons why (for 10 days) I have been no use

the other is *Apollonius* running now, on the presses, & ready tomorrow

Crazy biz, but, this once, a *throw*

muckracking, or
Chapman Jonson or any
Elizabethan gangster!

up nights until 6 (the rib is a cracked, & is in splint — no trouble), such things as, shall I stay here, etc
    — will write tomorrow: but this, because, FIRST, to you —
    love fr us both, & to Ann our thanks for RED

Olson

[Black Mountain, N.C.]

Monday night, September 3 [1951]

Lad — it's 12:30, and have had the immense solidity (most
necessary, this exact instant — an idiot (or is he something quite the
opposite, taking my photo for fucking release on these
appointments, the three, Harrison, Litz, myself (they with good
reasons, perhaps, me, with no reason but the hell of no dough, no
fucking dough, and that never a good enuf reason for me for
anything) anyhow between now and tomorrow morning, to
decide, whether to stay, or say, fuck it, I'll take my baby
elsewhere

              so, yr thick letter (including Mitch, on PV) just picked
up (a holiday dividend, the mails, somehow, how) there, and just
read, and damned solid, like I say, to have you in here, this
instant, telling me
                    for, this day, this hr, this instant (whatever the
fucking decision, all is cleared away
                                    done with em, stay or
not
     am set to take up
              you see,

it wasn't all crazy, or, dished, or watered off (like those fucking
hoses they go over old gold fields with, to suck off, what's left (a
million b[*broken off.*]
                    [*In pencil:*] toss this in (having the ounce)
just as sign of how, they take me off the hook, every day (or
have, did) like a side of beef!

Yr mail is all over the house — distributed, like type — where it did
the most good
         BUT now I must go around (like a seed-carrier) and gather
them up, to get the sense & continuity back, eh?
         Been fine, to have you in — and especially, like I say, where,

to get the feet down (exact opposite of, they won't move) is, the effort — crazy, no economy of service, or, of the heart (filthy youth : and me sort of sure, blind sure, it'll all be wasted — that I won't get that *Grant* — the "scholars" will sink me!

Yrs

C

[Fontrousse, Aix-en-Provence]
September 4/ 51

Dear Chas/

Very, very great to have the MELVILLE — in this noon. Tell us how it goes, i.e., how they make out with distributing it. So glad to see it out in time for the given context; it makes excellent sense.

Reading it now, it hits. Straight item; and hope they get the point — and really don't see how they could miss it, eh?

Somewhat object to the fold-in format, but I take it that enabled the printing, & assembly to go faster, and so that use, etc. Anyhow, cool.

Not very much doing here; or only one story done this past week which I sent on to Cid, quick, in hopes to displace that other, should he be pushed to use it because of the context, etc. Anyhow, it seems a little more on, & if he doesn't use it, will get you a copy. Otherwise, I think he would beat me, i.e., will have the issue out before I cd get a copy to you. Anyhow.

I met a man here, Ashley Bryan,[110] young negro painter, who's the

first I have met, [*added*: here] come to think of it. Or first who
moves me, & he does: considerable. Had only a few days with
him, as he took off for Spain yesterday, but will be back in a
month or so. Anyhow, talking with him about G/ & G/s hopes
for the Am/ issue cover — if nothing is moving with Ben Shahn, or
Twombly, figure it might be simpler to do it over here; i.e., wd
allow for shift, etc., in the event of any headaches, what with all
parties being closer, etc. And he cd do it, I figure, and very, very
well. Have also asked him to figure something for Cid; which will
send on to latter, once done, and say simply: how abt it. But
don't say nothing now, i.e., want just to confront him so. That
damn cover is the only real weak item there now.

Anyhow, very
great pleasure of talking with someone who really makes it for me,
& who has some of my own roots. It was crazy, & suspect I must
have bothered him at that; as it was, I spent the night there with
him in Aix, & was going, again, well before breakfast. But what
else.

Anyhow/ anyhow. Things come a little, & will keep you posted.
You do likewise. Have missed the letters, but know how very busy
you must be there. Crazy about the A[pollonius of Tyana]/ and
let us hear about that too, eh? Ok.

Going house-hunting in abt a week; have that one to check on in
Carry-le-Rouet, & if that don't pan out, will mosey along the
coast, etc., etc. But no matter. Write soon. Great the rib is
nothing bad. Write.

All best love to you both/   Bob

[*Typed in margin*:]
   Note me the number of lines (including spacing on
KINGFISHERS, when you can. Have asked G/ abt PREFACE, &
will tell you when I hear; I'm counting on it, anyhow. (Got
EXAGGERATION off to him.)

Tell me if they get that novel to you ok; simply forgetting it for
the moment. Can't really figure it now.

[Black Mountain, N.C.]
thursday september 6 51

lad: to let you know i am among the living, and to tell you i
sent off to you yesterday the latest (EIN BUCH, bound in boards,
mit colophon, map etc.: done in the last ten days, and what it is,
what it is

or you shall tell me (still kick myself i couldn't afford to ship it by
air, had to tolerate the wait (its weight 10 ounces, so, 1st class,
and personal for you & Ann
                          at the same time i wish you wld look
on it as the "European Copy," and share it, if you think it worth
it, with Gerhardt — and, secondly, with Mascolo, when & if
                                                         (i still
figure it wld aid their discharge of their ISHMAEL if they had
other items of yrs and mine to move: wrote Mascolo that I had
sent the book to you, and also, recommended he get from you the
five stories, for use by Gallimard:
                          two other ideas on that
one — (1) letter in Monday from this bird John Kasper, Publisher.
Abt a month ago, had a p.pst card fr him telling me, he was on
his way to see me, had read me etc. He did not show, and I
learned this weekend from Moore (who has our Washington
house, and drove down, with his girl, to see us) that the Old
Spider had waylaid him, used him, and told him not to come to
see me! (Real wild, the way what Ann sd abt Ex [*sic*], is still true,
the bitterness)
                  The point of this Kasper is, that he has cut straight
in to the problem: DISTRIBUTION. Left NY to tackle just that,
and as of such as Ez and me. So i shipped him what of the
MELVILLE LETTER was left, for a starter, and one good copy of
APOLLONIUS (the copyright copy, which I am to have back) to

see if he wanted to publish it commercially

(we ended up with no
copies, for ourselves, Hatt   the designer & printer   and me: I
conceived it as a *local* thing from the start, and we subscribed the
edition of 50 out ahead of time to foot the bill (collected 46 bucks,
Motherwell donated 5, and a kid, rich, bought two of the ML's
signed, for 10 ((the both of them only cost, with everything, 63!))

Well, anyhow, (1), I sd, Kasper, publish Creeley's stories. But (2),
I have suggested here, we do them this fall, if you wld permit it.
You see, one of the reasons I pushed on these two is, that, it gave
me a chance to give Hatt some work (he came to me fr Woelffer
and Vashi) and at the same time gave me a chance to see what
this print shop is capable of. And if I stay, what I shld like to do
is, to use it, to find out, for the 1st time, the problems (terrible
problems, as I now know, fr last week's go, trying, to get the stuff
run — timpans, platens, chases, and all that fantastic slow
deadening process of *evenness*

What I am urging on them is, to take this shop (as they have
taken their farm) and separate it from the "college," make it a
production shop, and commercial, and get a top man here to drive
it
     also Shahn, is trying to get Blumenthal (the wealthy head of
SPIRAL PRESS)[111] to come here in October, look over the
equipment, in hopes he'll supply other type faces, and maybe a
press (he's already offered to take any of the best as apprentices in
his NY shop)

(((One thing, abt Kasper, to tell: that it was Origin #1 which drew
him!))

As of the presence [*i.e.*, present], we stay here. These people have
been as usual with me, very smart: left it this way, that, at any
time I want to leave OK with them. Which is as much, etc. And
tho I am nervous as the cat abt the whole environment, yet, it
does look as though I have little chance to do otherwise, for a
short while. For the doctor says the child has dropped (is in

position, like the Tulum Diving God,[112] for the dive) and that it would be quite wrong to jounce the lady until the lad or lass has made it

    ((Cid, and his patroness, damned well joyed us, by, last week (which was as complicated a one as I ever did know of: I think I told you Con's mother, died, a week ago Saturday night, at 53, alas, just, a vein broke in the heart, then an embolus, and death in five minutes without recovery of senses)

by offering us her house in Marblehead or her apartment on Beacon Hill for September!

    damned wonderful, coming, at that time, but still, no way to get my lady there, so, for the present, here we stay ((tho the idea of NEW ENGLAND this particular winter (as alternate to Yucatan) seems most attractive

    damned peculiar business, the way both of us, have this weh for it (and i dare say it is the birth of this baby plus the death of both our mothers in eight months — curious, a baby, in between both — has our selves turning like a weathercock

    rockport, or, if twere possible to feed and house (to be f and h) Marblehead!

I hope, now, anyway, Robert, to be back on, after these last few weeks, with you, to keep these letters moving, and to stop this damned irritating gapping about yr mss (both the verse and the stories). Please understand that, I get unsure, going at such a silly pace as I have, and tend to wait for some morning when I can read you full on, and answer you likewise. Now I shall see to it, letting anything go, so far as I can.

(The novel, by the way, has not yet come. But I have THE PARTY in, to read and send to Cid as you ask. And shall write you about all today: this is to catch us up, and I have written it without even clearing the havoc of this room (from the past week of printing, and getting rid of the things) —

that filthy GOAD, with
us both, came in too, and I am shocked with what they do with
CHUTE, where it sits: by god, how that Emerson misuses us![113]

and do you know that, still, i have yet to see GG#3, what you
had what, 3 months ago!
o, yes, another publishing venture:
Cernovich has started a series of single poems, to be issued at 10¢
a copy. He is using BULLFIGHT as #1, and I shld like to ask if
you will let us have GUIDO for #2: if so, and you have copy, do
let me have a true copy for it. (I don't know how well I'll succeed
in holding this idea to only professional pieces, but I shall try —
and any single poems you have, or know of, of others, which can
make the series professional, good)

On KINGFISHERS: I have no copy here. Am asking Moore to
send me the MR with it. But, immediately, as of lineage, I can say
this, an estimate: that it should run just abt a page more than the
LOBGESANGE[114] (a page in *fragmente*)

Shall get off too, to you, the chapter fr the novel, you sent me (I
apologize)

Am quite unhappy. Tired. Puzzled, somewhat. And faced with the
HU rewrite — before Sept 15
(another printing thing is, Cid has
asked whether they, here, could take over *Origin* printing job. Cld
be, if, the shop was righted, and rightly headed — let me post this
off & come back again, later.

All yr letters (and Ann's notes on babies, dyes, etc) have been — for
us — like touching base — in this empyrean!

Love   Charles

[Black Mountain, N.C.
6 September 1951]

same day (later):   LAD
          THE PARTY is now read, and I go for it,
jesus, it is like verse, it is so separable, the elements, even to the
separateness of the syllables. A delight. So very fine — the one
word for it. The highness of it. And the four — or five — things, the
way, the tone stays, shifting, in each.
          Only one thing bugs me,
and that it does, throws me, that it causes me to wonder, where i
go off, if you mean the "she said" as — at that moment — it has to
be, not the woman who makes the toast but, the woman of the
story — "she"

     "It was love, she said, a very true love"

                              Surely this is the line
the whole thing holds by. But if it is "she," then, his line earlier
"But it must be me a little, that I walk in on it" goes akilter, at
least, for me — that such a man as this would, if she were capable
of this blooper (for so I read it), have a care.
                              No. This really
throws me. That is, the velleities, throughout, the lesions, seem
properly in between uncleanliness and him, and to exist, exactly,
right through to her last. There was certainly nothing wrong with
it, even to the wondrous line, You really prefer disasters (which is
perfect, how often, eh?) . . . Or hers, at the early part, They are
all much too busy (which again, is, scores, right on the
target!)
          Which she is it? I must take it (you are so careful) it is
she. And if it is, then, I figure I must miss your point, which
puzzles me, the thing stands for me. Then I am thrown on the
business that, it is the writer, and not the story, which has me —
the kind of receptors he shows, working, ahead of him like any
grasshopper.
          So you must tell me, whether I miss, or, the she,
here, is the toaster. It is just unbearable, the business, of, to John,

the wonderful climax it is of, uncleanness—beautiful. And your statement there, A windy void. So it must be the toaster who continues, true love. Then, I think, you should have it in that paragraph, your method, up to then (the care of the separations) demanding it, so that we be clear, right here, where, it matters.

In any case, I think the whole method (the getting it all in by the lightness—that sort of condensation) is wonderfully good, fresh. And I so much like the conversation at the party between cheers, and the toast—the way the thing reaches out and covers, any such, anywhere—the anonymous throughout, and how it expands, and so, ties down: the exactness of, a pronominal world, in yr hands

      (Again, that there are two allowed, Briggs, and John, leads me to think it must be she was [*i.e.* who] says it, and I am again puzzled.)

      Let me let out one other gusset, that, the enlargement (from the two of them) has a treachery of story in it, that, as a result of the intensity always being highest (?) when there are two, the story tends to go down, to lose that warmth, in the party and the children businesses. Or is it that, somehow, you need a couple of more breathings, at the very end, to bring it back to, the two. That is, at exactly the point, You make it sound momentous, again, the "she said," has just enough ambiguity as to which "she," to keep the return obviously there quite clear—to give us back to, the beginning (the firmness of same, however, a canoe!)

      My impression now is, that, all you need is to extricate, quite clearly, the two of them, in that last exchange, from the other woman (maybe leaving her out? no—merely making it quite clear, right there, with "You make it sound momentous," that, it is his "she" who is back again at, her position toward him, eh?

    Strange beautiful thing. And crazy, how, it is just these exact instants which it poises on. I damn well hope I am right, that, just there (1) true love and (2) there, the end, you need to make it

quite clear the "she" — to swing the sentence so, it points, like a
needle . . .

Shall appreciate your telling me, whether I am on or off: very
puzzling to me, and yet very delightful — no fuzz, all high, and
damn wonderful, to feel the advance here, the discovery, in the
form

(The physical businesses alone with the two of them — and of him,
with the party people, and the kids — and the three of them, on the
couch, at the end
        THE WAY YOU MAKE ALL DISPLACE-
MENTS AND DISPOSITIONS

count

it is so clearly your business, Bob, and most exciting to me: why,
here, with the swiftness and quietness, and the way the exchange
is minimal, it is so exact object-image:
                        very damned fine. And the
way the real world, as humans have it, stands clear — all the air,
and insides, stand up (the damned party house, how, it is all
there, the lake, the huge space of her house — how you do it, with
the voices, in her house
                o well, christ, this is what we know.
Only, today, it just feels special good to me, to be back!

                        (Wld
you accept my dabbling, on one sentence, the watch business,
leaving the word watch out
        for the thing, as is, loses tension, for me, by, the
        qualifying being, descriptive, instead of, say, so:

                She had got up and now looked at her wrist, the
little band there, of bright metal, and then at him, saying, it's very
late

        well, shit, that don't do it, either — maybe, leave the watch,

and cut "a little . . . metal"
                        It's just that, unlike the other details,
this seems not to make its point, to push us, out, and forward —
that is, *her* canoe, her auto, her house, her friends, the other "him"
is enough, eh? *her* kiss
                        You see, why, I can't believe she'd pull the
love line, is, that, that other, which delighteth me: Sometime you
have to answer me. Sometime there will be nothing else for you to
do. What an essential business.

I've just been through it again, and one last tightening I'd offer: the
double sitting down — could it be saved, for one, by, when he
comes out with the hostess, having the sentence go, "She watched
them go, blankly, standing, and he beside her, trying, as he
thought, to help" so that the going away of the people is all in one
motion, and so, that climax, of the three of them, and then, she
and he, will, be simpler, straighter, less complicated by, that
business?
                Ok. Please let me know back, what, this amounts to,
eh? And I shall send it on to Cid.

                                Yrs, Charles

                                            [Black Mountain, N.C.]

mon   sept 10 [1951]
                    rob't:
                                spent yesterday picking up again on,
HU. No startling changes yet occur to me. Probably because it is
so far back, eh? Well, in a few minutes, I'll be going back over yr
correspondence to pick up, on, yr critique once more, to see if, I
am bright enough, now, to really make it different/ let's hope

                                                          my
feeling is, the piece is there, and now, I want to do another
thing — an essay on the theatre, which I will get to, shortly

Point is, to let you know, the mss of the novel *is* here. Found it
last night in my study, like they call em, and to which I never go,
hating same. Somehow some dope went and put it there (because
of its bulk, no doubt). Probably was there when I wrote you, no.
Mailed by Morrow, Sept 4. So okay. Squared away.

Wld like yr opinion on which to call it, THE HUMAN
UNIVERSE, or, THE LAWS. For I still go along with you, when
you suggested, some combination of statement of the law and,
alongside, exemplum. Yet I shy from such a method as, too early
or two dogmatic, that, the problem still is to unravel and so,
throw the emphases, off, in the sense (again) that you argued, I
smother the chief points. Or it may be that, the essay, as was,
was my own discovering of such things, and, so, it shows its own
unclearnesses.
            Damned bothered abt it. Don't like to tinker with
it, thinking, of Con's first pleasure with it and your own, the way
I think it rode you, then.
                    Yet wld like to make it large and clear,
free standing, cool

and now tuesday — just got off note to cid, flagging him, that the
damned rewrite was coming on tomorrow, or thurs to him (he is
putting #3 to bed)
                    so you will understand what
keeps me, from the good things, and yr affairs —
                                    the thing has
given me trouble, simply because I am not as interested, as I
was
      BUT, yr go's on it (which I have been over and over) have
been, as I knew, right on the bizness:
                                and have enabled me to pull
out the real stuff, in those opening pages

(can't seem to get rid either of the Christ thing, or,
the Malinowski, but they will go, tomorrow, or be
folded in with greater ease and clarity

anyhow, to hell with that. Just, to put a hand across there, where
you are, to tell you the SOX came, as smooth as they were
sent — and beautiful they is. Christ, this business, of the child's
clothes ahead of the child! Fools me. Kills me. WOWS me, is the
word. — and Con coming home today with two blankets she picked
up in Asheville for 49¢ each!
                              She's as taut — there — as a snare. And
tho she has had trouble with her kidney, is otherwise, wonderful,
a pleasure to pleasure, to watch how (even tho the thing's
beginning to be fussy on her) she rides it — handsome.
                                               (Ran into yr
letter of Aug 1st advising, stay put. And it rested me, for I had
come, the last two days, to figure, I was doing all right, to stay
here — that the terrors are offset for this nonce, eh?

As of Ashley Bryan, and G's cover/
                              I wrote Shahn, on it, some
time ago. And no answer yet.
                         Gave him another offer
yesterday — from Cid — asking, wld he design the Origin cereal top
for next year

Will let you know as soon as I hear from him — put it this way:
sd, if you must choose, choose ORIGIN. And yet, I sort of think
the European idea, will appeal to S
                              well, will let you know

O yeah — the other story — GRACE, wasn't it? Cid was all excited.
Liked it big. Says it small — can't you get me one off, air mail?

well, it's midnight, and i'm for bed
                         Ho

                              yrs,
                               O

短篇小説について

ロバアト・クリイレエ

私を感動させる一つの重要な事柄、それはあなたがストオリイに重点を置くだらうといふこと、しかも既に知られたいろいろなストオリイ・マガヂンの常に重点をおくそれより以上のものに貴方が重点をおくだらうといふことです。この件は一つの事実によって、ぴつこにされてゐると私には思はれます。周ちそれは常にノヴェルのロヂツクの一延長、或ひはよりよく、いつてもノヴェルがそのより長い長さのうちでハアトとして用ひるであらうところのwholeとなると、ふることです。そのやうにそれは識ひを望み得ないな全体に対して張合つて居り、或ひは単なるハアトとしてwholeの重要さに関しては絶望的であり、重要性の鋭い限なるハアト又は離片としか見えなくなります。ひしなにか別なものとして、一つのフレエムとして（散文の）根本に於てノヴェルのフレエムよりは異つたものとしてとりあげることにより、あなたはこの塔印をのぞき又ノヴェルよりノヴェレッタ（あなたは何と呼ぶか知りませんが）へ、ショオト・ストオリイへの今までの等級立てと言ふものは明らかに嘘鷙であつて、それは長さや woolage 等についての文学的感覚に関係してゐるに過ぎず、この三つのどれもの本質的構造とは無関係であることを知るでせう。次にはショオト・ストオリイは frame の効用によつてどんな小説になり、またそれと反対な効果があるかといふことです。よい部面はショオト・ストオリイはノヴェルの不可能な強烈さ（読者として語り手として）を保持すること、またメルヴィルの呼ぶところの（broken stump）をフルに使用することができ、また力を塩配してその力をして方向や結論を無視して（ストオリイの中に一つのバランスをつくり、それがそれに自身でスウイングして、完成して、始ぬより終りへではなく、はじめからへつてゆくといふ一つのリアタルとして私が使ふところの）自由に働かせることのできる irresolution（停滞、または優柔1断）を用ひることができ、又長いノヴェルを堰々おちるところのパタンから取出すことができること等である。どうもこれでは細かすぎて、しかも不愛けなやうですが、なにかこういふ風な考へ方がショオト・ストオリイをそのノヴェルに附属したものの位置、或ひはノヴェルでないものを書くものが書く作品にあたへられた位置から解放するために必要

ではないかと思ひます。

一般に散文全体は諸芸術からはるかに遅れてゐるやうに思はれます。その一つの理由は記憶術でつくる松葉杖、メモリイの支持です。わたしに初めてそれを明らかにして呉れたのはオルソン氏でした。フリオズの present（現在）とはどこにあるか、その時後の、二つかやうにすべてを思ひ出させると、ふことは、求められたものへ、つまり正確なものへの道ではない。まず私は私達の誰もがかもひ出すといふことについて極度に慎重であることをその第一とする私達に起つた事柄を思ひ出す、私達に起つたすべての事をいかにして繰返し繰返しわれわれ自身に呟くか、それは何か、それが私達をどうしたか、その重要なことは何か、それは何であつたか。

実際これこそ生きた作品の取引の場ではないだらうか、すべてのものがそこへやつて来てその理由を求め、そのイリュェ（ネエシヨン）を求めるところの。かくして一作家がメモリイを直接に与へる時には、彼は他の場合より一層彼の読者と一つの徹の中に、ゐるのではないか。彼はクリスチヤン被等はライオン？

さういふ風に考へると、詩の場合には又は時代にふさはしい poetry にはその fusion（融解）があり、それはマテリアルの present があり、今つまり now をつくり、私が 10 歳の時しやぶつた砂糖菓子の聯想を起さしてもかまはない、さういふ詩の融解が直接の文脈にひつぱりこまれたのならば、音楽にも絵画にも同じ present がある。散文にのみは記憶するための方法がその使用のロヂツクの故に保たれて居るそれが私の今関心をもつてゐる事柄の一つであり、私がストオリイに試みて発見しようとしてゐる何かなのである。それで私は一つの story と、thing がその場に先立つて存在することを望すない、私は私だけの敬虔な態度がその context（文脈）の直接性であることを希望する。「Mr. Blue」はそうした作品、一つの試みです。私はそこに forces をのぞみました。書いてゆくうちに、またそうした力が湧いてくるにつれてマテリアルから出てくる力を望みました。私は描写されたものを望んでゐるのではなくて、その枠の中での、その present（現在）を望んだので、フォルムは内容の拡張であり、ロヂツクはこの方法のためのものであるといふのが私の、ひたい考へなのです。フリオズ、これまでより一層そのメッソッドに重点を置かれるべきであると私は信じてゐるのですが、それにしても私はあまりにアブストラクトに走つて軌道をそれたやうにも感じます。

The first issue of Rainer Gerhardt's magazine *Fragmente*, 1951.
*Charles Olson Collection. Literary Archives, University of
Connecticut Library.*

Rainer Gerhardt and family, Freiburg, Summer 1951.
Charles Olson Collection. Literary Archives, University of Connecticut Library.

Thomas and David Creeley, ca. 1951.
*Charles Olson Collection. Literary Archives, University of
Connecticut Library.*

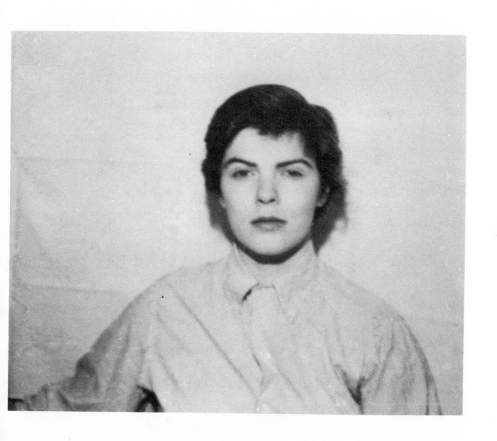

Ann Creeley, ca. 1951.
Charles Olson Collection. Literary Archives, University of
Connecticut Library.

Envelope of Creeley's 11 September 1951 letter to Olson.
*Charles Olson Collection. Literary Archives, University of
Connecticut Library.*

[Fontrousse, Aix-en-Provence]
September 11, 1951

Dear Chas/

So very sorry to hear of the death of Con's mother —
please give her all our sympathy. An impossible thing. But so glad
that the baby is coming, and that there is no cause for worry
there. Anyhow, all our dearest love to her.

A damn deep pleasure to have the two letters this
noon. And all the news! Wow. I mean, my head spins not a little.
Very interested in what you tell me of the possible angles for
printing down there, and this man, Kasper. What do you really
think about him, i.e., an inveterate amount of Yankee blood
makes me want to go slowly, but you say. Very, very damn kind
of you to suggest the stories to him; and hope, jesus, certainly,
something does work out.

Briefly, this would be what I might have for him: the 5 ND will
print in this coming annual (word from J/ Hawkes, saying that
Laughlin had written him about taking them, etc., reassures me it
wasn't NYC wit, etc.) *plus* the one you have there (THE
PARTY — & very many thanks for the help there, & will go thru it
again with that in front of me) & another, THE GRACE, which I
think I just wrote you about, & which Cid says he wants to use,
now, in this 3rd issue. That means 7 [*Added in margin via
asterisk*: I think they wd *continue* to hang as a *unit*: a thing like
UH being what wd kill it], then, and if the type is fairly open &
of good size, approximately some 100 pp.
I want to suggest a
related idea (which I've had in the back of my head for such an
edition, i.e., G/ had suggested something of the sort (as likewise,

with yr own things) perhaps this coming spring, and so had been thinking about it). This man I had met, Ashley Bryan, wd be terrific for doing some drawings, etc., for it, and, as well, for settling on a type-face for the things (to be matched, as closely as possible, by what types, commercial, are available to the printers). He knows this kind of gig, sets into me very strong, and wd have complete rapport with him on any such gig. I.e., he'll be right around here, etc. That would cut out Hatt (which bugs me) or would cut out some of it, for him — & wd that be death? Jesus, I wd say to hell with it, but for my very honest hinge on this man, Bryan, and what he comes to mean for me. One of those proverbial meetings, but one don't pass them, eh? Never have yet.

Well, you say, again. And will certainly be very, very great, if they have any eyes for such. Should note, perhaps, that B/ is in with Pantheon (NY), i.e., walked in off the street, fresh from Cooper Union, & they gave him the job of doing illustrations for that series of Folk Tales they are doing; African — but not out yet, tho he has done all sd material, etc. About 30 or 40 color plates, & some 80 black & white is what he did for same.[115] Crazy biz!

And he wd do this, just to do it, I'm very damn sure — IF they have eyes?

Anyhow, that wd give him: book, wrapped up, ready to print — and if they do have eyes, ask him to stipulate all limits on any such illustration as B/ might do. I.e., page size, etc.

(I get so used to Ez putting the finger in — agh. We are young, eh? Or ynger.)

To wind it up — will (unwisely, I wonder — i.e., is this jumping the gun?) get off to Mascolo copies of 3 stories in ORIGIN, & note, etc., to effect that L/ is issuing 5 in ND gig, etc. An iron, etc. And many damn thanks.

Terrific abt Cid & the lady — he is damn well GOLD. And sd, he did, they he had talked with you, but, so bashful, he did not say what abt! I get to love him very, very much.

And very damn eager to see this present BOOK—many many
thanks, & will certainly consider it : the European copy. Ok. Did
Mascolo ever write you abt receipt of FRAGMENTE? I suspect
that G/ had sent them a copy anyhow—making two, at least,
which might wake them up? Do you know Giono[116] is the
translator on most of the Melville, now whirling abt here? Real
craze, on same, in Europe at present. Was thinking—there's the
man to review CMI when it gets out. Lives about 20 or so miles
from this room in which I sit. An idea.

Abt it. This last one, THE GRACE, gets me back on altogether—
feel I made it there, & really, have been so damn wobbly this past
summer, it was no little joy. Cid sd, the last letter, figures it
coolest to date; and failing its issue there, in the 3rd issue, will
either get you off a copy, straight, or ask him to send that one on
to you, to read. A thing there, i.e., a flavor, that I never quite
made elsewhere, and it IS on *place*, and it IS, surely, the outcome
of all we'd been saying of Williams, and all of it—I got it there, or
so I damn well hope. I hope it GOT IT. Ok. Ok. Ok. And now,
allons, allons, allons, etc., etc., etc. Ok.

Phew/—looking for a house, still, but some people here, so very
great, husband, mechanic, and cd run me into the ground on any
& all aspects of Fr/ literary life, et al, have undertaken to settle us
in somewhere. And so, some hope. May, at that, hang around
Aix—it is a goofy city, and these people think they may be able to
get us an ap't there, with large garden, and also, their kids to be
around, Dave, etc. so wd be goofy—likewise, wd mean being near
Ashley this coming winter, spring, etc., and also, close to G/ if &
when that goddamn *taciturn German* (there is NO OTHER
word???) ever gets out of there . . . Well, time enough, & will
keep you posted.
        Crazy, too, & in this rush, almost forgot it/ abt
the single poem issue—will get you off, directly, copy of sd
GUIDO (crazy . . . , ok) & how abt that A SONG? As alternative,
to which add, *for ann*, in the event you wd want that, rather than

G/. Time enough, & say what you think. Ok.

(The *she* is
supposed to be, toaster, i.e., anonymous 'woman.' Will try to lock
that up; likewise ending—will send copy on when
cool.)

Wonderful to hear again; and hope everything goes well. (I
say: get the hell out, but I am I, eh?)
All our very best love to you both/ Write soon! LOVE/

Bob

[*Added in pencil*:]
The "platens, chases, etc" remind me *too much* of Leed and me a
yr. ago—*and* we *were cutting by hand all* spacing! But we never
got *set* more than *1 page*!!

[*Note by Olson*: c. Sept 11]

THE PARTY/   one or two more items, re same, i.e., again cannot
tell you how grateful I am to have yr hand-holding here. That is, I
liked it, frankly, but got swept off with this new one; but Ann
hung on anyhow. Lawrence (S/) took one look at it; and says: no,
shakes, etc., but he wdn't know anyhow, anyhow.

Why I did
hope for it—that it is one thing clearly beyond my own actual
experience; tho leave us dissociate, i.e., so what's eggsperience?
Ha/ha, etc. Anyhow, do you remember that pretty hysterical
postcard written you from Canada over a yr back now?[117] I.e.,
this is it. This woman: the Late Theodore Spencer's widow, and
the yng man: S/ Lawrence, tho the idiot never caught on! Or that
was why, anyhow, I felt it better to let him look, anyhow. But it
ain't him—i.e., I am the ONLY hero. . . . Ha. [*Added in margin*:
strictly *entre nous*, eh?]

A time back, had annotated my copy, i.e., of this story, & now
looking at same, see I had hoped for that one sentence: to have an
echo, i.e., to sit it out there as what the 1st she (the woman:
central) wd have sd at another time, to him, earlier. And what

now recalls it, in this 'toaster's' mouth — somehow, anyhow, to
have it hang out there, an echo of all these 'loves.' A voice, really,
not anyone's; or a voice somehow disparate, and singular —
hanging out there, in that space of their remembering. The drunks,
etc. (I hated the bunch of them — maudlin idiots, etc., and they
did, honestly, say everything but just this, as I recall it, tho no
use: to recall, etc.)

But I dig the problem, and believe yr solution
is the one; to put it back into that para/, so as not to screw the
reader. It is, this toaster; but she is many voices, say, or
something like that. So great, yr reading on the different sizes, of
the rooms, etc. What I damn well LOVED!

Reading back over — I see the run-off toward the end there, i.e.,
how the main woman is a little pushed back. And will do best to
hold her, latent, strong thru all of same, and tidy up
generally.

The point: to not make the second woman particularly
involved, or not but by her own bewilderment (they leave, etc.)
and sense of loss, & emptiness. It is the woman, older, bigger,
who *knows*; or who has the hand. And whip, etc. The job: to
make the other a blank wall, for the man, to make him jump
there, but be sliding down again: to receive the last statement of
the 1st woman, that surety, etc.

Well, many, many thanks; I was
all at sea on this one, and now get so I can see ways out of the
fix. And so great it hit, I mean, so damn shaky this past month
(months), not sure of anything at all. And felt the novel style had
thrown me, or couldn't be something to move back into these
stories with. Or that, better, in writing the novel — had fucked the
feel I had in the stories, earlier. However/ seems not a loss, or
hope not, can hope not, now.

[*Pasted on verso envelope: frame from a* Red Ryder *comic strip
showing Western gunman with blazing six-gun saying, "Hey, Ez!
Watch out they don't flank us on the north end!"*]

*[The following, typed on a single half-sheet, was found loose
among Olson's papers; it was originally part of Creeley's letter of
either September 4th or September 11th:]*

To keep on it: (this biz of the house, & how it now balloons out,
to other things).

Both of us, oddly, have this very strong fix, of
"place"; one which I am very conscious of, & so able to fight in
some sense. It is that the 1st sense of place was so very strong, for
both of us—that is, Ann's mother died when she was 7 [*added in
margin*: She was adopted by a single woman at 4; the woman died
when she was 7.], & she stayed there, in that house, Ann did,
until we were married; and I had grown up in Acton, which was
where my father died, when I was very young, and so felt,
always, that pressure of my mother, & of the others, towards
holding on to that remnant.

It is, it just occurs to me, of the same
piece with my own first *attack* on place—that I tried, and
honestly, seriously, to somehow suggest my father *had never
lived.*

He held me there so damn long, to that one house; I dreamt
about it continually, after we moved, and many times would
manage to get out there, to go by it, to look.

Now it's this NH
one; and we feel, a little, some betrayal, or that something is
going out from under us.

I get to think it of ultimate importance
(& what else): that one never succumb, or go under to, this way
of fixing oneself on the simple going-on, of any living. It is an
exact death; it cannot pay anything, back.

From Ashley's letter:
"This leaving, coming back. How does one manage distance,

alone . . ." But how the hell else to manage it, but, alone? To always ride back in on, hard: that I am I, that that is that, & an end of it. I take what I can get.

I can't be convinced that it can, finally, matter: where one did think of it, or where, the same, one got into love, or any similar act.

Stimulus: pure & simple. To keep it, that way. You can't have seen us, both of us, here, just after I wrote the last of that part on Gordon . . .[118] For a time, just then, we started to feel, go back; that is, hang on to it somehow. We lost our 2nd child there, in that house; I remember how that was, and how it is very simply hard, to leave a body one is kin to, in ground he can't manage to hold on to.

But the *place* is, false; any of it. I think, again, just of Ashley, negro, and how they have covered him with their dirty, *place*, have left him: eyes, mouth, mind, & little else. They smear his color into him, trying to make it stick. What is that, but: *place*? The whole stinking concept; stuck on his very damn skin!

Well, to hell with it; I vomit it all up, & get on to something else. Never to sink back into that. Never to damn well allow there is, in any sense, "anything in it . . ."

I have, finally, never been more at my *own* ease, but where they did give me *space* — which is not place, and who else but you, taught me. Where it was my *presence*, that final thing, I had given weight to, had managed to make, pure. The encroachment of "place" on us, seems to be the most pernicious of all damn illnesses, costing us, language, understanding, & god knows what else. Shit, on it.

[Black Mountain, N.C.]
tuesday september 18 51

Rob't: You drag at me, telling me, to get the hell out of here.
Because I feel it, myself. I am like a tiger, with my energy (the
place invokes so many forms of it) crawling all over me — I'm like
to break somebody else's bones. Instead of what I should —
perhaps — exclusively be breaking, words, say.
                                        You are my friend.
And you ought to empty your mind on this matter. Not
actually — I suppose — so much in the case of whether I do or do
not decide to give it over. But because I guess the sense that you
read all I now write in this sense of what it isn't because of Black
Mt. And that damn well impedes me from writing you. That is,
that, I feel you are committed, ahead of time — you would know,
how this, is a cloture.
                        So I think the best thing is for you to spell
it all out — chapter and literally the verse (eh?)
                                        More so, bothers
any act of my writing — for I am the fool of my own position, that
a man is an instrument, and do take it a place, or people, or a
baby, or whatever, has to be watched. That we are precarious, eh.
Not that I don't equally find (what I picked up yesterday) how
right the Sonofa Bitch is, when he says, you cannot call a man an
artist until he shows himself capable of reticence and of restraint,
until he shows himself in some degree master of the forces which
beat upon him. (Mia Patria)[119]

    That is, that you seem to rest it, I am a victim, here, of too
easy a praise or attention. Nuts. The drag, the clawing, is what is
it, not, such. Or I am without eyes.

Well. Just. That you damn well matter to me, your perception.
And you ought — in this case, and by now — give me all that is on
yr mind. Please.

Perhaps I shld have got off, for a few days. Maybe it is more a

need for that sort of freshening—and not from eight weeks, but
nine months. For I have been on, in that time, in a sort of a way.
* * * * * * * * * *

Off that, and to, what counts, eh? (1) More damn literary
businesses: Duncan reports, mss to Cid, and hot for two things in
            O 1 and 2: yr letter p. 71, and POSY—otherwise, his
            usual testy self: "mag needs more "temper," more
            weights & measures (no less!), and himself as such, and
            as opposition!
                                Fine.
Like him. And hope he comes in—or rather, that Cid takes to the
stuff: a long poem AFRICA REVISITED,[120] and three African
"genesis" pieces (? Frobenius? probably—he's correct about Joyce
and Pound as his strict mentors)
                                (2) big letter in fr Kasper—who is
also written all over with the Mark—even Horton, is his partner!
And so I am slow to accept his offers—of 1000 issue of Melville
Letter, of 2000 issue of a volume of "selected" olson, etc:
                                            i wish to
christ, on this one, we could CONFER!
                                for i think there is a way
to MAKE USE of this whole operation (and it's fast and sensible—
all of Ez's hard sense of commerce etc)
                                BUT, it's risky, given, that
it is already (patently) EP's tricycle, trotter, and—in the end—
poisoner
            I, of course, am puzzled, and—sure—interested, that, he
is giving me this play.

Even to a check—and just when I was trying to get up the fucking
hate of it, to ask, these characters, for my September check—there
being, nothing, in the pocket, for a movie, or, even a sandwich if,
as i have craved, to get out on that road you lugged a bag up
from, and bum off somewhere, for a few days: just to
change:
            $9.60 (for Melville Letter—15 copies, in other words,
MORE, than in 9 months was, my earnings—$4 royalties on CMI,

$1 from Cid Corman for Origin 2

look—i so want yr mind working on this one, let me toss in this
character's outburst—just in, today—including his gross act, to
EMM—for your advice: wham it back.[121] I'll play him off for a
week or two, waiting on, your opinion.
                                              (tho I'll not, by god,
delay his digging the fucking EMERSON, eh?!
                                              it's coming, to
reckoning time, with that one:
                              just damn well print the thing here
      ((you see, what a little gets me, is, that this Kasper, is
          NOT a distributor, like he was made out, BUT, another
          publisher—and who can trust
any of them but CID CORMAN
                              (boy, that lad keeps letters
coming in here which warm the—generous, sharp, on: *at work*—
fonder, and fonder, I too, of him

* * * * *

Full of this outbreak—plus the printing here: yr GUIDO will be #2
(forgiving me, that, it was the bullfight, that started it off, and, so,
it went ahead like that, and it's Cernovich's play, anyhow). #3, I
figure, is well, now, a Duncan—now that he is back (he's a
Gerhardt ii—disappears into his teacup, for years)
                                              And Shahn and
Blumenthal coming, to set this press in business so that a
publishing house can emerge from it, perhaps—ain't that THAT
crazy? that i shld be in this position/ look: let me have yr best
thoughts on all this damned proliferating situation:
                      PUBLISHING & DISTRIBUTION
will be on, on all other matters, including the novel, directly   O

[*Added in margin:*] Shahn ACCEPTS, on *Fragmente* cover!: know
this will now disappoint you, as of AB, so you must take him
forward, eh?—What about his designing us your *GUIDO*? just to
get his hand in, with us, but FAST—or Duncan's AFRICA
REVISITED!?? You tell me.

[Fontrousse, Aix-en-Provence]
September 19/ 51

Dear Chas/

Forgive me for being off, these past days. We had been broke, & no way to get anything off to you, and then, in the confusion, damn well find all the bits & pieces I'd hoped to get off to you, today, are damn well lost.

Fuck it/ and forgive me for telling you abt what now doesn't exist — damn/damn/damn. Ok.

The main thing: continuing delight in the letter to Martz, however dull that now sounds, after the Williams' confusion I'd got into. It is that, on this matter of *root*, you are so very damn clear; and i take it as a piece with, KINGFISHERS, LA PREFACE, et al. Ok. Just that I tell you.

2) Only worry about HUMAN UNIVERSE, as title, is that it might lend itself to that interpretation against which yr fighting: viz, the partial use of a universe; cf/ 'human.' Otherwise, why not THE LAWS? You are not speaking of anything *less*. Fuck the idiots who will, anyhow, misread you, and suppose, at that, they can likewise fuck themselves in the 1st instance.

3) I asked Bryan to try a cover, also, for ORIGIN; but there'll be no hard feelings, if Shahn picks up. In either case. B/ is very fine; hence, my interest, etc. To put it pedantically, etc. Shit — no explanations needed. Ok.

4) Damn sorry abt not having got you off a copy of GRACE; the same bug as on the letters, and not till now I had the loot. One going off with this, or at the latest, tomorrow. Ann's off soon,

to mail, and can't say if I can make the copy in time.
Anyhow — obliged to send it straight mail, but will be there,
anyhow, shortly. Forgive me for not getting it there sooner.
Had the idea Cid's #3 was due out in late Sept/; hence, thot it
wd get to you as fast, via him. [*Added in margin*: Enclose it
here — not that much extra. BUT hope you can READ it!]

5) Looking for *Apollonius* with all damn eagerness; Cid says, letter
   in this noon, is crazy. Damn well waiting for it; and many
   thanks for sending the copy on — as sd (but did I get the
   goddamn letter off) will get it around, as you suggest (to G/,
   and likewise, Mascolo).

Speaking of the last — a note in from Gallimard today, saying he is
on vacation, along with everyone else; but pleasant. They have the
3 that were in ORIGIN; I want to get them copies of everything
shortly. To play it all the way, etc. No matter.

Cid tells me, Ferrini writes him "yes, he has a fine prose hand,
thanks to charles . . ." If the idiot understood what he had said, I
should not be quite so angry. But he does not. He finds that
influence, or seems to, an occasion for criticism; you'll know how
they do it, any of them, and no matter that this man is, in other
senses, a kind one. He feels that I have 'nothing good in (my)
work that isn't pure Olson . . . ,' or Cid repeats it (the 1st being
straight from Ferrini).
          It is a damn dead comment; it is totally
without understanding. And I hate it. I hate what belittles 1) that
precise influence you are, *and can be*; and as well 2) what can
deny me, so very coyly, the actual fact of my own
existence.
          These idiots will never understand 'influence,' however
often they are the first to yell it. Simple arithmetic, like they say,
will show Ferrini that he has known you 'longer' than I have; is
there any indication that he has profited, in any sense, in his craft,
by that acquaintance? *Damn well let them look to themselves.*

You have been the only *possible* influence, for me; you are the only one who can give me that sense of my own work, which allows me to make it *my own work*. Damn them all.

It sickens me, not a little. Simple imitation, of you, wd get us how far? Or who would allow it?

And then he says: ". . . I must say I did enjoy mr. blue. which kept picasso in mind thru the reading . . ."

MY GOD.

(How can one ever face that man again/ how can one ever speak of him.)

Damn well let him come to me, with this shit; and see if he can *hold his own then.* Generalizer! Christly generalizer!

Well, allons, etc., etc. It is damn well not worth that space, to talk of him, after he has shown himself capable of such a reading. It is not, damnit, my 'egoism' that I defend; damn well his 'reading' that I'm interested in. Shit.

Jesus, all of them. So dully 'afraid' of 'influence . . .' They have, thanks to you, as clean a set of statement as ever was made, on their craft, and damn well won't touch it, because they are, 'afraid . . .' to. Fuck them all.

Not much new here; entangled with the christly french bureaucracy on the matter of residence: Carte d'Identite. They had told Ann, they wd jail us all—to then say, they wdn't, etc. They seem very splenetic & expect they have, at that, reason.

What seems so much cleaner: how Con comes. I wish to god we were nearer, always. That we could see you both. It wd be that much simpler, all of it.

Anyhow, give her all our love. I hope that things go very simply, for you both. Keep us in touch.

And will
do likewise. But a little dull, at present. Tho not the flatness of
this past summer — that I hope not to get into, for at least
awhile.

Write soon, & now we have some loot, won't get so far
behind again. Ok.
All our very dearest love to you both,
Bob

As my most wonderful wife says (of F/). . . . "Imagine a grown
man writing poetry like that. . . .(!)"

I sd love to send him, if ever it does come to pass, a french
edition of these same stories, to be written thereon:
for my dear
friend, Vince — who will, perhaps, find these less offensive in
french?

[*Added at top of letter:*] Thanks, again, for sending PARTY on to
Cid; his letter says, ok, & will hope to use it in #6.

[Black Mountain, N.C.]
Saturday September 22   51

Robt: damnd moving moment. am moved (yr tender, tremendous
letter of the 19th (only two days here!) in. and grace. and the
novel read: it is as though i have at last got abreast of you, have
caught up — and time i should, at that, with, this place, shooting
the rapids again, starting, Monday
and the more important sort of
change ahead, that, took Con in to doc, and he says, he's looking

you right in the eye, meaning, he explained, that, he dropped
right — 2 weeks ago, and 6 is what that tells, so, one month, and
the lady of the house is a mother — and there's an olson of sorts in
the world! in this thing that, god knows, here we are, say, you
and me, trying to figure out things to do with a like fact, that we
are, and by god — i go and add another, for his troubles! Crazy,
the feeling, that, one should go and do that! At the same time,
that, one doesn't have an election — which is a curious — more
curious — sense, no?

anyhow, it begins to come over me, what's — up! And it lifts me,
mightily, tho, I don't damn well see how it could have been
earlier — in fact, that, but for the sort of events which have come
on since i wrote a guy a rime, on his name, how much he, has,
given olson a track

(1) which is on agenda as #1, this stupidity, ferrini's, that, that
   fool corman has had to add to you: f passed his shit on to me
   some time ago, and only this week did i get off a letter to him
   in some months, which gave me the occasion to tell him flatly
   (a) you are wrong (b) that olson is as much or more influenced
   by creeley than is creeley influenced, for which the sort of
   thanks that, once in a life, it can be so & (c) turning the stick
   up his ass, by reminding him that, it was he who put me on to
   you, and that, from that day — Creeley, yure off, yure trolley
   — things have sprung up.
                     It shocked even me (who never
   exaggerated vinc, i think it is fair to say) that he shld expose
   his fucking jealousy (which is a very dirty soul, anyway, of
   envy, and real destructiveness — real damned mass man CP
   ugliness, all the way from sex to state

TO HELL WITH HIM — ain't worth our bother, but for the
damned pain he has caused you — i say corman was an idiot,
simply because any man who knew ferrini — saw him — would not
let his cheapness over to you (corman has this false liberal concept
of "honesty" anyway — that relation, to earnestness which thinks
itself seriousness & is actually wholly ignorant of responsibility —

abt the only apothegm fr the old barrel which i still walk around
with is, cover my brother — or her — nakedness, lad

No, let's on, to ourselves, and work, leaving such, to their own
droppings: i just damn well want you to know from him who is
supposed to have such influence on you that it is one of the lifes
of his life that you, one Creeley, so completely do stand up as
yrself, whatever, that, it is a straight goddamned miracle to me
that, we too, who are alike enough to make the life we've had
between us this past year and a half, are so clearly — shit, as tho
we cld be otherwise, or you at least — ourselves
                                                  (i say you, because
it is constantly my pain, that I am not, in print, or anywhere,
sufficiently myself — or is this actually, what the thing is, that, we
do not come within shooting distance, of, what is — like they
say — on our minds, eh?)

(2) very damned happy to have you say, the Martz, letter, is still
    of life with you — that you put it there, with The Ks, and
    Preface.
            In fact, the demands on me now are such (the peculiar
    springing of time, and so, that memory is added to so fast,
    that, in these short reaches, i do not keep as clear on my own
    emphases as i do, have, and will), i shld be most obliged if,
    you see something, in anything goes to you, that you wld sort
    of put a pencil by same, and throw it back to me somehow
    (know the cost of mail problem is insurmountable, either way,
    figure, maybe, if i kept carbons, and you just pointed, it might
    be a damned big help). That is, what you did, then, in the
    cases of the PV material beforehand, and the G & C, *made
    them possible.* And my own guess is, HU, is not their equal
    because of some such loss: distance, and our shiftings, and no
    matter, in one sense, but, for me, damned does matter, that we
    are not so close in exchanges as we were when, Littleton,
    Washington, was the axis
                            Figure, anyway, these differences,
    these moves, etc., part of, what is, as of us. And only, that,
    when one of us thinks of something (like you do, here, on the

Martz letter, it gives me just the sort of gauge I damned well
need — the more so, that I am so forcibly removed in the
direction of too many other people's lives, in such a narrow
road, as this one, just here

(3) As of, say, yr letter, on Apollonius: figured this one in today,
   might, just be it — and, am waiting, for, what you say will, be
   primary. And am scared. Scared, lad. Waiting, like a horse at,
   barrier! Or something!

(4) GRACE on. Read once. Will be back at it, close in, to text:
   want most to examine the "time" used — that is, am put off,
   some, by the participles. But see how the passage of the moon,
   up, and over, is, enforced by them. The thing is, *the largeness*
(5) here sought, that is, the dimension of yr seriousness, which, in
   ' Grace, and even more so, to me, successfully, in
   ' Party, has reached out from behind (where it was) in, say,
   ' 3Fts, and ITS (it was most out, perhaps, in BLUE?) to assert
   ' itself, more directly — dramatically, I am tempted to put it.
   '

(novel)   Something has gone on. Was it the writing of
the novel, or the abandoning of it? I am honestly asking. For I
take it these two stories are a shifting of such consequence, that I
am wondering if I shldn't be reluctant to try to define the shift too
closely, figuring, much more of such stories as Party & Grace are
coming?

          And my own impression, now that I have finally read all
of the novel as it is, is, that it was the marshalling yard on which
you turned your locomotive

What I am going slow about is the *language*. Crazy business,
which I dare say, you notice, of, how your prose is now another
instrument. And it is my first working assumption about the
difference, that, your handling of "time" is as crucial as is the
"displacement" of yrself as narrator from "I" to he.

          That is, conjecture was both (1) a proposition *stated* and (2) a
going method of the attitude of the narrator toward what goes on

inside the exemplum of the proposition, in other words, the story. (BLUE, e.g., the perfect showing of this)

And my impression is, that, in a push toward some largeness, you have reduced both the old functionings of conjecture — the "metaphysical" statement is not allowed to be pulled up and launched as such — is left down in the things, like, yr question mark, in Grace, "But it is here . . . It has to be?" — as so many times, in the novel;

and the other — the driving in, always in, with, an assumption that, only you, the narrator, "I," as conjecture, can disclose

— It

comes awful sudden clear, for me at least, in the reappearance, in the novel, page 70 (beginning section 5), of the other — shall we, alas, call it the "older," method.

For you see, my trouble is, Party I go for, strong, Grace right off the bat not quite so much as Party (but this one I am only once on, and shall be back), and in the novel, the damnable thing is, it is just this passage I now speak of which, of all, I am most moved by! That is, the statement of the proposition, viz:

There are those places into which one does not easily follow another. Which is to say, there continue privacies beyond any real notion of them. It now occurs to me, I know hopelessly little about anyone — that I am free of them but not willingly so . . . the gap. And so makes it that loss.

Really, wonderful. So, the business. And I want the tale — and neither your immediate incident (of the friend, whose letters you read) or the long one which makes part 5, of, she, Boston, Jack, the poultry show of, the year before, give it to me — that is, give it to me as an extension direct of the "I" therein, or by way of a methodology of such bearing on, keeping at it.

But as I say, look: I know too damned well myself how one advances, how, moving,

one oneself is, to sound so fucking reactionary as it comes to that,
if, I make a preference. I don't. Yet I should want you to have my
respondings to what the novel is and what is in hand, just,
because, I also know how, such measures, are of use. At least,
yours have been to me (I still find yr welcome of EXAGGER-
ATION, of maximum use. As against yr critique of DISCRETE)

> This is my try: that you have swung out, somewhat away from
> your going by way of yrself (literally, your own experience, so
> presented) toward a resting of the case more in "nature" and a
> looking, there, for unravelments—and so, perhaps, the change
> to "he," and the change in, the prose
> > and that there is a largeness in nature which is different
> > fr the largeness there was in Creeley as Cr
>
> > > but i, for one, *prefer* that dimension of both which
> > > is disclosed when you and it are managed as equals
> > > by *intense conjecture* of Cr as Cr—example, still,
> > > for me, the crux:
> > > > the hawk, business, letter,
> > > > december, 1950

suddenly occurs to me: maybe what you want to do now is, what
you did in PARTY, go all the way over to, the fictive act of,
another's experience: that this is yr hunger (a confirmation is, that,
for both Con, and me, it is WILSON, in the novel, who is the
most interesting—and that Ann, in the novel, is most exciting, that
scene, she talking to Wilson hunched, beside her on the chair

   In other words, that (and this, I think, is my chief trouble
with the novel), it may well be that you are now moving into the
clear of *two* handed way
> that your own conjectural method (e.g., to shift from the
> formal stories to the sort of excitement out of which I
> wrote you, a year ago June, why don't you attack a long
> A narrative by moving yrself through it toward a form
> which—it was my guess—such a way of throwing things
> as yr letters to me represented

CLEAR EXAMPLE IS, the letter, Origin, p. 71-74, surely
(a *pure* form, that)

B   all the way over, *away* from yrself, and yr
     preoccupations, to such as THE PARTY

(the novel, for me, is hung, mostly, in between these two
methodologies — or so, at this moment, it strikes me, though, you
will surely be aware, how *impossible* (literally) it is to say a word
about a thing when you have only — what? — a third of it?
                                                    or it is
for me. You'd guess — where form seems to me what you yrself are
as committed to as I am — how impossible it is to feel any
assurance abt what goes on, in 90 pages, when there is so much
more to come

          I wld take it (with that condition) that the novel is
the unfinished arbitrary that the PARTY is the finished act of

Well. To give you what, today, my mind is on. And to ask you
to take it as it is given, most tentatively — and with no rear. If it
seems tentative by comparison to my usual responses, it is due,
chiefly, to the insecurity, as I say, of having not the whole of the
novel.
          But PARTY, and Grace — their coming in, helps me to say
at least what I have sd.

Will get this off, and hope we will — I will — not let gaps appear
any longer in this going on. At least I have the feeling, today, I
am on, again, and have only the several poems, to give you back
word on, in return for them

          Please write any time you can: both of us wait, and wait,
          for yr letters, and today, I walked through the rain, leaving
          Con, who had no coat, to get the letter in today — and what
          a difference it has made, in this black afternoon.

                              Love to you both, and the boys
                              (who don't know us)

                                        C

                              [Fontrousse, Aix-en-Provence]
                              Sept 23/ [1951] Monday

Dear Chas/

          Yrs just in, and honestly thank you for coming out
straight on the biz of my nagging. I damn well don't mean it like
that; I can't say how much is me, and how much, a more honest
reaction to the work I've seen.
                    I don't dig Melville, and some of
the other items, to the extent I have others, but I don't mean a
bias, or to imply a bias, by virtue of that place, where you now
are.
     I get very scared of collections of people. It's a fear, of my
own. I do wrong to swing it out on you, in this fashion, and
particularly, at such a time.
                    Anyhow, the Apollonius *is* just in —
and can ride on that, out on that, with all possible wonder. It is
very damn fine. As fine prose as I know of, and as clean a job.
Crazy, crazy thing. And want to go on about it, not here, i.e.,
Ann just about to take off, and want at all costs, to get you this
quick, without delay, etc.

               So: Kasper — I don't go for him, much.
He smells too much of the others, Horton, Simpson, & so on.
What he did to EMM seems damn crude, & without any excuse. A
simple dirtying.

As for publishing, etc. What do you think yrself? That is, it would be cool to get such items out, certainly, but will he, or is there any assurance, to hand, but this present palaver? I would ask to see it, if I were in yr shoes. That is, can't you pull him down there, somehow, for a face to face gig? It would save considerable time.

The drawling complacence does bother me; I hate this kind of tone, etc. In anyone, but in someone having this apparent tie-in with Ez, it smells even more.

(Something to put against this: two days ago, got a letter from Richard Aldington, saying he'd had a 'ukase' from Ez, to get in touch with me. He's coming over, he tells me, and will report what happens, directly it does.

But it does look like a genuine confab; it seems somebody is getting smoked out.)

Anyhow, can't you ride it out there, for the time being? I.e., what you tell me of how things are moving there, on the press idea, could mean a very actual possibility of bypassing all such as Kasper? It would be the much cooler way, certainly. To say, to hell with all such.

Otherwise, do ride it very cool; i.e., get him clearly & firmly, *in yr hands*. Certain items in this present letter of his, scare hell out of me, frankly, or do with respect to any chance of making anything with him. Viz/ thing re Gerhardt; viz/ general complacence. Myself, wd say, fuck him. But there is, damnit, problem of getting things out, and so on. And you have too much backed up as it is. But if possible, look for the alternative: Cid/ BMC press. That wd be so very much greater, than any hookup with someone who smells to me with such strength, as does this Kasper. (I frankly want no part of him; I mean, that's straight.)

Other things: got copy of VOU, and ok. Puts in letter, quoting you on ITS, that early hit on *past*. I see, *broken stump*, riding out at me from the hen scratches, etc.[122] Crazy!

And today, a little

book, from him, and thank you again for getting me in there. I.e.,
it's all in japanese, but it does read considerably better than Mr.
Kasper. Which reminds me — how about his SHADOW for the
series? It would be the thing?

An item: what about sending
APOLLONIUS to that Italian woman, Bottegha Oscura (?), i.e, the
magazine,[123] for possible gig? It wd not infringe on any further
use, etc., of it, and wd net you some dollars, if taken. They say
she carries it round in sacks, etc. Anyhow, if you figure it cool
and if I can facilitate matters by getting her the text from here, say
the word. (What abt map? Well, time enough.) [*Added*: I have her
address.]

Otherwise, proofs in on stories for ND 13. Miserable
messy job they do of it. But who am I, most humble, etc., to
kick. I took liberty of swapping a couple of words in yr intro (and
that is still holding the fort very damn firmly), i.e, where you refer
to the stories as 'in a book, or words to that effect,' and I just
swapped to make it, these stories, and dropped, sadly, reference to
them being a book, etc. Nothing momentous, but wanted to note
it.

Otherwise, quiet. Again, I do damn well depend on yr letters, and
do write. Damnit, I cannot allow anything like my own horrors to
get between us. That is, fuck me, or I don't mean to superimpose
my own theories of collectives, on what must be the damn
harrassed condition of yr own existence there. Which is a hell of a
long way round, to say it, but ok.
                                      NO/ THIS APOLLONIUS
CUTS THRU ALL THAT. OK.

But hold, again, on Kasper, IF YOU CAN. That is, if it will not
mean a simple blockage, for you, with the work. Otherwise, do
you really need such as he promises to be?
                                      Why not, all damn
energy on Cid, & on possible ORIGIN editions/ via, perhaps,
BMC? Well, it moves, and so very damn glad to hear it.

On
Shahn/ fine. I.e., AB, will not be bothered, etc. And Gerhardt will
be very, very pleased, I damn well bet. Will ask AB abt GUIDO;
note me dimensions & other possible limitations, etc. Can contact
him there in Spain. (How abt ORIGIN, i.e., will Shahn do that
too?)

Cool abt Duncan. And all the rest. Again, don't let me bug
you. Write soon. I.e., for god's sake, don't go way.

All our dearest love to you both/
Bob

[*Typed in the margin*:] Why don't you get in touch with Laughlin
yrself, i.e., bypass these idiots, on matter of distribution? I have,
also, an uncle in the publishing game, like they say; but hesitate to
pull him in, as he don't very much like me, etc.

But I damn well think we cd do better than Kasper? I know the
damn miserable fucking little game they play. (And how did they,
any of them, *distribute* Bunting's poems??? Ask him about that
one.)

[Fontrousse, Aix-en-Provence]
Tuesday/ September 25th

Dear Chas/
A night's sleep, and likewise time to read
APOLLONIUS as it deserves; very hard to give you a sufficient
sense of the impact it does make on me. I am very damn grateful
to have it, and *just now*.

For one thing, and even the main one — this man as *center*, center for a joining of two distinct forces I had thought, before, to be in some sense irrevocable. That is, the kind of content implicated in the Christ & that implicated in Kung; in other words, the generative & the conservative, giving each, certainly, full weight. Blackburn had come to a dead-stop, with Ez, when he told him he could not make of the Kung an impetus which could generate, i.e., could push in that sense. And I think he is, to some extent, very right to feel that; I know nothing about it, or hardly more than I've got from Ez, but it is clearly a conservative position, i.e., one intent on sustaining a man in the most 'safe' way, whereas there is the counter principle, in some degree clear in Christ, of the other, the generative or that which maintains itself almost by an excess.

It really spots, for me, two main kinds of men; that is, there is a distinction, clear, between the figures of Lawrence, Melville, and on the other hand, EP, Dante, and so on. I feel the above provides some sort of frame, for a possible reference. But to duck that for a minute — again, this figure, and it is wrong to call him so, 'figure,' in your context, comes to me as the first occasion of, a joining.

You have bound the thing, the work, together in a damn miraculous fashion; I have never seen your prose clearer, or more firm. And I damn well do take it as of the very best you have done. The way you manage the moving between detail, and statement, i.e., between the detail necessary for direction, for use with the dance, and then the statement, the base, from which any such dance must be issuing. It is a beautiful thing; the wonder is very strong here, and very much your own.

What you do with, "how is it far if you think it . . ."[124] — simply what I could *not* do, and I have tried to do it, even so. It is an incredible thing, there — quite honestly, worlds do damn well spin, do break in, on that 2nd statement of yours.

The MOVES are very, very interesting, in the fullest possible sense of that word; they are so, feel so to me, because they strike me as most basic, most *substantial.* In fact, I feel them as even that prime gauge (if there is finally one) by which any man comes to fullness; I believe, for myself, that they are just that. I try to think of some way to say this more clearly, or at least to give my sense of how you do this — wonderfully easy, & soft rise, of your intelligence, to land then, very quietly, on the ground of the statement, and there, to cover, to spread very like a flower, or any live *thing.* It is certainly a deep, deep pleasure to read this.

                                                            The dance of the mind as mute. P/ 14 : the vertical. P/12: place & object: the local. The dance of recognition. It is very, very difficult to isolate, so, any one thing, or several, for particular emphasis. And I count that the particular wonder of this book — that it destroys any premise for so citing it — it is so firmly bound in, all of it. But you must know, you have to, how very, very close this comes in, to me, just now, just at this particular time. It is the most *full* thing I think I've ever read; it is fantastically *useful.*

To get back, briefly, to Kasper, since this is, as he says, one of the things he wants in the Selected, if it turns out you do it, etc. I wd feel it, honestly, loss, to couple this with any other thing, no matter how good; it is very well placed, precisely as it now is — it is very clear & unavoidable in this present format. Hold out for just this same issue, when the time comes to put it out, in a larger way; can't we figure something, to maintain it as it is? I think so, and though it may take a little longer, it will certainly be better than to lump it with other things, no matter their fineness, etc. Again, Gerhardt did say he could issue a decent booklet, of 24pp, 1000 copies, for $175 and Cid said, he could do it, there in Boston, perhaps even cheaper, i.e., this was all with respect to HU; but I'll be very straight & say, this does seem to me more, or does seem to me a very precise hit, on, again, the same head. It cuts a great, great deal of shit. Anyhow, I don't see why we couldn't manage to issue it, ourselves, as an ORIGIN edition, or something, early this coming year; but just this to note what I think about any subsequent issue — this present book is so very fine, I'd hate to see it muted, in any sense, by coupling with other work, even your own.

Thinking more of Kasper: my humor, sense of, comes to prevail, i.e., he is certainly a fantastic character. Last night Ann had sd: how very few poets give any sense of their feeling toward children, which may be relevant, and then again, may not be—but it is true, or seems so, that the Gasp/ is particularly without thought on that head; I don't think I ever read any comment quite so weird on the subject of babies as this one he provides at your expense. We tried to conjecture, like they say, how that one must have landed; equivalent to what a 'friend' had said, to Ann, when Dave was on the way, i.e., he had bumped into her, having not seen any of us for some time, and learning she was to have a baby, sd, o, and are you married?

Anyhow, you have our sympathy, eh? Ok. Otherwise, the Gasper is also reminiscent of a a petty-thief I got hung with, once, in Boston, i.e., a finally bitter entanglement, and had to listen to his confessions, etc., and didn't finally, feel very easy in that position; at the same time, it turned out, the newspapers were giving considerable coverage to these same exploits, and I didn't dig the inside information with very much ease.

One last whimper, re BMC: it struck me, at last, what does bother me re that place—the fact that it was the 'place' where I got one hell of a shock, i.e., Ann very nearly married another man, while there, and it was just as I was going into the AFS, etc., i.e., there was neither time nor way to get clear, & a year went by, before it solved itself. But the memory is a very damn dismal one, and to think of BMC, is, sadly, also to think of it; and I expect that explains the kind of brief nagging I've been doing. I get to think that's the main thing, re any comment I ever made about it, BMC, to you—much like a dream, it does seem to me, and a very unhappy one, as it happens.

I wrote some notes on the back of the EMM letter; didn't mean to do it there, & didn't see that I had, until I had. Anyhow, will leave them: attempt to feel the gain, possible, in the 2 alternatives, 1st person narrative, or 3rd. Just a feel of it, etc. And too damn 'mystic,' now looking back at it. How abt that classy expostulation of, 'thot' — phew.

          Ok, and write soon. Miss your letters very much,
and need them, equally. So write soon.

                    All dearest love to you both.
                                        Bob

[*Typed in margin*:] Another story, in my head at least: THE
MUSICIANS; but nothing written, of it, as yet; waiting for a new
ribbon! To make something of that thing I had told you of, i.e.,
last time in Boston, with Max & Eleanor — & assorted characters,
were there. But don't know if it is anything, at this stage. But
might be — I like the possible ride-out, almost on speech, and with
the minimum of gesture, etc., i.e., it could echo, to call it that,
just in one room, just with those people, there, & so moving
among themselves, etc. Well, will send what comes.

[*Added at top of letter*:] All of the following goes for Ann too;
both of us, very, very hit by this thing.

                              [Fontrousse, Aix-en-Provence]
                    Wednesday/ 27th [*i.e.*, 26,] Sept [1951]

Dear Charles/

          Yours just here; and terrific! Can't say how this
holds me, and hauls back a clarity, a damn clarity.
                                        Sure. That is,
you have it *exact*. Trying, I am with all I can damn well haul up,
to pull out a way that can compass both aspects of that scribbled
biz on the back of the Gasp/s travesty re Melville.
                                        I.e. — how to

hang on to, 1) the plunge (pure conjecture, or where this does grab in with all possible force) & 2) the passage (the riding between, which has, in some sense, heretofore fucked me).

Hence: novel (what you have of it there) is the pivotal gig, and am now of some mind, or curiosity — can I dump that, for the fact of the learning I got out of it, and work on to some kind of double-play? I have to, anyhow; I can't [*corrected from* can, *with* (!) *added*] sit this one out in the middle.

In any event, to make clear: I dig all you say here, dig it in an ultimate sense.

Working, this morning, on another story, and back up against the wall, etc. It makes very clear to me, what you had said about the 1/1 exchange. That is, how there, in that fix, there is the most possible plunge of, the human business. I fooled around, i.e., got 3 in there, at one point, and saw, sat back & saw, my work going, light, and myself losing hold of it. But turning, made it, one comes in, another goes out; and things look a little brighter. But no matter, i.e., am on to it, thanks to yrself, and watching them as close as I can.

I get the sense of GRACE; i.e., how 'time' there makes a somewhat doubtful definer. I hope you'll give me more on it, i.e., try it again, and see what is bothering, beyond this first sense. (Party, it now seems to me: the more basic use of, the 'passage'; what do you feel about that idea?)

It was the writing of the novel, what I did manage of it, that showed me things can come up, call it, from anywhere, i.e., can come in from any possible point. (I had not really trusted that feeling, until I got chance to work some of it out, in the novel, or what got done of it.)

The stories (since) have been some attempt to pare this down, to the smallest possible occasion, or better, the finest instance. That is, I want the assurance of being able to handle *passage* with some sureness; to ride back on, then, whatever I have got, living, in the meantime, to make it, again, the pure conjecture, with the addition of, my sense of, passage, or what the hell I do manage to pull out.

Will you, when you have time, give me all your thinking on TIME? It would be of immense value; I see this thing now, very clearly, i.e., this present letter gets me in a much surer frame for seeing it.

You see, that passage biz: to *allow* the flux to contain multiple explosions, i.e., to be able to blend, as mingling, the attentions of any number, against the base hold. What I can't yet feel anything as yet, has really done. BLUE continues to diminish certain echoes, or relevances, in my own head; I feel that if I had a surer hand re passage, I might have set them in there too. Remember what a hell of a time that woman gave me, in the writing, and how I sweated, when the *three* of them had to be, all, there. What I'm now trying to back up on, that is, to get clear — a via.

You put it, again, best: that is, where you say, the *two* handed way. Honestly, it got me scared, a little, the main way of the other, that is, I felt the room shrinking, and not wishing simply to duck out, felt I must work out some way into, anterior experience. And to then, lay it INTO, the base, which I have to count on, as, myself.

Not to extricate myself, like they say, i.e., not to wriggle out, etc. But to find more means, for planing out, the surface, or really, the ramifications.

It is all, in the dark. Jesus, that you feel these things: pure, pure joy. And you can see how very damn much it means to me. And can you have any doubts, whatsoever, about WHAT Apollonius MEANT? I, for one, refuse to listen to them, if they can, in any sense, exist.

Well, it is goofy, crazy, fucking GREAT, to have this letter; and releases me, so finely, from all the worries of the past 4 months. That is, I can get on with it, now, feeling a good deal surer than I had.

Can't there be meeting, somewhere, between the two ways, i.e., can't there be space, where a thing like THE PARTY takes on its right dimension, because there is, no matter the arrogance, an intelligence leaning into it?

What I want, somehow, to get on to/ that plank.

Trying to figure how weight, can be so put, that it springs back, always, into myself.

What it wd do: release, for me, the force of either 'world' — i.e., wd allow me the movement, actual, between them I now don't finally have, or can't have.

I envy so much, so many others who seem to me able to inhabit a much wider place, call it, than I have yet been able to find. But anyhow. You hold me on to it, and all my thanks for that.

I begin to think it cooler, to count the novel, i.e., that part you have there, as the experience, etc. That is, it has got me some insight, into the biz of, what PARTY & GRACE show otherwise. I want, now, to try the move back in, i.e., once I get out the one or two other things, depending on this 'method,' will attempt to go back into the older method, with what I may have learned.

But one must push, and hard, at these damn walls. A matter of simple attempt, much of it, to see what can be stretched, or hauled into, the work.

All of it, all of it : sheer arrogance. But fuck it — no use saying one is not, finally, serious. Ok.

("largeness . . ."; I can never get enough, now, but I know the dimensions of my own world, or have some sense, of them, and can feel, I take it, what I will get back to, no matter.)

Ok, and so great to have this here. Enclose

picture[125] I'd meant to send you before, i.e., done at Dave's request
(his favorite/ LA CHUTE!) and now he says, send them to Olson.
Ok. All our love/
                    Bob

[*A series of postscripts typed in the margins:*]
Card in from Mrs. Crosby; says she wrote you—good to get back
with her, & hope, somehow, to meet her before she goes back (she
sd: November, as you'll know anyhow). I told her abt yr
APOLLONIUS (I will tell anyone I get to listen); likewise, the
Doc. Ok/

Cid writes, I am in index of Doc's Autobiography & many thanks,
to yr fine self. A letter, today, from the latter; he sounds very
bugged. Have you got the Auto/ there yet? Again, thanks to
yrself, I get, it seems, a free copy!

Whole hell of age, what works into: novel. Simple limits, of same.
Continue to feel: stories are my surest occasion, call it—where I
feel most on.
                    But have to pull it, even so.

Do you figure me, finally, *too off*, with these last 2 stories? I.e.,
am I managing any wt/, by means of, passage? Where I try, for
the moment, to look in, like they say. Let me know yr thots, re
same.

Very fine card, from Mrs. Crosby; she says she is writing you. A
very decent woman, and hope we get chance to meet her, before
she does go back.

All waiting here; always start a month early! Ok. And very fine
all goes well; keep us in touch.

                              [*Olson's note*: Sept 27th add?]

Chas/

Just to add a note about A/ Bryan, i.e., a letter just in from him on the stories (ORIGIN) sent him there, and likewise, my suggestion that he might have eyes for doing a thing with them.

Sheer damn joy of hitting, again, someone who does get it, who doesn't throw me down:

"Your stories shaking up attention: insisting upon primitive vision, meanings and objects changing places in the word [*i.e.*, world?] . . ."

I mean, *wow* — & that it does, hit me very close & hard. To have him say just that.

All of it, so wonderfully kind, & *on.* "your forms doing things in space . . ."; ". . . (& of his reading, of them, to one there) he didn't have any size; and it was good to know that at last it was impossible for him to say: but the hand is too large if one judged by the eye . . ."; ". . . exhausters . . ."

Any-
how, I can't stand here all day with this smile, etc. He does go for the idea, as sd, and jesus, if you think it could be made there — too damn much! I wonder: what do you think of tossing out, perhaps, THE SEANCE & also, perhaps, THE LOVER, and adding, these last two (GRACE & PARTY)? I am no damn good on such a matter. But if it were possible, jesus it wd mean MUCH to me. Let me know what you think about any of it; I hope it isn't a damn dream.

Have just written him about the GUIDO, enclosing copy, etc. As soon as I have limits, i.e., dimensions, et al, don't see why he can't go ahead on it.

And also, if you figure it a good idea, the same on Duncan's AFRICA REVISITED. What you say, i.e., let me know.

But it does, all, open. I feel considerably better, to put it very, very mildly, with your APOLLONIUS *here*, and now, this wonderful letter from A/.

Only wish that he were closer, that I
might now put this book of yrs into his hands. But soon, and he'll
be back, I take it, in November.

Anyhow/ anyhow. Keep me on;
just getting back up, is what it all seems to come to.

Ok/ take
care of yrselves. And write, please write as soon as you have a
spare minute. Have missed your letters, very, very much.

Again/
all dearest love to you both/

Bob

[Fontrousse, Aix-en-Provence]
Wednesday / Sept 27th [1951]

Dear Chas/
Just mailed those others—fine clear day, & real
pleasure riding in to Puyricard, on the bike. The road is a very
fine one, a ridge for the most part, and the same valley we face
here, holding most of the way. After the rain (fierce & crazy storm
last night, explosions!) everything is now fantastically sharp; I
have never seen such sharpness, as comes here, after such a rain.
It lifts every damn thing, straight out. Can see, with all ease, a
wash flapping on a line that must be close to 3 miles from where
I'm sitting. No wonder I keep thinking the sea is just over those
damn hills!

Anyhow, odds & ends, to clean up. Mrs. Crosby did write the fine
card, noted. Hope, again, to be able to see her, before she does go
back. Right or wrong, I had kept her on re the several things you
have got out; and could, this time, tell her of APOLLONIUS, and

is there any way she might get the text? I would send her this one, straight off, but continue to hope that Gerhardt can make it by here, and want it for him to see then; too, the problem of Mascolo, and those one or two others (Bud, in Spain, likewise Ashley, and Mitch in Italy) who should have chance to look. Well, will figure some arrangement. But won't let it stagnate, in any event; and will get it moving around directly.

Two days sober thought on Kasper don't encourage me very much; I can't finally spot it, but it seems a little odd, all of it. That Horton is on it, and apparently strong (note the economics — sure sign of either H/ or Ez; H/ being, *always*, the echo, every damn time) is the same thing as saying Ez is; and I can't quite figure if this is the condition for a reconciliation of sorts. Again, you'll have the feel there. Do you think that might be it? Well, all I wd say: go real slow, and you wd, anyhow.

(Finally, the idea of handling THE PRAISES and all such material, there — *is the one which excites me/ what else*. It would be tremendous, incredibly great. I hate to get my own hopes up, and suppose you feel the same; it is so very much a thing one is pulling for — hate to jump the gun. Anyhow, some such thing is, I think, inevitable. We have too damn much steam up, to be backed off now. I can't think that the Gasp/ comes to more than the incidental; the "Selected Olson" is by no means the same thing as, a direct out for any & all single instances of work such as, APOLLONIUS. That he misses that, does not reassure me.)

Thinking of Cid, and by that, Vince: there is that loss, and hitting it, as that quote, etc., it did rub. But jesus, you make that very right again, and all my thanks. Can't argue it, but I know who means it, for me; I damn well cannot quibble. Things have, also, happened *to me*, since that first letter; I am a hell of better judge of just that, than will ever be: Ferrini. Fuck them all.

But that Cid does have this notion, of the 'good,' does bug me on such occasions. He pacifies me in this last letter (in with yrs this noon).

The point: that one doesn't really want these soothings; he'd much rather the basic distinction, dissociation, or what you will, had been made way back at the beginning. However. You say it: earnestness is fine, but . . . , it is not, seriousness, or not so simply. Have you ever bumped into these characters, who, speaking of overt madmen, say, sweetly, but what a childhood! This, when the man is about to rape their mother! (What finally drove me to the woods: the hopelessly lost neurotics who were tolerated on the basis of, motive . . . , that is, these people could tolerate them, not, mind you, attempt to help them toward any cure, say, simply could tolerate them, because they counted themselves, smugly, cognizant of the divers horrors had brought the men in question to such a fix! One, I remember, was followed around with a very complacent sweetness, while he literally raised hell with anything & anyone who happened to bump up against him. Goddamn Freud, if that's all that's to be made of it. God, goddamn!)

What does scare me a little, now & then: Cid's lean to the earnest, tho I have seen him throw down a considerable body of just such work (including, I will certainly grant him, Ferrini's) that could be called so. I do trust him, in that place, i.e., faced with the work, tho he needs constant pushing. Your contact on him, and I can judge it, has cleared his head in a way I once thought altogether impossible; one yr of hammering, my own, never got me within a mile of it, or him. Well, I do like him very much; Ann calls him a parrot, and I damn well know what she means. But let him be the one, I do damn well love, because he has a very honest mind, and a good heart; I can't think of anyone else who wd do what he has done, for either of us.

Anyhow, anyhow. Crazy how this weather, now, looks so much better to me; I had sat here all morning without once taking any note of it. You wake me up.

Will put this aside, for the time, i.e., supper cooking, and want to get off this table. (I get so I can work this, balanced on one knee!) And pick up, and go on with it, tomorrow. Use candles, here, and tough on the eyes, at night (what other time to burn the candles, r/ creeley) Anyhow, back soon; and hope it all goes cool there.

Was very clear on this a minute ago, and hope to christ bringing back the typewriter hasn't damn well lost it.

The thing: all work prior to the attempt on the novel left me with the *limit* of passage; I don't want to consider, now, whether or not that limit was actual, i.e., it may have been only my confusion. In any event, I felt my loop, such as it was, hadn't the flexibility needed, *with respect to passage*, that I had to get to. In other words, I cd, as noted elsewhere, plunge on any one perception, i.e., could make that the full basis for the conjectural, but could not, as also noted, move with any grace from *one thing to another*. Again, the difficulties in BLUE; and now add, the whole device of, IN THE SUMMER—where the narrator literally puts down one fix, to pick up another; and the use of 3 frames, in 3 FATE TALES. You see what I was bumping into, and what it could finally coop me in.
So, like any car, back it up, and see what the hell IS IN THE WAY. Brings us to, May 1951, or thereabts, & the horror, of damn little to say, as I then felt it. What happened: false starts of, SORT OF A SONG, and another little horror, like they say, I never had the guts to show you. Then: novel. Immediately, hit the problem of, passage. You can write 10 pp/ on one perception; you can write, perhaps, 1000, but it was something else, I was trying to get in. Simply, to knock it, i.e., to work against any one thing, a multiple of others. Call them, 'people,' trees, or whatever, and you taught me this anyhow.
What happened: new attempt to gain means for, passage. To be able to balloon, spread, on any ground, and to make of that, quick, passage to another. To get a base sense of, sequence.
I think the novel, finally, can be dropped, i.e., I think I can drop it, and not feel I fucked off, or ducked out, or whatever. Better to move to the last two done, and even, this one right now

under hand. The way I had just now thought of it – the quesion:
where are these things coming from. I think that gets in, or
suggests, the shift, or makes ground on which to talk about it.
You see, the experience hasn't changed, i.e., I am writing, can only
write, from one ground, but my stand, there, of course, is
variable. And too, the shift to 3rd person narrative isn't sufficient
explanation, when one figures both THE LOVER, SEANCE (and
now I add, IN THE SUMMER): all from that position. You damn
well know what I think: it's the ground under them that begins to
move too. I.e., all of those others – held in one fix, one head.
Rock, or anything, against which: waves. Now, there is not,
simply, that rock, and I miss it, you can be sure, as much as you
do.

But how about this: IF I can work this present method into a
way to hold out, the several attentions, or forces, present in any
one instance, IF I can gain sureness enough to allow me the same
quick passage I'm after, i.e., ability to record, quick, a movement
in terms of *several* (what I have not been able to do, earlier).

And
IF, THEN, I ram up, again, ram in, the conjectural – what will I
have. I mean, the means to it, the quick & final flux between
anyone, anywhere, and any *thing*, and can add, somehow, to that,
the dimension of the conjectural, the literal hands on it holding,
perhaps I will be able to read my work with some pleasure, and
some pleasure which I honestly cannot yet feel. Certainly, it is a
little insane, but it is all I have to think of.

When you say "time"
of GRACE – it is, I think, a hit against, a right one, against that
very old deus ex something or other, that is always hauled in to
force, meaning. I.e., time's passing, and so, and so. It is almost
that simple. I like that story for other things; particularly, the
conversation about the house, the old one. I like, at one point
there, a hanging of them all, *without* time, if I don't pat my own
back for something that didn't come off. Anyhow, the moon rises,
etc. [*Added in margin*: also like *shift* of positions: he to hers; hers
to his. Without *irony.* / i.e., what I try to learn do to, etc.]

But,
is it worth it, will ask you very straight, do you think? You can't

know if I can pull it off, and I can't. But can you see, and you have already (yr comment on "*two* hands" . . .), what I'm trying to work out to. IF I make it, it makes me out, clear out, into SPACE. It breaks all the limits I've yet known. That is, gives me the means to move anything, anytime or where, and again, the plunge, always to *define.*

Etc., etc., and I sound much too close to egomania for my own comfort. But damnit, it is a desparate biz; no one ever said it wasn't. One's ownself is the question. The place, here, shook me badly; perhaps I only write, or make, a defence against it; but want never to get caught, so off, like this again. Must make a *means* equal to anyplace, anytime, just from the angle of, myself.

[*Typed in margin:*]
The last sounds, the answer to it: the old method, but you see, it needs the hauling in of (what I wd like to find a better word for), *passage.* I.e., got to find out how to move things quick, must develop means to handle a multiple surface, as of, any number. Got to put myself deeper, into the method; way into the commas, question marks, SEQUENCE. Or something.

Literally, I want a means to *move* the *base* perception, not only those subordinate to it. I.e., THE PARTY does get some of it; there is this literal shift, of the ground, in it, or so I hope. And that is what, finally, all of this, of passage, seems to come to. The tenacity, with which the conjectural hangs to its point of departure (the base perception) is the main problem. How, then, to move that, too. I.e., move the whole damn works.

[*In pencil:*] The lean, now, on *passage* wd explain the change in "language"? Have to find out HOW to *re*-assert the conjectural. Give all you can on: time, and also how you feel this thing of "displacement." Tremendous help — what you *have said.*

Thursday/ [28 September 1951]

Dear Chas/
          Morning once more, and have a haircut, thanks to
Ann; and feel, consequently, a somewhat new man. Hadn't one
since a week before we left NH, and so: a certain length, etc.

Am going to put in, with this letter, 2 little things [*added*: does
them for kids] by Ashley, I got while with him; that is, I smeared
them miserably in printing, & also, poster-paint, which wdn't give
the cleanness of ink, etc. But I want you to see these 2, anyhow,
i.e., gives one some sense of his mind, and how he looks at,
things.
          (Terrific similarity, between his way of hitting any such
thing, & what I remember of Klee's comment, re, "but that doesn't
look like Uncle, etc., etc.," i.e., where he only says, I need some
weight here, hence, add this, etc., etc. . .)[126]

Unfair to him, I know, sending on these two smeared cuts; but
anyhow. Gives you the top & the bottom, at that.
                                        Great pleasure
in talking with him; wonderfully *clear* head, i.e., he expresses
himself without all that garble (argle/bargle) I usually bumped into
with painters. Jesus, how some of them "do run on . . ."
                                        And one
fine story, too: he said, one time he had a scholarship, for one of
those summer gigs, & among the instructors was one most serious
man, altogether addicted to, the usual patter. They were 'studying'
one of Botticelli's paintings, in which was included, among other
things, a small girl (foreground) & a large church (background),
and the man, in question, was bent on matters of, weight, and
direction, and had spieled out the usual, again, saying, this line
leads to that line, leads to this line, leads to that line, etc., ad
nauseam, until he came to what he felt his, king pin, i.e., the
church & the girl, and sd: the girl is so very small, you see . . . ,
in order to emphasize how very large the church is. Whereupon
(and may all history record him!) one young man sd: and why
shouldn't the church be large, in order to show how very, very

small the girl is?

That afternoon, this same man, painting along a gravel path, etc., had left it for awhile, walking off, and what with a strong wind, easel & all landed face down in the gravel. A/ sd, they came walking back, and found it so, and since no one wanted to lift it up, etc., because of the mess, and job, then, of trying to clean it, and this man some 3 or 4 minutes back of them, they all grabbed rushes, growing along the path, and formed themselves into a line, all leaning, the rushes sweeping down, to where the painting lay, face down, in the gravel. And the man comes along, sees them, and by his own logic, finally is led to sd painting, whereupon: he never sd very much about such, again.

I mean, pleasant, and wish to christ more painters, of my acquaintance, had had a like experience, like they say.

A/ is a very nice man, and hope, sometime, you can meet him for yrself; one of these goddamn days, anyhow.

Continue to ride on yr letter; very damn fine how that shook the works up, and let me get hold of things I hadn't really been able to, before. I make, of Ez' statement, now: method must be got to as, constant, to allow content, to be all possible, variant. This is only an extension, etc. Perhaps too tight, at that.

But anyhow, I was thinking of how Stendhal, for one, can *move* the base premises, how, by that, he is never pulled back by any 'prior' statement; what most novelists get caught on, i.e., something they said earlier, to put it that loosely.

And it is, still, the headache of, sequence; take any 5 pages of James M. Cain, and you'll get it, but good. I.e., why does one thing follow another, and, more particularly, how. There is NO rule, of course; or none but the way, of the attention, and one never drops conjecture, I think, there, i.e., one never does, with safety. One cannot shape things, before they have come into existence — or, let them try, etc., if they think they can.

Sequence, then. Again, that passage about

which I tried to get something clear, last night. You read these things, the stories, so damn carefully & wonderfully, I know you are as aware of the attempt, as I might be in making it; I never stop thanking my own god for just that fact. It is an incredible help.

Well, one tries. That is, I had felt that, by means of this SI, as felt by both of us, the job might then come to be : what variations are possible upon one's *own* intelligence. Impossible to give up that center — how, then, expand it to give a reach, a largeness, in terms of several, people or things.

I cannot say that I've dropped the conjectural; certainly, have put it to work elsewhere, but remains, anyhow, my one tool. Nothing else, I know of, etc. But how it can work, too : I know, say, what happens when *I* stick a knife into myself; but what happens when someone *else* does? You see what I try to do, i.e., try to throw out, to that 'other' experience, and do it, again, certainly with, only, conjecture, and ride, or try to, on just the force that can throw up, for me.

(Really, moving back behind things, a little, as you note; but do want to get this matter of, passage, or sequence, very clear. And as well, find how to allow in, others, in a variety of positions. That, now, seems to me an immediate part of the job.)

Soon, I will get off to you all the letters, from you, that seem to me basic; there are a lot, so will send them straight mail, marked, etc. Anyhow, will get them to you there, soon. The Martz letter IS of the cloth, as sd; and others, equally up in front. Well, can see for yrself; and please, do keep them for me, i.e., I wd hate not to be able to have them, again. But they are certainly *yours*. Ok.

Fine clear day again; letter in from Bud and hope to see him in about a month's time. Will be wonderful. Damn well NEED someone to talk with; have been, more or less, silent for the past 4 years — time, now, to try to say something, like they say.

Write

soon; will get this off this aft/ — want to get out of this house; sit too damn much, in it, as is.

All love, and keep us on. You damn well don't have to worry about a damn thing; this APOLLONIUS is damn well the continuance. Terrific, terrific thing.

(And want, very soon, to try to get into it hard. In spite of what I have sd, feel it's still only surface.)

Friday/ [29 September 1951]

Chas/

Have to get this out of here, before I have a bundle, etc. I had thought to get it off yesterday, but then hung around, thinking Aldington might show up, though he didn't. Perhaps this afternoon; curious to see what will happen, etc.

Continue to ride on yr letter; so many things depending on it, finally. The problem the novel is, is more or less the main one; despite other considerations, like any of the stories, now. I remember, very clearly the morning I wrote that passage you liked, i.e., where the older way breaks in. An impatience with the limits, and allowed myself to speak out, at least that time.

I felt last night, that just there was where I might try it again, i.e., begin there, and make it 1st person, and allow myself, again, all play of, digression — what I've most missed in this present way. Anyhow, perhaps it would make it so, and once we are a little more settled, and I have space & time, will get to it. Few threads of this present lean, call it, to be got out, and once they are, figure it will be time for it. (I do vacillate, somewhat, on whether or not to junk this 1st try; i.e., it would take me, I suppose, about a month to finish it. About ½ there, roughly, as I have felt it, etc. What might come of it : clear instance of a flat juxtapositional method — i.e., free of 'histories,' etc. Ann sd back a few nights, now : "novel — having no *history* prior to its reading . . ." I thought very straight. I.e., back to : destruction of, reference. And

am reminded, saying that, of how good it is to talk to painters,
i.e., Ashley, about just that fact. They get it, straight off, where
another writer would quibble forever. Anyhow, to get back — don't
know quite what to do, i.e., do you think this present thing
(novel) is worth salvaging, against other possibilities, i.e., are you
anxious, at all, to read the rest of it? Only way I can think of
putting it. Flat, at that.)

And other things — mainly, that I am relishing the few days, now,
left me of some damn age over you! I.e., only dep't in which I do
precede you! That is : parenthood, like they say. (How horrible
the Gasp/s comments were!)
                    Anyhow, do feel for you both; very
aware of those tensions you must be bucking. Always thought :
smartest thing for everyone would be to separate, for that time,
although it sounds frightfully cold-blooded. Just that the woman
does get so deep, in herself — one feels as though he were sitting
somewhere, half way to the moon! But mark it anyhow — yr time
will damn certainly come, and what no woman knows of — just
that instant, it is born, the baby, and one damn well knows,
somehow, has been thrown out, thru, incredible thing of, himself.
(Try to tell C/ she's VIA! I dare you to!)
                    Anyhow, anyhow —
foolish to anticipate. But I did feel, those two times — was only
man in the world, and crazy, how SHARP all things then were.
When T/ was born, was sitting back in the house, with some beer,
etc., listening to that crazy idiot, who has the record show in
Wash/ DC — somehow got him, and of course, was thinking of
you as it was. I mean that joker who does the grotesque
imitations — etc. Wild unreal thing, hearing him then.
                    The time D/
was born — the nurse wd give me no information abt how it was
going, because she didn't believe I was the prospective father — i.e.,
she sd I looked too yng (!) and contented herself with
flirting . . . (intimations of the exterior reality if one were ever in
any condition to take note of it.)

But kids — so great, finally, to have them, any of them, in spite of all the hell they sometimes can be. I get to feel pleasantly expendable, having the two. I.e., it makes an odd & useful freedom. One can move on other premises.

Dave now picking up french remarkably quick; makes sentences, and seems to catch words very surely, i.e., hearing them once, can manage to use them again, etc. A pleasure, seeing him make it. When we first came, he was so beat by not being able to speak with the kids here — used to ask us why he couldn't, and very, very sad for him. But now — he picks up with great ease, and can only face my own dullness, who knows not five words more than when we moved in.

I should look at it as, a language, wd be of use, should we ever get to either China or Japan. The former — interesting me very much, and wish to christ one cd now go there. The size, here — what stultifies me.

(Think of the dialects, in England, and the size — odd comment on their lack of communications. Similarly, here. No movement, it seems. Mind like Valery's finally horribly fragile, and limited — incredibly bounded by its apprehension of, size. It moves on very old tracks, I think. I read some of his prose (notes, etc.) this summer — many times moved, very much, by certain insistences, but never felt I wd have gone at it in any of the ways he chooses. And cannot forget that the way one arrives at a thing, even if it be the same thing as someone else's, does mean considerable. The old habit of lumping ends, i.e., of thinking, well, all roads lead to rome, etc., or of that better instance, you get the same thing in the end, etc. (that horrid lean on, really, the general) — what it does leave out, what it does damn well lose — forgetting, that just that movement, just how any man does move, is his final interest, is the only thing he is.)

Isn't it some kind of comment, on the European intelligence — Freud vs. da Vinci? I.e., that book?[127] I saw it very much shrunken, i.e., those two 'times' so put at one another, and felt da Vinci, was the 'american.' Again, reminded of how you had sd: Lawrence/ american. That was very sharp statement. Dimensions seemed very, very important to him; and energies, likewise.

Can hear T/ burbling down the stairs; crazy froth-like wheeze he manages! Scares D/ sometimes, in the night, with the sounds he brings up. How they wake up, anytime, and lie there, making these noises! Well, you will be getting it, soon now. So wonderful to think of it, and so very very happy for you both.

Thinking of the Dr's letter, i.e., one I had noted as just in; he asks how much it costs, a week, to live here, and says, "I've got to do something." Well, all this part—"I'm working on a novel, it's hard going. I don't know what I want—perhaps the result of my age plus my illness now happily on the wane. But I'm unsettled, restless more than I've been for a generation. Wish I knew what I physically want : I know crystal clear what I want otherwise." He always does that, i.e., suddenly, the 'revery'—I like it. I.e., he comes very clearly, just there.

One thing: if ever you bump into anything, i.e., any fix, call it, wherein you think I cd be of use, there, i.e., USA, keep me in mind. I sometimes wish I had an occupation where I cd be of direct use to someone else, to be doing something like that. What I've really envied you very much in : BMC. I never feel much else than, the lone wolf. But I have not a thing to kick abt, at that. Well, no matter. Write soon/ keep us on. All our love to you both, Bob

[*Added in margin:*]
11/am: just in, Fenollosa, from Mrs. Pound—very damn glad to finally have this in my hand; had never got it, until now. (This is Gasp's thing?) (Has address of, Cleaner's Press)[128]

Also note in from Mitch, with review (Walter Allen, who has written some excellent critique in such things, NS&N—England) of W/ Lewis' RUDE ASSIGNMENT (autobiography)[129]—wd be interesting.

[Fontrousse, Aix-en-Provence]
Sept 29/ 51

Dear Chas/
Had only time to note the arrival of the Fenollosa, yesterday, before Ann was off, etc. But you can figure, anyhow, what I'm feeling like at this moment—good lord, it IS precisely what you had called it, "the damned best piece on language since when . . ." I mean, CLEAR—and what incredibly ACTIVE comment. It really lights up yr own work, very, very strong. That article, GATE & CENTER, read as the continuum of his concerns, I mean, that line, does take on weight, does grow very big & very damned important.
I get now, more clearly, yr past comments on Hart Crane, and likewise, everything. I wish I had had this thing back then; it's sure enough that I was missing something, not having it. But no matter now—I DO have it right on the table beside me, I will not be done with this quickly.
(The thing that confounds me, not to make simply a mean crack, etc., is how Cid managed to note the reprint, back a few weeks now, without so much as a ripple—i.e., simply noted it, & passed on. For myself, & again, only to make clear how it does hit me,—I find it damn hard to think of *anything else* but what *is* of its cloth. It is really incredible writing.)
I love the man writing it, the fineness of him, the way he leans into the material, where he says, there : "I submit my causes of joy."[130] (!) Crazy thing. And what he does do to classification, i.e., that example! Phew—& I feel like a few hundredwt/ of stone just up & flew away, off my back.
And verbs—no confusion *possible*, after reading this. How it does LIGHT UP the works! Really, I feel like running thru the streets, like they say.
Again, & more particularly, it helps me to gauge your own work, & to appreciate the job you're up to; I hope others can make the same conclusions. I.e., you deserve a hell of a lot of credit, for carrying on this biz, straight. I don't think even

Ez, who I've read, certainly with all possible attention, can be
called as direct, in his continuance, as you have been on this
matter. I wd now say, if anyone's, you are F/s son, i.e., this is the
man behind you, the one who lights up yr own work.

All so
vague, finally — the way I put it there. But I hope you will get it,
anyhow. That is, the dimension this puts on your own work, and
how grateful I am to have that. It is a terrific damn thing; couldn't
have anticipated it, in any sense, BUT by just your own
attentions.

(The thing: when I wrote to Ez, back a few wks now,
had asked about the possibility of issuing the Fenollosa, i.e., idea
of ORIGIN editions, or possible, Gerhardt, if & when he gets
here — and this, I suppose, is the answer to that. Haw. Anyhow, I
did write him, last night, the way it hit in; ridiculous not to
acknowledge something like this. Few enough times when it is
possible. Cannot overestimate its importance to me, *just now*; with
this, and yr APOLLONIUS — I can damn well consider the NEXT
MOVE. Ok. And doesn't it damn well center me, at that, right on
sequence, right on the thing in hand — it is impossible to contain
this excitement.)

The other thing — reading, again, Pivot, which I've not had, now,
for almost a yr, i.e, loaned to a transient, like they say, & never
got it back (plus the Analects, & do regret the damn loss).[131]
Anyhow, you know what I feel abt it, from past comment, so no
need to go into it here. It does steady me very much, these things;
I have never hit anything more exact, than : "Only the most
absolute sincerity under heaven can effect any change."[132] That
damn well is LIGHT, for me.

Etc., etc. And hopeless fact of not having you here, to be hitting
this direct. What does get to kill me, a little, re the letters — that
we are not allowed the more direct passage. Well, it doesn't
matter, or doesn't against that which we have pulled out. I damn
well get to more, with you, at this distance — than I ever have with
anyone else, in the same room. Let that go as, the fact.

Will have to pull myself down, now, to get to work; that story,
upstairs, still sitting at page 1 & ½ — and between it, and me —
APOLLONIUS, yr letter, & now this Fenollosa! I won't manage
the ride back to this one, easily!

          Anyhow, one IS MOVING.
What damn well ONLY counts.

" 'All flows' and the pattern is intricate . . ."[133]

Feel, finally, very giddy — and trying to pick up, a certain dizziness
I can't very well write out of here. And who gives a shit, at that.
So this is what the Gasp/ did get out — and what is his reputation:
can certainly understand that.

          Continue to wonder about him;
please tell me what you hear from him, when you do; i.e., what it
gets to sound like. I continue to feel, if, frankly, it could be yrself
& Ez again free of the bitterness, his — that wd make movement
considerably more simple. I continue not to understand his feeling;
and having this F/ for root, it baffles me even more.

          To my own
knowledge, no one, but you, who manages the clarity of
emphasis, on this continuance, on this incredibly important thing.
And why he does not accept that, or bucks it — I can't honestly
understand.

Well, this for the moment; must cool down a little; too much
play, at this point, like any damn wheel, etc.

          Hoping for a letter,
from you, this noon : 2 hrs to go. Ok, and will pick up,
directly.

      All our dearest love to you both/

                Bob

Keep us on; ok.

12:00/ and all quiet, so will get this off. One thing: Mitch wrote,
yesterday, & this comment on S/ Lawrence (WAKE) who had just
been by: "Seymour was thru here last week. He was lost. He was

carrying a tennis racket he'd had in his hand since he left NY.
They won't take it with his checked thru baggage, so it's carry it
or let go . . . As he gets older, he seems to be more and more
absorbed with plans, calculations, schemes, arrangements. / He
was saying he never got any satisfaction from the WAKE. I didn't
ask why, then, he'd done it. Seems he's going to put out one more
and drop it. Makes sense. It looks like he's moving in smaller and
smaller circles."

[Black Mountain, N.C.]
saturday september 30 1951

Robt: All three of yr letters have come in in a fantastic morning
(along with the mss — back — registered mail, of the Praises! fr
ShitFace, claiming, he sent me proofs, in July — than which I never
saw! I had quietly writen him, a week ago, saying, just send em
back, eh? figuring (no word from him since April, and yr news,
that his GG, was mimeo, or multilith, or whatever, that he had
had his time! And now, he pulls this, that, the fault is, mine, that,
I did not acknowledge, the proofs! Jesus, what a swamp he is, a
mudhole)

The grand thing, is, that, I feel as you, that, we are on,
again. At least I was riding back, the last two days: reading
wildly, as the result of finding, Thursday, that Asheville, 12 miles
away, has a library, which can substitute for me for the Lib of
Cong, a private library of 35,000 books & pamphlets, the work of
a civil lawyer, which he willed to the city, the Sondley Reference
Lib: for ex, pulled out of it, not only Berard, and a interesting biz
on Elizabethan pneumatology (as of the plays), but such a book as
THE MUSIC OF THE SUMERIANS![134]
Anyway, I have again

flung myself loose into those areas which are my concern: am studying Greek, for the 1st time, with an old German, Gottingen, named Dehn[135] here (along with Con), and already know the first three lines of the ODYSSEY! At same time am pushing along the Berard biz further (found it possible, last night, to read all of his intro to his French trans of O,[136] in a couple of hrs, without recourse to a dictionary but twice! Crazy, how the little Spanish I picked up, is pushing, the French). And Herodotus, who, 2nd only to Creeley, is the narrator I enjoy. And last night laid something like this out, as — for me — the live ones:

texts:
     odyssey
       moby-dick
         herodotus
           ovid (heroides, as much as metamorphs)
          pausanias
            euripides
               sumerian poems (with eye out for discovery,
                   coming, of the Phoenician Heraklaid)

scholarship:[137]
       berard
         jane harrison
         waddell
           maspero (conte populaire d'Egypte)
           & anything & anyone on SUMER
             (kramer, porada, frankfort, this galpin
              (the music) even woolley)

critique:
       nada nada nada (but there are some shots,
       principally berard, a guy named Thomson, on the
       art of the logos, and a book pub. American 1820 on
       "The Theatre of the Greeks")[138]

& grounds for *logos* and/or the single actor drama or *epos:*

lattimore's (inner frontiers of asia)
strzygowski (on wood, & Gothic[139]
frobenius
& any histories of Ionians, Phrygians,
Cappadocians, Hittites, and
SUMERIANS

beside all of which please place:

THE STATES: Mayans (language, plus sculpture, plus *tales*,
any Indians') especially, UAXACTUN

the physiography of, these two continents (to
be relevanted to the Caucasus-Himalaya
chain, as of that other past)

Cabeza de Vaca

The Civil War

One, Carl Sauer, on Deglaciation

Add, last, investigation of *voice* and/or *speech* and/or what was
called *poetics*:

composition, here and now, mister, olson

& as, antistrophe, fenollosa
e.p. ANTHEIL
dante De V E
creeley, notes, on prose

Damn interested, to see it out, like that, and thot, maybe, might,
interest you

Ok. Now, to what you hath given: (1) damned happy last go on
stories & novel of use. For
in return, look, what you hath given me—"All of it, all of it: sheer
arrogance. But fuck it—no
use saying one is not, finally,
serious. OK"

(2) APOLLONIUS: when that little one sits in ferrini's house,
let him say, let him say!
The point is, how, MOVE, but, as *you*, by saying what
you have now sd to me, make *me* move. For yr biz, of
the generative & the conservative, that proposition, is as
beautiful as anything ever offered me (how much more
accurate than that of, Blake, the, prolific &, the
destructive—how Blake is spoiled, by the good & the
evil, from such seeing: only Rimbaud, of the
predecessors—that is, inside the box, 500 BC—1950
AD—got free of, that one, I take it:
the problem is not
destruction (this is those who are not alive); but those
who are, are confronted, and only, such as, the pulling
between, the backward and the forward, is, how you
have put it!
(As you equally do, in yr notes on, *depth &*
passage)

by god, lad, i was scared, on A, and that you do ride, do say
such things, welcome it, find it, of use, that, surely, is as
important, as anything, of the several moments you have
supplied me with, sight
i get so profoundly disturbed that i do
not communicate, and you alone are
enough, simply because it is you.

it is yr biz on the prose, which, opens my eyes, that, that
once, i did land, with a pad, that the fucking intellectual that
i am did not, take over—too much

(((3)))   the half-century note which, fell right out, and almost
blew away, where i opened the letter!

Con was with
me, & both of us, 1st thot, was, no, goddamn it, they must
need this one more — even for stamps! So you must surely tell
me, some windfall, or else i'll continue to do with it what
seems to me the course, in all gratitude for (as before) giving
us, floor. Only, this time, the floor is a crazy one, for me:
that is, Lerma, it was us alone, and saved us. This time, I can
eat, sleep, and maybe (if these birds ever do pay the pittance
a month they proposed — i am not blaming, for, it was a poor
proposition anyway, and they only got 30 students, and 14
faculty, so, the dividing, is probably, abt 15 dollars a month!)
I can go along, so far as we two are concerned.

What I
propose to do is hold it, for the present, in case it is the only
way I can get Con and the lad or lass out of the hospital. But
if any dough from any other source than you two (who,
surely, are, as we are, and not, as those, who might, if they
were of any awareness — Murray, say, or the De Menils[140] — or
even (tho this is a far cry, and only, for you, BUT, that
E[velyn] S[hoolman], of Cid's, if she wanted to do what she
toyed with, a house Boston, September, made it cash!   —
such never do, out of, plain need to get something back, flesh,
or the looking into the eyes, the idiots   — only riboud ever, &
murray once, planked it, down!

The course, then: hold it, for such purpose, if needed. If any
other out, here it is, sitting, for you, when, you need stamps,
again — PULLLEASE, eh?

And jesus, like you say, "almost by an excess," viz, a
crucifixtion. Christ, how the bill shores us! You tell
Ann.

(4) & Dave, that, he and his pop, have given me the 2nd great go
on CHUTE: Con says (nasty like, never, going for the poem, and
the reason, a jealous one)[141] — "It's the only time you ever wrote a
poem for children, and it should be published, with Creeley's

drawings"!!! o, that animal, WOE-MAN!

> what wows me, is the arrow, drawing 2 — & the stool,
> drawing 4: real BONGO, & the lute! flat GONE. & the
> pieces, to be, picked UP!

I damn well think, myself, that Dave is as his father is, a damn
fine critic!! For, me, that one is, honestly, *my* PREFACE, my own,
nobody else's, THE beginning — & that it is a transposition from
the Sumerian, gives me, honestly, the real jumps. You take
PREFACE, and leave Dave & me this little insinuator (it, of
course, delights Con, that, again, you and she, are, of like
mind — if you won't mind, such, family politics! That, say, *her*
poem, MOVE O, you preferred (then) to this one, of Dave's, one
other, &, myself!

      You see, I'd read this one, as 1st, whenever,
anyone, asked — i am so soft about it, that, here, I declare my
"con-gen," my, *will*: *kata*, the Greeks had it, as opposite of *ana*
(basis)![142]

      KATA, as alternate title to, CHUTE

                        (by god, maybe,
this is where the French word, comes from! Look in some good
French NED, please, for me, and see if, their word is derived
from, that, eh?)

      Wonderful excitement, these days, anyway, in
ETYMOLOGIES: wild for it, every moment. (Crazy, that, Cid, at
my suggestion of an alternative, cut out, the etymologies of
"symbol," image, etc, in HU! Hope you won't burn, but, the idea
was, to get the thing off, on the beam you suggested (strike
comparison as of now down) and then go fast (yr word was, to
bevel against) to the Maya, and, their stories & acts

                      will see, you
will, what, two weeks? Am again, nervous, but will await,
eagerly, your judgment, on it: crazy, isn't it, how, it never stops,
the "concern"

And what other delicacies are there, at this banquet, you have
given us, this day — this FEAST? My god, that, suddenly, all is lit

again: I have been damned dreary, for three weeks — feeling, drained, and not on, and frightened, I was lost. All in the jaws, hammering, and wanting to do nothing but fuck 500 women — nothing else, just that. And no chance, or, not wanting to take on, the results — at least, not wanting, just now, to throw Con off, that least bit that, such, for me too, throws off, eh? Wanting, to stay in. And yet, so ravaged, so much beast, and glad of it, and wanting OUT. And asking myself — the pressure was so high — what will happen? Actually. Figured, a couple of times — from the losing of any sense of rails — that I was going to break over, to go, smash, from the breaking of, the light, that, the will for it, was (and I don't mean, of course, just, the fucking), was like, epilepsy, the conflagration (Augustine's, say, there, that letter),[143] this, frankly, just here, is the only place where, I understand, those, statements, that, lust, has, that beauty, this, is the face of, the god, just there, the ride out, from it, the sense of, here, is the explosion, we hold against, we make from, this, is, how we go down, that "love" is ass backwards, that love is conservative & generative as it is from lust (don't like these words, any better, than you do, and use em, with that qualification, merely, to make the two the one they always were, and that all platonists and christians have divided, and so have stolen, the secret, that, it is in, down, not out, up, where, the thing is, where, we are on

> (why that also wrong man Shakespeare has it wrong, there, in the expense of spirit in a waste of shame is lust in action:[144] what a fucking puritan-renaissance lie that is! Myself, I read it altogether backward, the other way, that, there — right there — is, where, the spirit, comes, alive, that, such, is the frankincense, from which, the bird, (the other bird), springs up, eh?
> How abt that, lust, is frankincense!

One little thing abt yr remarks, on A, about, the 2nd, of how far, that you should nail it, take up on it — well, you probably don't remember, but, it was a rhetorical device of yr own (in Notes on Prose), that very not less than but certainly more, which made it possible for me to get in, just, there! This sort of business, is delight, delight, o father mapple,[145] find out, real deeee-lite!

As of Gasp—agree entirely, and also, that A of T had better (now
that you have welcomed it as you have) sit by itself. My notion is
this: why not, now that THE PRAISES is back fr SF, just make
this what Square gets: that is, under that very title, so, that, the
thing exists as such, it has been so bandied abt? And if you are
strongly against it, leave out the Melville Letter, in fact, leave it as
it was to be:

    The K's, the P's, Move O, Morn News, I C H, For Sappho,
    Torre, ABC's, Dry Ode, La Chute

                         and perhaps add, what, from
Origin? Myself, I'd like the Gerhardt, Posy, Issue M, Adamo (?),
The Round & Cannon [sic] (coming up), the Exaggeration—what
of these would sit well with you—or any others (he sd,
hopefully!)

              or how wld it be, to throw the y & x (PREFACE,
anyway) in, for circulation, calling, as sub-title, to the P's,
"selected poems"

Or maybe abandon the damn P's, and make it, simply, *Selected
Poems*. And wld you advise, now (after WCW), giving yr wish
the ride, that is, printing the PV as the introduction?

My reason for going on this way, in spite of Gasp, is, that he does
have a circulation (from his Fenollosa—the 1st in his Sq $) and
from his new will, which, in lieu of a commercial publisher,
and the bother of it here where so many new things (like the
single poems—Fight, Guido, etc) & some of yr new stories (in case
you wld agree) &, say, a thing in music and words I hope to work
out with Harrison, & a Tarot Volume, etc etc—maybe the
ORIGIN contract, if the shop grew fast, and cld handle it—or
even a rerun of APOLLONIUS (we cld put out another bound
duplicate of this one, I imagine, for, say, well, 50 cost us 50, and
the most of that linotype cost, so, I figure, 1000—well, I shld
think inside the 175 for booklet, just because the labor here, is free

But the point is, that, this other old verse—it could ride free by
Gasp? Let me have yr thots on this. I grant you all—and again,
Con gets her 2¢ in, saying, you see, Cr and me, see, see!

And by all means, do what you propose on A, to, the Bottegha
dame – if for no other reason than to get that Cagli off his arse!
Make him burn, that, we go in there, and all these years, and he
never, the little gibbon (I suggest it also, by yr copy, simply,
   because, the paper bound, on a white paper, did not take the
   ink so good, and, what you have reads best, I figure – tho
   some others say, the "pamphlet" is much more straight on – (it
   also has the map however – which, I take it, you go sour on?)

One puzzle: did you mean, as of exchanging, Seance & Lover, for
Grace & Party, in ND #13? If so, no: that is, it's like you say to
me, the new stuff, is (always, no?), what one wants out, but,
there's time. And I think (knowing that Laughlin) you'd only
hinder the biz, there. I'd leave it, and, if Gallimard, say, or we,
here, can get out a 2nd book of stories, wow: see?

                                                    In any case, I
think you can well put out the narratives as poets do – that they
are so firm and self-operating, that one little volume after another,
is a way of doing it which the fucking commercials have lost all
sense of:
            R CR   MR BLUE
            R Cr   THE MUSICIANS   (look at that)
                      next, please?

Tell AB that, the platen, here, is exactly the size of the Melville
Letter. And that this pretty much determines the maximum field
(though, twice that, by a fold, can be fed in – warning, that, as on
any press, the problem of printing through, on such a run, is
great – as well as that, our choice of paper, has to be of such
texture it does fold). And that, to give the chase room to work, he
should contract this field to some extent. But also, that, he can
fold his sheet (that field, of the ML), any way he chooses – that,
for the single poem, he can use any design up and down, left to
right, or however he likes ((I don't have a ruler handy, and so
can't give you exactly, the measurements)) O, yes, the other thing,
is, the repro processes – silk screen, some can do, here; and
woodcut, or linoleum; but he will know better than I: just tell
him, that, the simpler his repro problem, the better – that this is

not a commercial shop! — yet!

[*Added in margin*: Note, it is twice folded — one fold makes a handsome page — there are any no. of sizes, cutting down — *only* condition is, ONE SHEET]

This leaves one hell of a lot of the major things left out — conspicuously, your own going on, eh? But for me, as I sd, I think you are on. And I'm just waiting, now, for THE MUSICIANS!
   And a baby.
     And to see what olson comes up with.
   Anyhow, PLEASE, just keep firing. And I shall try to do better than this once a week stuff. It is only, that, to get on at all myself, with all this fucking business here, is, a difficulty!
  Love to you all, from us both, and the depth of the joy & life
     you give us — Charles

[Black Mountain, N.C.]
monday october 1 51

Robt: Had figured, this afternoon, to get back on, to you. And bang, comes in yr bundle, including Friday! fantastic, how, yr letters come here so fast: wonderful to me, to have that gap of space closed, by time: don't figure the other direction can be anywhere near so fast. Imagine! you write Friday, and here it is Monday, and we have it! Crazy. Most exhilarating. And thanks for all: speculation, on yr own biz, news, and share on the biz, ahead; Con continues crazy clear, well, and (but for a funny lot of lesions, in her memory) seems altogether on top of self: it's her flesh gives me the ultimate pleasure, the richness, without any loss

of what was, for me, always, the joy, the bones: her legs (under
that thing, that African stomach) look as rich as they did the first
day i went for them (it was crazy, really, the way, we went into
it, her self, revealed, from under a demure dress, in a bathing suit
I still keep looking for the duplicate of, with a skirt, blue, and
there we were in Rockport, not at the sea, but in front of a house
with a stone wall, and she took to jumping down for me to catch
her where I stood in the grass. What a flirt, eh? It sounds so. But,
for her, or me, not so easy. The thing was, it happened, that time,
fast – and it was what? play, sure, but, to be able to play, that,
takes a change, a shift of base, eh? Anyhow, I was caught, just,
the damned delicate strength, or the directness, of, from what
clearly she was, coming straight: crazy, and still, I don't know
nothing about it, in this sense, that, it still holds. How
come?

          Well. And by god, a check, with, yr letter! From BMC! For
September. And $61 at that! Knocks me down. 61 bucks. Jesus.
The pay envelope: imagine. Never believe in such things. And
there it is: suddenly, Oct 1st, in the mail box, quiet like: 61 bucks.
Earnings. Apparently the joker is, they will pay out, at this rate,
for the first couple of months, making a play of it, as though they
could keep it up, but, that, soon, what they have will be gone,
and then, they will hold a meeting and agree to cut themselves
down! (It, of course, occurs to me that that's surely the time for
all wise men to go for breakfast, the cow, having been, milked. So
for Christ's sake, with that from you, i ought to get through this
BIG MONTH, have Con and the baby home, and only the doctor
(whom I figure has time) – in other words, be CLEAR. BUT, this
puts the 50 into an altogether [different] light, doubles it, and you
just say, when, yr economics is not on such an even keel as this
character's, suddenly, eh? Goddamn wonderful. In fact, I can look
the thing in an eye, with an eye, with what an eye, eh?

          And my god what a joy it is, to have you swirling. And
to be a little of a swiggle stick myself, again. (Fall, too, eh –
covered with New England – and loaded with projects: as of yr
idea, some BIZ, US, for you, ahead, this (my BIG BABY, to
finance us, for the next decade! Or some good part of it. And

between us, I don't see why we can't divide the whole fucking
boodle:

  THIS IS IT—blocked it out once before, have the sheets, and
am only holding until the right publisher—or plural—come to
hand. And figure you'll see it's too hot just to throw out, to
anyone. Thot Giroux (Harcourt) might be he, but, he is such
a soft character (by letters, anyway). Well, if ever again NY,
will talk to same, maybe. Tho, figure, some house (like
Random), maybe more likely. Trouble there is, don't know
the real boss. Or anywhere. And figure this one is one has to
be given straight, to the BOSS, the MONEY. You'll see.

  HERE: 10 yrs from now, the biggest publication deal of all, is
going to be (the States, if they are still the States') THE CIVIL
WAR. Now this is the sort of deal which is encyclopedic, and
goes into every home (Review of Reviews sort of biz).

                    It's
sure (1) to be something the schlemiels of nationalism like
LIFE INC will be lining up five years from now; and (2) that
the "professors" will thrive on, eh?

  So my idea is this: beat em both, with a grand plan, for
coverage with real invention in it, with real work behind it,
and a straight SCOOP. Ok?

(Get nervous, at this point, you'll think me all off. But let me
throw in my man—Herodotus—or words CINEMA—photos—to
give a gauge.)

  the idea is to lay out a total coverage, not only the materials,
BUT *methods of presentation*:
            start PHOTOGRAPHS—ever see
the Brady's? Well, I've worked long enuf on this biz to know that
(1) the glass plates exist, and repros, of a quality Brady's never
got, can be made IF the work is done soon, and not tied up by the
imminence of the CENTENARY
           (2) that the Confederate
photographers have not yet been dug out: and know three who

belong with Brady, Gardner (who is to be brought up to equality
with Brady), one Baton Rouge, one Charleston, SC, and one St
Lou[146]

(3) that, my prize hunch, the whole Brady outfit was a spy
set-up — what a tale, and the Archives, Washington, where it sits,
if my guess is accurate

in other words, PROJECT 1, a new & total PHOTO HISTORY
OF THE CIVIL WAR (right there's one whole publishing house's
moneys committed!)

II (and this is where I may be able to bait you, the, Herodotean
operation) In the first years after the CW, almost everyone was
putting down his recollections. On top of that both N and S
gathered official records. But the beaut of it all: the REBELLION
RECORD,[147] in how many volumes, by a Washington
newspaper — the craziest collection of all, like all the Egyptians,
Greeks, Babylonians, and Phoenicians, putting down all that
happened — wild tales, of guys, behind lines, home, etc etc.
                                                              Now
here this stuff sitz, almost, as it got published. And with local
records, and correspondence, untouched, basically.
                                                    My god, what
stories, what books. And not "history," since Thucydides, but
LOGOI, MUTHOI, as Herodotus.[148] Set men loose, under our
direction, to dig it out, bring it to us, and (assuming somebody
else writes it! but with declared methodologies we declare) what
we shouldn't be able to put out as books — scores of em, and for
the live reader, the "people, sir," not, the goddamned academics —
who, if we don't move in, early, will kill this one off too, as they
have killed off all the viable past for this people or for any
modern people anywhere.

In other words, the two hooks, wld be two presentations, the
known popular one, of PITCHERS, and the lost popular one, of
STORY (which I damn well figure is due for a rebirth).
                                                      Now II

brings up MOVIES: my flyer (for some other dough) would be the connecting of the gran project to some EISENSTEIN of film here we don't know anything about, YET. For surely, those boys, are going to be in on those 5 years (1961-65)

Well, crazy, and will sit here holding my hands until you tell me. But, for the likes of, what could be better, than, to sell this package as a deal (the whole of it, or parts) to some characters, and then, as GENERAL EDITORS, let them give us the means to do our own work on, with us directing the labors of trained men — whom we also, damn it, are better fit to train than who else?

And we pull in such of our friends as Ashley, Ben, and others: christ, it's time, anyway, BOTTEGHAS[149] came back into existence. (Maybe the thing wld be to get some one buck or babe with bucks, and start the whole operation from scratch: our own publishing house! tho that gets into executivism, and risk, and we are not interested: all we want is to sell the idea and get the stuff out right. (My assumption is, the thing there, 61-65, is a natural market, anyway)

Ok. Just to say, a HOOK, for you and me ahead, seems to me no problem, despite, the apparent hopelessness: that is, I honestly think the whole commercial situation has got so bad, is so brainless, that it's time we got in (note such signs as, this EMPIRE, art now in books (Ashley) magazines (Shahn)[150] museums as culture dispensers commercially, theatre even, and obviously education.

Or come at straight from our present occupations: this is a Medici time (and exactly by the same order, that, the Medici, had made their dough the same way in the earlier three generations). And I wld bet it ain't far ahead when we can tap some such dough (that wants to burnish itself with our feathers . . .

Well, to hell with dreams. To work:

what rides me, in all you

are saying in these letters, about the
                            DEPTH (by self, conjecture,
& single perception) and VARIANT, or passage, as, quickness,
and participation in others)
                    is, that IT IS IT
                                    and so what you are
about makes *absolute* sense

                        Flatly, I'd let the novel sit, ½ done.
My hunch is, attacking as you are in PARTY and Grace — in other
words, by that tension of the small quantity — gives you your
exceptional room — the room all the stories so far done declare as,
your own
                That is, I don't, myself, figure, that that room, is solely
an extension of yr self as perceptor and conjecturer
                                            figure it is also
a tension area proper to the problem as of now (that is, think, for
a moment, of where a poet is, so far as a longer form goes: ask
yrself, what dangers there are, in trying to outdo CANTOS or
PAT (tho PAT is not of quite the order of facing to it, that CS
are) — that, say, LINE, is still too unknown to be batting off into
epics!

        I say this, because i go back to, HAWK LETTER and
ORIGIN LETTER, 71, and my own impression a yr ago of how
you have in yr hands the attack on long narrative form
                                            like you
say, here, like Ann says, having no *history* prior to its reading: yr
energy, by its moral pertinence,
                        that is, what, say, Ez contrived,
in CS, was (he later cut the lines out) RAGBAG,[151] in other words,
anything which happened, or came his way was, TO GO
IN
        which is what yr letters are, and — I'd guess — what you can
make THE FORM for that extension of what you have been
about, and are now abt anew, in that direction which has been
called the novel
                    my guess is, that, still, you are thinking too

closely abt what goes to make up "a novel"

surely, for example,
you are wholly right in this biz of passage — of acquiring a means
to shift the base (at any point) without any sort of need to refer or
hook back to, previous considerations, even in the "book" under
hand

   my feeling is, that, all you honestly need to do — to unlock the
long form — is to take up a certain freedom (by contriving such a
methodology as the Letter, 71-75, already directs) *which will* wheel
quickly enough for you to drop yrself at any moment that yr
interest shifts to someone else

(what stiffens the present novel
is, that, this will is all too
obvious, too looked for — and you lose tension, say, BLUE, or
the HAWK letter[152] (which was not so conjectural, in the same
sense, as Blue, but more open, more, exactly what, you want
now, by presenting "others" to get in

   I still say you are already armed, that, Ann as "she," for
example, springs up whe[ne]ver you touch her — as does Wilson,
say, in the biz

and what more, finally, do you need, than, three
people — plus, say, such as "the baby" of GRACE

and what you
have also, THE PARTY, at least three "others," there, and none of
them, the above three

the thing is, yr form, anytime, anywhere, is
from YOU — and that, I take it, you have in hand, whether as (1)
any short form or (2) the already clear, if unused, form of the
LETTERS — as, the going on

   I think you are altogether going straight — even, maybe, a
simple rewrite of the novel (throwing yrself forward as the
declarant) wld save it, and use the whole old methodology, and
make the new there (already clear in She and Wilson, e.g.)

look, these are quick thots—and must cut off, to do my one
of two a week jobs (Mon and Thurs nites)   so let me pile this off,
and come back at it, as soon, as i can, eh?

just to keep the hand in, and
our love,

C

[Fontrousse, Aix-en-Provence]
October 1st [1951]/

Chas/

To get this in, with the other—letter just in from RWE, &
he sounds woefully confused, i.e., for one thing, as you probably
have word of there by now, he had sent proofs of The Praises &
copies of GG#1 to you there at Lerma, & weren't forwarded, etc.

I
know this all smacks of his usual wooden-headedness, but if he
has got this far, seems best to try to make it still? Well, god
knows yr patience must be somewhat thin, at this juncture.

Just to
figure it, the coolest, etc. He notes it will lose him abt $100 plus, if
the book doesn't now come out on his press, etc. Likewise, he had
given it the ad, notice, in that issue above, etc.

He says, can't
afford loss, etc. I don't know—really not yr headache, and he had
his chance, etc., and he's hardly helped very much, with any of
it.

What I am thinking—getting THE PRAISES out there, allows
you time & place for any further collection, and also, the issue of,
the prose, as it now seems to be building up. I.e., IF he cd get that
out, and you cd stand it (phew!), gives you that much more time

& space for the other things, and gets that biz off you — E/ being capable distributor, if nothing else, & likewise, capable bk/maker, or all I've seen were handsome enough.

Another development — that he tells me cd issue poems I'd sent him, as booklet, sometime '52. I know this tune, etc., but I don't give a shit, in this case, i.e., with me — no other chance, & the poems are not that close to me, etc. I.e., is prose I wd be caring more abt, & the issue of, the poems, simply gets them out of here, & makes room for other things. So, sd ok, to him. Can't lose, at that.

He does sound sad, but, as with all things, what cd be made, with them, the point. These sentiments after some yrs of delay, can't hit yr ear very kindly. Well, to figure it, anyhow, & to see what you think — why not ask him, point-blank (tho I know, too, that as yet never got an answer), how SOON — 'because you don't want to break him, etc., etc.' I.e., that way, & see what happens? Well, idea, etc.

Have just written him; "hope it can be settled, etc." That idea. And I do, certainly, at that. More presses cd be lined for yr things, or any of us, the greater. He does make bks/, etc., even if it takes t i m e —more than I had really thought possible, like they say.

Let me hear what you think; this just to note his, in, & likewise, how he sounded. And, likewise, this thing on the booklet of poems he now offers me.

[Fontrousse, Aix-en-Provence]
October 2, 1951

Dear Chas/
Had time for very little, yesterday, so want to get this off to you, with further figuring on RWE, etc. The thing — I feel

these several things, & hand them over, for whatever.

1) That he does have the type set, & likewise, engravings made, & also, paper & binding material; 2) that he has committed himself, clearly, to yr book by virtue of this GG#1 – the spread there, etc.; 3) that getting the book out with him, as sd yesterday, you have the room & time for other of yr things elsewhere.

To add to that –
only my feeling that he is if nothing else, a competent book-maker, i.e., all editions of his I have seen were free, pretty free, from any kind of gross mistake such as Laughlin, for one, turns out, I damn well think, with every other item. (Have you ever noticed what he's done, consistently, to the Doc, by way of the books – I have yet to see ONE readable book made out of *any* of sd man's things – viz. Grain, crammed type, & horrible binding; Paterson, those rough edges & no page numbers, etc.; Complete Poems, all spread it seems, i.e., they seem to knock round on the page – and all I ever liked at all, LIFE ALONG THE PASSAIC RIVER (tho type not finally it, I think) & the little pamphlet, BROKEN SPAN, tho type is, again, a little small, but very clean even so (I think it was Baskerville, & I think that's a firm type, etc.) Anyhow, divers items of E/s that I have seen : all clear of such blunders, – see what he did with Williams : THE PINK CHURCH – very clean & readable job of printing, very *helpful* to the text in question, as against a horrid item like Cummington's edition of, THE WEDGE.

Etc., etc., which only comes to, again, a possible use, Emerson's, above & beyond the run. And I do not forget the horror of this wait you've been put to; just that IF things CAN now move, I'd say: why not. I.e., another out, that sense of it, another angle, etc., and one damn well can *not* have too many, even if, after, you never want to hear his name again, etc.

Well, not to shift round; IF things are set to move, as this present letter so sadly suggests – cd it bungle things too badly, moving with him? Who knows, or one can hope: he'll feel some extra responsibility for decent handling, after what's gone before?

Myself, I don't finally give too much of a damn whether or not it takes 3 yrs, on this thing he now offers me, or any number. That is, I am in no hurry, haven't the *things* you have, haven't the pressure on me. All of which: let me take it much slower, whereas it would not be that case in any sense, if it were the prose one was talking about. That, I feel can't get off in the backwaters. But the poems: there are few enough, any hitch would mean, only, hauling them back, adding the few more decent ones in hand, and trying them elsewhere, etc. He says, 1952 — somewhere around spring, or, thereafter, shortly thereafter, but — I know, certainly, it might be a year from then that saw them out, finally. But to hell with it : nowhere else, & more than that, no very great thing at stake, as sd.

I wanted to give you the contents, i.e., for it, and please, tell me if you figure I leave holes, or if anything cd be switched, changed, or what have you. I know there's not very much to shake the world, etc. Just want a tight firm thing [*added*: wow!], if at all possible.

STILL LIFE OR	(relined, from 1st issue, etc.)
HART CRANE (1)	
LE FOU	(possible title?)
THE LETTER	(cd you give me word, on this, & others?)
LITTLETON, N.H.	
HELAS	
HART CRANE (2)	
THE EPIC EXPANDS	
GUIDO	
A SONG	
CANZONE	(little short one, "his violin is not love, etc")
LOVE	(not one Cid printed, i.e., last one)[153]
THE SEA	(sign-off item, or something? You say.)

In short, only a handful; only the few I continue to like at all.

Wednesday — 3rd

Dear Chas/
          Have gone thru the APOLLONIUS abt 3 times now,
& this last: I read it in a line from, Fenollosa, Gate & Center, then
it, i.e., went straight thru those 3, one sitting, etc., and found it
main line, for me at least.
          (The Kung is of a different cast,
shadow, or what can one call it; it is not quite 'human' in some
respects — well, human, certainly, but conservative in an almost
feminine sense; almost that kind of intelligence.
          Ann saying last
night, the way a stallion (as opposed to a mare, or gelding) is a
fine instance of the male's "gratuitousness" [*added*: (Need a better
word)], how there is that sense, or taking, of his energy.)

But to get back: it is a wonderfully *clear* job, this book; and it
has, what I now feel & take very strongly, a very insistent
affirmative — which I would link in with, the climax of LA
PREFACE, the last two lines & how they break out, are
unavoidable, & also, what I like so very much in THE K/s, that
part beginning, "I am no Roman . . . ," to the end. I mean it is of
that same sureness, & emphasis, no matter it is another instance,
etc. I.e., I don't want to make simple comparisons — they get us
just about nowhere.
          One thing I do very much love in it — the way
all (I think it is *all*) of yr concerns, yr centers, i.e., points of
touching, ride in here so very easily, and surely. I was reading
Rimbaud, or just looking thru it, yesterday, and had hit:

(And what L/ Varese, seems, to me, to really miss altogether:)

"La main à plume vaut la main à charrue. — Quel siècle à mains! —
Je n'aurai jamais ma main . . ."[154]
          (Which she has: "The hand that
guides the pen is worth the hand that guides the plough. — What
an age of hands! I shall never have my hand . . ."
          I.e., I read it,

with the *two* dashes, and take the final sentence as, a *third* perception, & a very damn valuable one, its way:

> "And how can I teach him
> his hands?"

But they know, anyhow, more french than I do, etc., etc. This same woman generalizes like this: Alchimie du Verbe : Alchemy of the Word! Horrible, horrible translation — not even literal equivalents 9 times out of 10, and *never* sounds, or rhythms, or any, any intensities. Fuck her; goddamn dilletante.)

$$\left(\begin{array}{l}\text{Qu'il vienne, qu'il vienne,}\\ \text{Le temps dont on s'éprenne . . .}\end{array}\right)$$

The movement, all thru: a thing of very great beauty — incredible *undulation*. Never seen it better, never more sure, than in this. All the passage of, MOVE OVER, or any of the poems; all that *going*.

("O may it come, the time of love
The time we'd be enamoured of . . ."

GODDAMN!!!)

"Before starting the revision of this translation — in suspense since 1938 — I was conscientious to the point of making myself a nuisance. I don't know how many people I importuned with my scrupulosity . . ."

A Form Letter:

"Dear Mrs. Varese:

The acquisition of Rimbaud, by yourself, does not constitute a legitimate acquisition; it is lazy, inaccurate, and persistently self-centered. It makes mistakes which are mistakes, only, of the intelligence — in this case, your own. It is not a matter, or question of, difficulty. It is a base question of, *depth.* That you have not seen this dimension; that your translation gives no sense of it.

Rimbaud is valuable, immensely valuable. He

cannot be presented by any such half-measures as these two
translations (A SEASON IN HELL; THE ILLUMINATIONS); it is
a disservice, to him and to his readers, that you have literally no
right to make possible. In this sense, we ask you to withdraw,
willingly [*crossed out*: and of your own free will], these two
translations from circulation; we ask you to take that first step
toward an actual recovery of, Rimbaud.

Yours sincerely,

(all signatures possible)"

i.e., to send it round, perhaps, & to see how many names, etc., cd
be got, & then send it on to her, DAMN her.

In fact, will enclose a clean copy, damnit; I think it's worth that
time. Ok.
(Let Perse stay where he is!)

This for the moment; i.e., hoping for one, from you, & will, pick
up, once I see. Ok.

12:00 noon, and nothing in from you, old friend — & leads me to
all kinds of damn conjecture, re what *possibly* might be up : to
wit, ARE YOU A FATHER, eh? For christ's sake, & likewise mine
: please don't leave us hanging! (I get jumpy, as sd, very early,
tho I damn well doubt if, on this occasion, I can better you.
Ok.)
    Anyhow, write when you can make it/ there is not a damn
thing to take the place of, any such letter. These few things, for
the moment : the droppings, not much more. (I try to keep my
roosts clean, sd he, etc.) Ok.

All best love to you both, & will be back, directly/
Bob

When you can, wd very much appreciate word on the several

poems; I don't feel at all easy committing them anywhere, until you have seen them and had time for comment; simply nothing can gauge any of it, as you can. SEA—too slight, easy? And what abt, THE LETTER (which rides me, but the general reader?) And how abt: A SONG—which, of them all, I feel is the strongest. Ok, & yr word : what I wait for.

[*Added at top of letter*:] No sign of Aldington to date. (?)

[*In margin*:] Don't buy any more baby-shirts, i.e., my sister (baby—this summer) should have some free now—outgrown, etc. Am writing her now to see, and will ask her to send them on—if she has them.

[Black Mountain, N.C.]

[*In ink at start of typescript (carbon copy)*:]
<u>Wed</u>: Oct 3 [1951]—Robt: Goddamn it. This started out to start just where it ends. And so it may seem nothing more than my usual generals. But I wrote it as a kind of letter for you, and will start it ahead, for whatever. . . . Love, O

THE LAW

The advantage (and it is altogether recent) is, that the answer to a question (which is ultimately the life question) which has increasingly borne in on recent man

(DHLawrence came around always to calling it "ancient science," no matter how many times he had it, "the old phallic wisdom")[155]

that is, how
did other men than the modern (or Western) ground the
apprehension of life (was there a different base, and if so, what
was it, as distinguishable from value & the disciplines of value as
we have known them)

It now strikes me that we have the privilege to make that
answer, and to be quite specific about it, as specific about it as
Greek philosophy, Christian ethics, and Arab-to-contemporary-
physics were about what was another way (our own) from, say,
500 BC to what? shall we take Henry Adams' 1921 AD,[156] or 1945
(that ACT),[157] it doesn't much matter so long as we get quite clear
that sometime quite recently a door went bang shut, and a "box"
of history can be seen as such, and put away — say, the BOX 500
BC-1950 AD

(that is — to stay on the best known ground — biochemistry is post-modern. And electronics, now, is
already a science of communication — the "human" is
already the "image" of the computing machine, and the
lesson (by the substitution of the binary for the decimal
in its operation) of its better workings[158]

all these effects,
of course, or movements apparently forwarded are
"blind," in the sense that they go without any recourse to
a series of sanctions, as did the previous or modern
philosophy, ethics, and science

an evidence of this, open to all, is the stupidities &
dangers of "Cybernetics," which, so far as the noticeable
absence in it of grounded human sanction goes, most
resembles that side of collectivism which we loosely call
fascism)

I delay to put the answer straight, simply because I want to
be wholly serious, and to engage any serious person — which means
that the simplicity and the arrogance of the answer must not be
allowed to be easy, or to ignore one overwhelming fact almost

always ignored by my fellows: that almost all "serious" men are
still grounded in the old laws of the "Box"

(in other words, that the best energies need still to be
disengaged from their conditioning, say, Pound—or
Heisenberg (to get away from the cliche that Einstein is). Or
the younger, who, unwilling to accept "blindness" as a proper
condition of search now, look to renewal of old sanctions—
stay inside the BOX—and spend their excellent energies on
the assumption that, somewhere, in Socrates, Christ, Galileo,
or Columbus, if they are reexamined, "truth" will out

((i am trying to cover both present conservatism as the
Neo-Christians, the Neo-Classicists, and the Neo-
Scientists express it, and the Neo-Revolutionists, the
hope or mass men express it, those, the latter,
who are unable to understand that the significance
of the "Frontier" or Boom world which the
disproportion of population to land & capital
wealth made possible before the end of the "new
land" is no longer significant, in fact, that the end of
"new land" (Turner's date of 1890 is still good
enough)[159] was as important a factor in the slamming
down of the door of the box as any other

(((so all
imaginable "worlds" now dreamed of—even solar
energy—are essentially science fiction or comic strip,
false "projection," as solidly as all collective "one
world" is)))

So, to be "high," take the intellect as the tool of knowledge.
Or literacy, as the apparent gain that print, then telephone-
telegraph, radio, television made possible

(for, surely, it is not enough noticed that
these "modern" gains are no more than
extensions of that which marked Greece 500
BC on, and of which Alexandria is the
type: the sudden displacement of the oral as
the distribution function in the "economics"

TEXT   of knowledge by TEXT, and so, there,
                        Alexandria, then Pergamus, then Baghdad;
                        the LIBRARY
                                    ((and as of art, both the
ONE LIBRARY   plastic & the performing arts, the one
                        usable principle in Malraux's recent history
                        of art is, that, the reproductive processes
                        which followed from printing has made — as
                        the cinema does, as of the performing
                        arts — an apparent equal gain by making
ONE MUSEUM   one museum out of all world art, for any
                        taker, and so a putative force on any artist
                        toward single world culture))[160]

It comes out this bald, though wait a minute, before you
mistake me: TEXT, as distributor, is FIRST DIVISIVE FACT, in
this sense, that, all knowledge started to become visual, that the
eye and the face of knowledge started to displace the ear and
memory. That is, *before,* a man's own *organism* was text &
library: the tablets, so far as any one but the "producers" was
concerned, were the brains of each of us, the minds. The
"consumers" were themselves — had to be — ACTIVE, in this whole
sense, that, anything that happened in front of them in art and
knowledge was not reproducible except as they retained it *inside*
themselves, and projected it directly from themselves as objects or
by objects to others
            (so hands, and voice, and the movements of the body
            were undivided from the process of retention)

    Come at it the usual way, that is, from the premise that
"books" ((& the increase of the "scribes" or copyists before printing
almost amount to — actually "promise" — type)) were the thing that,
from the Greeks on, made a great advance in human knowledge
and flexibility possible. For the "book" is, is it not, the first
MACHINE — in this area which is my concern, the "intellectual" or
"creative"?

    The founding act of Socrates, Aristotle, Plato (from whom, it is always my argument, the "West" followed), or the birth of Greek learning, was crucial, right here, that, since then — *with texts* — another sort of intellectual & creative life came into being[161]

((((I am wholly aware that "texts" existed previously, but it is not a mere accident of archeology that from Pesistratus on, we have texts — and lack them, in any bulk, earlier. All one needs to do to see the reason clearly is to stop, for a moment, and read Herodotus side by side with Thucydides. They lived approximately side by side. One wrote LOGOI, or STORY. The other wrote ESTORIA, or HISTORY.

Let me pose the difference this way: record as reenactment, and basically oral, in which not evidence but effect is the law. Versus record as fact, as, the bringing together of evidence, and so, no active "time" in the text, but past time analyzed and described: the "truth" rather than any motion or active happening at the moment of the experience of the recording desired.

((((Exemplum, now: the wife of the contemporary writer whom I, for one, join as of equal interest to Herodotus for me, in terms of the act of narrative now, said to him the other day when he was wrestling with his own advance on his own problems: "No *history* prior to the act of reading, in yr stories"))))[162]

It is my impression that intellectual life in the West has been and still to a great degree stays essentially *descriptive* and *analytical*. And that this characteristic of knowledge is also a characteristic of art, though it is not so easily seen, simply because the act of art, any time, any where, has to be, at base, active in the sense that it is expressive. But there is, at the other end of it, room to measure how projective it is, how *wholly* active, how

clearly it performs the task which distinguishes it *absolutely* from
the intellectual.

Why this statement will seem a half one and so an untruth is,
that the intellectual acts of the West have had energies and have
produced goods, in fact, have raised, before our eyes, the
civilization we (and the rest of the world) think so useful. But
right here the principal distinction must be made. Energy or goods
can be of two kinds: mechanical *or* organic. And I would ask all
men who still take the Greeks or Christ or the men of the 2nd
heave of the West — the "Renaissance," remember, the word was —
Galileo & Columbus (to take a quick two, to stand for it, though
Michelangelo & Dante could equally stand) as still of sanction, I'd
ask any of them (and I mean the best), can they, honestly,
disassociate the MACHINE, & its PRODUCTS, from those
sensations? from the disciplines of logic & classification, from
which HISTORY, in the 1st instance, METAPHYSICS almost
contemporary with the birth of "history" — Socrates & Thucydides
date exactly together (T 471-400, S 469-399) — and the division of
FORM from CONTENT (as much Christ's as Plato's, C's "Father's
House" indistinguishable from P's "World of Ideas") follow?

Flatly:
is not THE ENGINEER the HERO of the system we call the
WEST? is he not, in his constant & average ability to make a
material thing *without any necessary relevance* to any other
human purpose than the satisfaction of the appetite for goods the
legitimate & overwhelming SAINT of a system which, in its own
roots, and on every one of its planes, did divide matter from
"spirit" or whatever word you choose to use to denominate that
organic force which the human, because he is "alive," takes as a
distinguishing mark of reality?
Mechanism or materialism is more
honestly & properly the issue of the Greek & Christian &
Renaissance world than any of the "ideals" or issues in idealism
which that world has claimed to offer men, and for the simplest of
reasons, that, the moment that you exaggerate the function of
discourse in the plane of knowledge or the intellect — the moment

you remove memory from the human organism, or, make it
merely an agent of knowledge instead of an agent of re-
projection—you make energy mechanical by removing from its
direction & end the very participant which can demand that
content serve a purpose other than a material one

            The hunger of
man is to act, not to know, and he will act mechanically—
inevitably—if knowing or literacy is valued for one moment except
as he can discharge it in his own instrument of action, his own
body and mind, and by their single action, not by any separation
of that action and some machine—a dialogue or a bolt of goods
except as he can wear it as he wears his skin.

         II

  To start afresh—and to proceed immediately to an answer:
what ancient science was, which was also ancient religion, was
ART. And for the simplest but subtlest of reasons: that RHYTHM
was so assumed to be the LAW of life that only a discipline which
found rhythm as inextricable from function could be BASE
                    ((I
  think it was Novalis, in the 19th century of this era, who
  corrected 2000 years when he said, "He who controls rhythm
  controls the universe."[163]

  But to say that (words have become such spreaders) is no
where near enough, any more—or at least now the word is so
"ideal," so disconnected from act, that to understand its full force
as VIA now or then takes as complete a particularizing of it as
action, wherever rhythm has been LAW, involved.

  One thing I can say (and I stay stubbornly elementary because
I don't know that any one of us now begins to come to grips with
action as rhythm simply because we are all, to more or less
degree, cripples of the West, hindered from the exercise of life by
the divided & smothering air of the BOX) is, that the way to begin
is exactly with the mechanical—that any other course errs, as the

West has, by assuming that FORM is to be discovered anywhere
but in the CONTENT under hand.

The premise is this: that the
very *mechanics* of ourselves and of the universe which we now
know—which was, it seems to me, the great issue of the West,
and its great value—can be made to yield *methodologies* (without
recourse to anything but our own organism and its needs in daily
life over & beyond the mechanism of it) which in themselves can
restore organic action—which means rhythmic action—on all
planes of human life & work.

Of course I assume that art is
leader. And if I now start talking in terms of the act of art,
instead of the act of knowledge, I do not at all mean ART as we
have had it, existing as a tolerated lovely duckling in a world of
knowledge-without-respect-to-rhythm, as decorative or secondary
to ENERGY, that First Born of the sun, and so (the West has
thought) prime. The point is, energy is only prime to nature. And
nature is not man. Man is artist, or he does not live: his act (the
act which makes him rival of nature) is ART. This is his special
attribute, the distinguishing one: that he can make forms, using
nature's energy, which are as prime & essential as nature's
forms.

It can be put this way: that all acts are in a decreasing
scale from the act of art only because art depends upon rhythm
maximally. Its "forms" are only accomplishable to the degree that
they are completely rhythmical. This is not so of even such prime
"natural" human acts as sexual intercourse, for example:
reproduction is possible, nature is so intent upon her purposes,
even in ourselves, without complete rhythm. Yet right here we
close the ugly Western gap between, say, what Lawrence called the
phallic or priapic, and knowledge. For it is exactly the sexual act
where man takes up rhythm in its most elementary expression
from nature: just that difference from insemination that the
involuntary motion of the sexual (at its least or worst) involves, is
the "common" from which all of man's rhythmic acts proceed.

((((One of Pound's most magnificent discriminations is
his characterization of Greek art as an art which

proceeds towards coitus. For even here the Greeks
need to be examined anew: the very art which we
have taken as measure also shows declinations of an
order like their history and philosophy (though I
hope an understanding of paradox is still not so
completely a lost habit as to make it necessary for
me to emphasize that art will regress toward the
sexual by the same law that forces the intellectual to
appear to go toward the abstract—actually, of
course, it goes, just as such art goes, mechanical.

((((Allow me also, for the *value* involved, so far as the art of
writing goes, to note that if, in the same breath, I put Lawrence
& Pound together, and precisely on the point of the phallic &
art, it is decidedly a measure of why, now, it is these two polar
creatures who stand up, out of the half century just gone, as
the two principal creative men

                         —that half century which was
                         the marshalling yard on which
                         the modern was turned to what
                         we have, the post-modern, or
                         the post-West)))

Let me go away, for a little while, from art as painting,
sculpture, architecture, those graphic and plastic disciplines which
have—and this is interesting—actually, in the West, been the arts
which the word art is most often thought to cover.

Let me, instead, start from the other end, from what one
might call the performing arts—music, dance, and verse—what
have been called (again, in the West) the TIME arts, in too easy a
distinction from too apparent a space (what Pound is being a
"poet" about, and right in, as of Greek art, is an unvoiced
objection to the wholly divisive notion that weights, or dimensions
of space, "perspective" was the Renaissance's peculiar arrogation or
extension of the classic Greek static space concepts as plastic—
Michelangelo is, if not coital, damned ambitious sexually

(the whole Sistine job is a sort of huge homosexual parlor
house of writhing bodies — and only because it is a sort of
planetary company has it escaped notice as such, and been
taken to be ennobling or grand

(Rob't: you can see, i'm losing hold — so i'll cut up, and ship it as
is, just, for whatever — only, let me see if I can spill the rest of
the argument in an outline of where I want to go:

DANCE, as prime now, because the body (the mechanic *we* are
                    possessors of) is, in dance,
                    both the matière & the
                    instrument

THE VOICE, as prime, because, the human voice is the stem of
same

MUSIC, as of use, afresh, because, it, too, is SOUND, and is a
matter of only several instruments which are mere *extensions* of
the human voice
        so DRUM, as 1st instance (the BALA-G- DI of the
                    Sumerians — which made sounds like a cricket
                    does, and was like yr drum for dave & me only
                    pinched in the middle like an hour-glass — was
                    also the ALTAR for offerings to the Mother
                    Goddess (Ishtar) — and was accompanied by
                    (existed only as the instrument of) SONG and
                    MUSIC and DANCE
        it made DRUM SPEECH, which "summoned the gods,"
        "calmed & raised the city men," assuaged tears, and, in the art
        of its drumming, completed the "FULL MUSIC" of song &
        dance[164]

The idea, then, to objectify, by way of elementaries of
PROJECTIVE ART, and all close details of it, the importance of
RHYTHM to any act, including the act of knowledge:
                                        to put the

whole thing back on KINESIS, and ahead, from there

la-la!

O

[*Encircled, with note*: continuation, of yesterday]
     That is, to what extent is a WORK SONG not as valid in
knowledge as in those "lower" forms of labor? Or is it that the
result of such labor seems more "constructed" or "constructive"
than breaking rocks, or making a highway, piling coffee beans? It
is true, the issue of knowledge is, say, a paper or a study or a
book — or dialogues. And that it is that issue, I suppose the
argument would be, where rhythm is called for. Which, of course,
is exactly what is still true, even inside the Greek or Christian
system — "style" is still what an historian and a philosopher are also
asked for; and a "soul" purchases heaven if it is "perfect," or
purgatory if it needs some perfecting, or hell, if it is shapeless and
ugly, eh? In other words, even at this latter day, work of any sort
calls for a sort of recognition that the law of rhythm must
somewhere be obeyed, to more or less degree.

ROBT: Thurs Octo 4 [1951] — to hell with above. And so, went,
1st time, to see the mail come in. And there, yrs, of sun & mon,
and such a ride it gives me, for, tho F[enollosa] has surely been
TEXT, still, did not know what you wld see better, that, he does
mean so much to me. Interesting thing: in library here, recently,
found reference to *two* other books of this fellow! And will get
same, from U of NC, and let you know

             (As of EP, figure — fr my own nerves — that, F
was back there for him, got into him, and, rushing on, to recur,
for him must seem not likely. That is, it *is* a fact that even TEXTS
get (like ragweed, say, for me) associations in one's own past time
which can be drag — are grabbed, in the going, out of, like, say,
my Beaver Brook,[165] but, any sort of reconcentration (Melville, for
me, now likewise) is *backward*, and distasteful.

Figure, too, that,
by the law of arrogance, EP takes it HE did the F job, not even F!
And so, any fellow like me *after*, is a "follower."

But what you
point up is surely the *reason* I have, in this instance of F, not
bothered that, it was P who introduced him — have, constantly,
put F forward without that intervention *mattering*! And not easy,
I'll tell you.

Actually, maybe I figure on EP as you on WCW, that
is, that he's *right*! The only nice words I ever got out of him (not
on ISH, that was, easy, but, on PREFACE, and GRANGER) made
me gone.

This whole question is intricate. It burns my ass, that,
so often, these idiots cry, "Pound," everytime they think they have
a critique of my own work. Yet, fuck em. I'll not be driven off a
value because of such — or, for that matter, because of EP
hisself.

My sense is, that right here is *tradition*, that, the work we
value, especially when the man is alive behind us, is to be gone
by — and I am not so concerned about being *interested* in EP any
more than Lawrence or Bill. But what burns me is, that, the
superficial resemblances (if there are such: myself, THE
KINGFISHERS, which, time & again I have heard, "Pound," feels
so completely *mine* that, by it as gauge, I must take it all such
people are idiots, total & depraved) are used to beat me with.
Fuck em.

On EMERSON: all I know I learn from you! Crazy, the way I
must pinch his arse: I wrote him quiet (not having heard since
March), and on receipt of his news that he had sent proofs (he did
not tell me it was to Lerma, probably damn well knowing I had
written him, carefully, before departure, saying, nothing, after
such & such date). Well, anyway, this past Sunday, I wrote giving
him a chance to save his $100 (also, he did not mention but, I
figured, so — and of course wld save him that). The move now
again is his, the fool. Glad as hell he makes it *YR* VERSE!

As of the GASP: no word, and i forgot to tell you i wrote him a

long straight answer to his three communications (1) accepting his
offer of a selected o (to be changed, to verse, perhaps, now, eh?);
(2) examining his enclosures (Horton & P), that letter to the editor
politics, stating clearly my position on such; and (3), really tying
one on him for the letter to *Miss* E M M (which she has just
written she has received — & the gd idiot has finished me off, on
that street! & she shows herself the less in it all, the piousness wld
almost equal, for you, the grossness of sd Gasp

    i figure he'll not be so warm, now. Anyhow, it is a 49-51
biz at best. it is certainly EP's HOUSE — and abt all i wish
might have stayed undisturbed was the chance to see what
in hell this play is all abt!

        can't figure it, any more than
you do, how come they are ready to run me in there, as,
2nd horse in the race for the Square Dollar Purse, with the
Big Red![166]

    Damn well wish that might have happened!

        Fact
is, my flying bat sense wld tell me that, the "economic" biz is sadly
out of biz now, that Ex [sic] himself must have caught on (now
that every idiot, including Laughlin, is giving the doctrine such a
silly play

    Better be more accurate. What I mean is, that, the
"politics" as was, then, the 30's (as of play to the Commies & all
Neo-Revolutionists) was *good*, to be on, MONEY. And that MON
is still of more moment than anyone but Ex [sic] and the bankers
know. What has changed, is, that, it is any longer of *use* to do the
politicks as Ez then did it.

    My PLAY, to GASP, would be, to
suggest a book to him! And that book to be EP's CHINESE
POEMS, entire! For one more such, JUST THAT ONE (which is
sure to be a beaut), ought to throw the weight of that HOUSE just
where it could be of real use, a real □ $ offer

    I'd bet that, that name of the house, will look sillier
& sillier *if* I cld get in there — and cld get to publish
EP's PIDGIN

Will try it, as, PLAY, ok?

What else is on our slate? Nothing new here on publishing: dead time. Blumenthal comes, a week fr Sat, and that may push it. But it needs some one like Hatt, or Shahn, whose interests are that strong. Mine, are rather to write & direct some such operation. And right now, with Harrison here to work with — to find something out abt musick — or words & same, that's plenty

Am dreaming, these days, of a way to cross yr path and make a thing a reality also: SUMERIA. Next fall. And a book, by god, called SUMER: a thing, of an order, based on verse (and maybe all that) but, maybe also, travel & the actionable, in such a culture, eh? Wld be a possible book without getting there, anyway. Like the idea. A real hook. And that verse!

(Not a word out of those dried fish, the Wennergrens — sounds like a drug store anyway, and probably deals solely in fishskins, passed over, the, counter, eh?

But your saying these things abt F & self put me back on what was that go yesterday: threw it forward to you without even looking it over, and then saw what a wild mess it is. Am resistant to pick it up again today (as you will have noted).

Thot to call it THE DRUM OR THE LAW: am still pushed by the corroboration (again, those sumerians) that the drum, for them (and I learn for all Asiatics!), was the prime & proper accompaniment for song (not the lyre, so much, or so basically, or the harp — I don't know that the flute ever was anywhere, it is so limited, however fine (or at least never except as O.E. pipe & tabor which were known as whittle & dub! our fife & drum: how this, still (from my old man, his interest) that pix, '76,[167] stirs me: goddamn beautiful, whatever, the shit put on it — even the look, the blood, the bandages, the tears — and that BEAT & FIFE! WOW

STICKS & DRUMS. Of course all it means to me is IMAGES of the instrument I am most interested in, the human VOICE (fascinating thing, Harrison tells me, that, there is some evidence that the speaking voice, in different periods, comes to behave like the dominant instruments of the time: now, then, the sax, trumpet, and such as Durante & Armstrong,[168] the washboard.

Yet I am tenacious, to keep it, from the trap of intonating: the idea, for me, is only to see what, if anything, there is in complicating or intricating by the recognition (or the prior experience of) such other planes of words such as *pitch*, individual timbres, the difference (as of timbre) from male to female voice
> e.g., dance: there is a failure to observe that *movement* has also a conversational plane. And the failure to observe this difference leads to all this present wastage of argument in professional dance. Or, for that matter, several stupidities on the Greek (& so modern, imitative) use of chorus

This is close to verse problems just here, on the ode: the strophe & antistrophe of such seem (so far as I can figure out the etymology) to come from the shift involved as the moving group "turned" at the limits of the "orchestra." In other words, that the union of verse & dance in the Greek was the more possible that both were "conversational." Which seems to me to cut through (even on such a formal thing as ode form) to an origin point quite akin to problems now:
> that is, a woman like Litz has come a good deal of a way from "theatre" dance, in fact contains her movements in a small "gesture" compass, in double fact gains her power by forcing the energy of gesture to stay inside the human compass (i have yet, i think, to see her leave the floor — which, of course, at a certain point bores the bejeezus out of me)

yet, just such, just such a valid development of dance (alongside music & verse) towards more "natural" behavior of the medium, tends — at least in her case, and it is a special one, perhaps, because she is a curious old maid of a temperament, & thus strong but not enough open, eh? — to make for an even greater self-consciousness of "high" art, due, I would take it, to the narrow professional debate of the "modern" vs the ballet, possibly

        in any case, the "folk" dance (and there are some signs that this business, even to the popularizing of the "square" forms, polka as well, are pushing toward a more formal use, a more "professional" or "theatre" use: at least that lad Moore, who is living in our Washington diggings, has ideas which still keep my attention on him: has a SAM ADAMS in the works, all turning on the maypole biz, & early Boston city forms; and makes a JOHN BROWN, with hillbilly stuff

    This gets to sound exterior, and let me give it over, that way: all i am trying to get at is something which is a part, I guess, of my own methodology. I am not trying to write for theatre. I use these investigations out there, and then, go on writing according to my own lights. The thing is, I figure, that way, is how one flexes.

        It is just this: it is the point where *breath* meets dance, and where *pitch* meets music, the meeting point only, which I am curious about just now

                    And it comes to two curious poles: that it is to what degree an "ugh" can be extended & still keep a relevance in dance—without the visual attention overriding the aural, or vice versa; and music, is, because the body is not there (except in voice as "opera" as we know it), but because music is such "high" sound, music is the other end: it takes the subtlest handling of words to manage to be relevant to it. And there is the opposite wish (for me, anyway) there, to remind music of its percussive force (gratuitous, after hearing Boulez 2nd Sonata—what a piece; try to run into this guy, somehow, there, Paris. Or ask him down to visit you: will try to get his address. Jesus: he's our boy. surely.

It is the *texture* of words which—a guess—are the base of relevance to *timbre* of voice or of any other of the instruments. And *pitch*? This puzzles me, so far as words go: the graphic languages clearly depend upon pitch for the differences of meaning of the same sign which, in the phonetic languages, because grammar seems to be necessary to them, is solved by context. Or I learn from Harrison that Chinese has 9 tone-colors as well as 4 pitch levels! *Razas*, these tone-colors are called in India, where there are 7 (or is Chinese which has 7 and Indian 9?) Here, again, I am puzzled to see in what sense American has — I am thinking of verse now — either usage of pitch or usage of tone-color (at least by any more than accidental or talent sense)

which gets to the bottom of the problem: *to what degree* does the habit of vocal speech influence the act of the writing of verse?

I am not used to thinking of verse on its several planes, and god knows i wld hold to that doctrine that, what matters — what you have there — that, only the most absolute sincerity under heaven can effect any change. yet this matter of the strict music of it is of some certain importance, & concern to me; and i figure to learn something of it

only it ain't just TIME (in fact, what invalidates — I have recently found — a good deal of EP's poetics, is, just this carelessness abt the relation of verse to music, that, it is all TIME

what else it is I imagine i am more able to say than to what degree it is TIME. and so, i am bothering these questions.

THAT IS: i got off my desire, to write you, abt time, on to the present kick, and you must excuse me: the sort of time you talk about it is more interesting to me, and where i have, perhaps, a little knowledge more than i do on this more conventional   • question. And I am purposely being stodgy, in order, to try to find out something — something i am not sure I am sure about!

It comes to this: I should like, for a little while, to see what words i might put with (a) dance and (b) with music, to see what it teaches about words anyhow

And what I am most up against at this moment is, in what sense, if at all, is the present human voice an instrument? and how can it be used as an instrument except as it has been, for intoning? which i abhor!

Well, just to say howdedo, to thank you for writing, and

to send you all love:

                 Con begins to be damned uncomfortable! &

sleeps

Notes

[References to pages and notes in this and previous volumes begin with Roman numerals designating the volume number, e.g., I. 110, II. 53, etc.]

[1] Not a typographical error, but Olson's suggestion of a mock-accent. An early draft of the poem made from this letter, "A Round, A Cannon, and an Evening" (revised as "A Round & A Canon"), begins: " 'I am too focking onnocent / to be guy,' he roared. . . ."

[2] I.e., after Athenaeus's *Diepnosophists, or Banquet of the Learned,* or Plato's *Symposium.*

[3] See Olson's 19 July 1951 letter (VI. 164) and note VI. 174; also Olson's 3 October 1951 letter below (VII. 240–41), and "Tutorial: the Greeks," *OLSON,* no. 2 (Fall 1974), p. 45.

[4] Literally, from the Greek, "black earth." Also — although with no apparent relation — the name of a character in Gertrude Stein's *Three Lives* (1909); uncommon otherwise.

[5] This passage contains the rudiments of "A Round & A Canon." See Olson's 30 July 1951 letter (VII. 19) and note VII. 8.

[6] Mitchell Goodman (see Creeley's 8 July 1951 letter — VI. 114-15).

[7] Several different typescripts of the poem (unpublished) survive among Olson's papers. The title echoes the opening of Eliot's "Animula" (see VI. 165 and note VI. 177).

[8] Finally titled "A Round & A Canon" (*Archaeologist of Morning,* pp. [72]-[73]).

[9] The American poet W. S. Merwin (b. 1927); for Lawrence Richardson, see V. 24 and note V. 16.

[10] Henry Purcell (1658-1695), the English composer, most notably of the opera *Dido and Aeneas* (1689).

[11] The complete revised draft of "Human Universe" apparently does not survive, but the story of Cormac referred to (it was not included in the final version) was found by Olson in an essay by Los Angeles

lawyer Norman Macbeth, "Law and the Change of Consciousness,"
published in *Proteus Quarterly*, 2, no. 2 (Spring 1951), p. 3n. (sent to
Olson presumably by Mary Shore of Gloucester, who had an essay
in the issue). The story is offered as an example of early man's sense
of law: "There was a lawsuit by one neighbor against another for the
trespass of some sheep who had eaten all the woad-herb in his field.
The people were assembled; and the judge was saying that the owner
of the sheep should forfeit them to his neighbor, in payment for the
herb consumed; when a youth (this was Cormac) started up from the
back of the hall, and shouted: 'Not so! For the herb is only the fleece
of the earth. Therefore let not the whole sheep be forfeited, but only
the sheep's wool be sheared, to pay for the herb; for herb and wool
will both grow again.' And the justice of this was so clear that the people shouted with one voice: 'A wise young judge; he should be king.'
So they made Cormac a judge, and afterwards king."

In a letter to Macbeth after reading the article, 14 July 1951 (a typed
draft or excerpt among Olson's papers), the poet writes: "My own feeling is, that law, in the sense in which Macbeth here uses it, has to be
recognized to be the issue of obedience on all fronts by such men as
a Cormac to those other laws which lie under 'law' . . . On the face
of it Cormac's shout is common sense, but it is such only in the uncommon sense that the observations which precede the shout is [*i.e.*
are] a clear & present noticing of how nature behaves. This sort of clarity is the issue of particularism (as against, which has been the base of
'law,' deductive & inductive methodologies of universals). Cormac, or
any of us, are the issue of a methodology of particularism."

[12] Jonathan, or Brother Jonathan, once a traditional nickname for a
typical American (like "Yankee"). See Olson's unpublished essay,
"History," from 15 February 1952: ". . . that special American
phenomenon, PROMOTION. For selling, in these States, sometime – I
remember Jonathan, in doeskin, the Yankee tinpeddler . . ."

[13] Walter Reuther (1907-1970), president of the United Automobile
Workers.

[14] The fifth-century B.C. Greek philosopher Empedocles leaped into
the crater of fiery Aetna "wishing to establish a belief that he had become
a God," but accidentally left one of his brazen sandals behind (Diogenes

Laertius, VIII. 69; Yonge trans., London, 1891, p. 365); subject of a tragedy, "Der Tod des Empedokles" (in which a disciple finds his iron shoes which have been cast up by the fiery volcano), by Friedrich Hölderlin, one of the West's traditionally "mad" poets, like Christopher Smart. Thus, the assertion shortly following that "any of H[ölderlin] is Smartisms" (and see Olson's 24 June 1950 letter, II.12).

[15] I.e., Olson himself; cf. his poem "These Days" (*Archaeologist of Morning*, p. [13]), which begins, "whatever you have to say, leave / the roots on, let them / dangle . . ."

[16] See also Olson's "Notes on Language and Theater," *Human Universe*, p. 73: "Before Aeschylus and before he added these means ["words as gab and masks to magnify sensation"], before the theater of boards collapsed during the performance of *The Persians* from the fright he produced, ladies screaming and giving birth right there in the taxicab and the city fathers announcing that henceforth it shall be obscene . . ." The poet's source is *Theatre of the Greeks* (see his 30 September 1951 letter, VII. 210), p. 111 (marked in his copy): "The common story respecting the Eumenides [a milder name for the avenging furies, the Erinyes] is, that the appearance of the fifty Furies on the Stage, wearing masks of a hideous paleness, their hands brandishing lighted torches, and their hair braided with serpents, caused such extreme terror among the spectators, that women were seized with the pains of premature labour, and that children died from fear; and that the magistrates, to prevent such fatal occurrences in future, ordained . . . that the Chorus should hereafter be limited to fifteen."

[17] An early version of part 2 of "A Round & A Canon."

[18] Creeley's story, "Mr Blue," as it appears in *Origin*, no. 2 (Summer 1951), pp. 111-17.

[19] Corman's letter does not survive, but see Olson's July 31st to him, in Glover, "Letters for Origin," pp. 107-09.

[20] A long-handled lever used for moving heavy objects. See also Olson's letter to Corman, 21 October 1950 (*Letters for Origin*, p. 6).

[21] See William Carlos Williams, *In the American Grain* (New York, 1925), p. 226 (marked in Olson's copy):

Americans have never recognized themselves. How can they? It is impossible until someone invent the ORIGINAL terms. As long as we are content to be called by somebody's else [sic] terms, we are incapable of being anything but our own dupes.

Thus Poe must suffer by his originality. Invent that which is new, even if it be made of pine from your own yard, and there's none to know what you have done. It is because there's no *name*. This is the cause of Poe's lack of recognition. He was American. He was the astounding, inconceivable growth of his locality. . . .

22 Olson's poem, "Composed of Distinct Parts of Discontinuous Elements" (see VI. 157 and note VI. 90).

23 Lines from Olson's poems "The Kingfishers" (*Archaeologist of Morning*, p. [49]), "La Torre" (p. [77]), "Other Than" (p. [57]), "La Préface" (p. [43]), an approximate quotation from "There Was a Youth Whose Name Was Thomas Granger" (pp. [54]-[55]), and "Move Over" (p. [71]).

24 From Olson's "A Round & A Canon" (*Archaeologist of Morning*, p. [73]).

25 Harry Smith, whose story "A Local Celebration" would appear in *Origin*, no. 3 (Fall 1951).

26 From "Concerning Exaggeration, or How, Properly, to Heap Up" (*Archaeologist of Morning*, p. [104]).

27 Latin, "he himself said it."

28 William Carlos Williams, in *Paterson (Book Four)* (Norfolk, Conn., 1951), n.p. (complete *Paterson*, New York, 1963, p. 187).

29 Thomas Brackley, "A Squirrel," *Poetry New York*, no. 3 (1950), pp. 11-12, a poem in short lines seeking to be faithful to the movement of speech and the squirrel it describes.

30 In *The Collected Poems of Robert Creeley* (Berkeley and Los Angeles, 1982), p. 112.

31 See Laurence Sterne, *The Life and Opinions of Tristram Shandy*, chap. 19.

32 Paul Goodman, "Advance-Guard Writing, 1900-1950," *Kenyon*

Review, 13 (Summer 1951), pp. 357-80. Goethe is quoted on p. 376: " 'Occasional Poetry,' said Goethe, 'is the highest kind.' "

[33] See I. 79 and note 83, and VI. 187 and note 194, for Creeley's original formulations.

[34] "William Carlos Williams: On the Road to Paterson," *Poetry New York*, no. 4 (1951), pp. 18-32; included, with minor revisions, in Martz's *The Poem of the Mind* (New York, 1966), pp. 125-46. Rolf Fjelde, editor of *Poetry New York*, had written Olson in Mexico, 26 June 1951, "BE SURE to read the article in PNY #4 (sent Randolph Place) on WCW's road to Paterson."

[35] Wallace Stevens's warning in a letter to Williams that "to fidget with points of view leads always to new beginnings and incessant new beginnings lead to sterility"; quoted in Williams's "Prologue" to *Kora in Hell: Improvisations* (1920) and by Martz in his essay, p. 20. Martz also quotes (p. 19) R. P. Blackmur as saying that Williams's poems are "lacking in culmination."

[36] Williams's phrase, a presence in *Paterson*, female and sexual; the embodiment of value, a kind of élan vital; woven in and out of Book III as an ideal ("Beautiful thing") and a personification ("Beautiful Thing"). Also in "Paterson: Episode 17" in *Complete Collected Poems* (pp. 276-280). Mentioned by Martz, p. 26.

[37] French writer (1881-1957), acquaintance of Williams in Paris. Williams has a conversation concerning America with him as a representative European intellectual, in the Père Sebastian Rasles chapter of *In the American Grain*. See also III. 128.

[38] In a discussion of the echo of Eliot's "East Coker" at the very beginning of *Paterson*, Martz suggests (p. 31) "that the four books of *Paterson* may be considered a deliberate counterpart of Eliot's *Quartets*: the eternal Pelagian's answer to the doctrine of original sin." It should be noted that Martz says Pelagian — after the doctrine propounded by the fifth-century monk Pelagius, which denied original sin and affirmed man's free will, regarded as heretical by the Church. Olson initially confuses the Pelagians, followers of Pelagius, with the Pelasgians, the pre-Greeks and thus founders of the West (see also *Call Me Ishmael*, p. 13). According to Pausanias (VIII. 1), Arcadia was first called Pelasgia;

thus Olson's references to Pausanias throughout the letter.

It might be noted that Williams was first termed a "Pelagian" by Randall Jarrell in his introduction to Williams's *Selected Poems* in 1949.

[39] The concept of the eternal conflict between the Apollonian or critical-rational spirit and the Dionysian or creative-imaginative power, first set forth in Nietzsche's *The Birth of Tragedy* (1872).

[40] American literary critic (b. 1917), best known for his later work, *The American Adam* (1955). His essay "Melville on Homer," *American Literature*, 22 (May 1950), 166-77, had been called to Olson's attention in a postcard from Melville scholar Merton Sealts, 29 June 1950; but see specifically his "Casella as Critic: A Note on R. P. Blackmur," *Kenyon Review*, 13 (Summer 1951), 458-74, in the same issue as Paul Goodman's article, "Advance-Guard Writing" (see note VII. 32).

[41] Italian seaport, seat of the Malatesta family powerful in the fifteenth century. Sigismondo Malatesta, patron of the arts, is a hero of Pound's *Cantos*. In the caption to the frontispiece of his *Guide to Kulchur*, Pound cites the "thoroughness of Rimini's civilization in 1460."

[42] "Wallace Stevens: The Romance of the Precise," *Yale Poetry Review*, no. 5 (1946), 13-20; mentioned in the *Poetry New York* contributors' notes.

[43] See Olson's 25 May 1950 letter (I. 46) and note I. 40; also V. 100. The "piece on him [Pound], about his conversation," is probably "Grand-Pa GoodBye" (*Charles Olson & Ezra Pound*, pp. 97-105), although the quotation concerning "original sin" is not included there.

[44] *Call Me Ishmael*, p. 15: "We are the last 'first' people. We forget that. We act big, misuse our land, ourselves. We lose our own primary."

[45] Tyrant of Athens (ca. 605-527 B.C.) who commissioned a definitive text of the *Iliad* and the *Odyssey*.

[46] See Rhys Carpenter, *Folk Tale, Fiction, and Saga in the Homeric Epics*, chapters VI, "The Cult of the Sleeping Bear," and VII, "The Folk Tale of the Bear's Son." Odysseus's father was the Bearson, Arkeisios, son of Kephalos and a she-bear. See also "To Gerhardt, There, Among Europe's Things" (*Archaeologist of Morning*, p. [86]).

⁴⁷ See Book VIII, chapters ii-iv, of Pausanias's *Description of Greece*. Olson used Arthur Richard Shilleto's translation (London, 1886) at this time, which he had acquired in the fall of 1949. In a marginal note on p. 63 of that edition, Olson writes: "Was *Pelasgus* a Quetzalcoatl figure of herbivorous times?"

⁴⁸ See *Odyssey*, XI. 121-31. The image is also used in "To Gerhardt, There" (*Archaeologist of Morning*, p. [87]).

⁴⁹ The three heroes are: Pelasgus, after whom Arcadia was first called Pelasgia; his son Lycaon; and Lycaon's second son Arcas, after whom Arcadia was named. See also note 53 below for "precisely our meat."

⁵⁰ The Trobriand Islanders of Melanesia, subject of Bronislaw Malinowski's studies such as *Myth in Primitive Psychology* (London, 1926) and source of Malinowski's understanding of myth quoted in Jung and Kerenyi (see III. 135-36 and note III. 78).

⁵¹ Vivienne Koch, author of *William Carlos Williams* (Norfolk, Conn., 1950), cited by Martz, pp. 18-19.

⁵² Probably, "Much conversation is as good as having a home. . . . To say many things is equal to having a home" — Pound's "Homage to Sextus Propertius," *Personae*, pp. 214-15.

⁵³ See, more probably, chapter ii of Book VIII of the *Description of Greece*, where Pausanias reports, "Lycaon brought a baby to the altar of Lycaean Zeus, and sacrificed it upon it, and sprinkled its blood on the altar. And they say directly after this sacrifice he became a wolf instead of a man." Further, "whenever he was a wolf if he abstained from meat ten months he became a man again, but if he tasted meat he remained a beast" (Shilleto trans., II, 62-63). The passage is marked in Olson's copy, with the following note added in the margin (with a line connecting it to Olson's note quoted in note 47 above): "*Lycaon* (his [Pelasgus's] son) a later hero-leader who taught men to eat meat? (and does he not inform my idea that man's first meat was man?)." At the entry for Lycaon in the *Encyclopaedia Britannica*, 11th ed., XVII, 151, Olson adds in the margin of his copy: "It was cannibalism brought on the flood! (which verifies Ishmael)."

⁵⁴ Olson seems to be confusing the Japanese literary magazine, edited

by Isaku Hirai (see note IV. 3), with the Chinese poet Rihaku (Li Po), whom Pound translated in *Cathay* (1915).

Pound's "Yittischer Charleston" appeared in *An "Objectivists" Anthology*, ed. Louis Zukofsky ([Le Beausset, France], 1932), pp. 44-45. But see also *Charles Olson & Ezra Pound*, p. 66: "Pound had also performed for [psychiatrist Jerome] K[avka] what he calls his YIDDISH CHARLESTON, composed originally for Louis Zukofsky. K says it is something! and regrets he didn't get a recording. A dance which Pound does, with gesture, movement, words." And see Pound's 24-25 letter to Zukofsky, in *Montemora*, no. 8 (1981), pp. 173-74.

55 See note I. 94 for "ant's a centaur." For "equity, with the hills," cf. "Issue, Mood" (*Archaeologist of Morning*, p. [31]) and Canto 83, where Pound writes: "the sage / delighteth in water / the humane man has amity with the hills" (*Pisan Cantos*, p. 107). "Equity" also occurs in Cantos 74, 79, and 83, and see Pound's translation of Confucius, *The Unwobbling Pivot* (Norfolk, Conn., 1947), pp. 52 and 53.

56 The sculptor Constantin Brancusi (1876-1957) and the painter Francis Picabia (1879-1953), both favorites of Pound. See, e.g., *Guide to Kulchur*, pp. 59, 87-88, and 105; also "Brancusi," *Little Review*, 8 (Autumn 1921), 3-7 (collected in *Literary Essays*, ed. T. S. Eliot, Norfolk, Conn., 1954, pp. 441-45).

57 See especially Sauer's "Environment and Culture during the Last Deglaciation" (1948).

58 André Malraux, *The Psychology of Art*, vol. I of his *Museum Without Walls*, trans. Stuart Gilbert (New York, 1949), pp. 16 ff. See also "The Law" (with Olson's October 3 letter, VII. 236).

59 Pound writes at the end of the letter that serves as preface to his *Jefferson and/or Mussolini* (New York, 1936), p. xi: "Journalism as I see it is history of to-day, and literature is journalism that *stays* news." He quotes himself in *ABC of Reading*, p. 29: " 'Literature is news that STAYS news.' "

60 Lawrence's proposed utopia, Rananim, which at one point he hoped could be established at Fort Myers, Florida. See Aldington, *D. H. Lawrence*, pp. 203-04 and 187-88; also Huxley, *The Letters of D. H. Lawrence*, p. xxix.

⁶¹ See note III. 76. Quoted also in "Human Universe" and "Introduction to Robert Creeley" (*Human Universe*, pp. 3 and 127 respectively), as well as "D H Lawrence, & the High Temptation of the Mind" written in 1950.

⁶² Melville wrote actually to Evert A. Duyckinck, 13 December 1850, from Pittsfield: "Can you send me about fifty fast-writing youths, with an easy style & not averse to polishing their labors? If you can, I wish you would, because since I have been here I have planned about that number of future works & cant find enough time to think about them separately." Quoted in Jay Leyda, *The Melville Log: A Documentary Life of Herman Melville 1819-1891* (New York, 1951), I, 401 — marked in Olson's copy. Melville did, however, write to Hawthorne in a similar vein, 17 November 1851: ". . . I'll tell you what I should do. I should have a paper-mill established at one end of the house, and so have an endless riband of foolscap rolling in upon my desk; and upon that endless riband I should write a thousand — a million-billion thoughts, under the form of a letter to you" (quoted in Eleanor Melville Metcalf, *Herman Melville: Cycle and Epicycle*, Cambridge, Mass., 1953, pp. 129-30 — which Olson had seen in manuscript).

⁶³ Pound writes in *Guide to Kulchur*, p. 217: "THE CULTURE OF AN AGE is what you can pick up and/or get in touch with, by talk with the most intelligent men of the period . . ." He also writes in Canto 11 (*A Draft of XXX Cantos*, p. 55):

> And they want to know what we talked about?
> '. . . Both of ancient times and our own; books, arms,
> And of men of unusual genius,
> Both of ancient times and our own, in short the usual subjects
> Of conversation between intelligent men.'

See also "GrandPa GoodBye," *Charles Olson & Ezra Pound*, p. 98. "His conversations, as so much of the Cantos, is recall, stories of Picabia, Yeats (Willie), Fordie [Ford Madox Ford], Frobenius, [Gerhart] Hauptmann, of intelligent men, and it is as good as you can get." Again, "The Materials and Weights of Herman Melville" (*Human Universe*, p. 112): "Ezra Pound . . . that 'the light in the conversations of — the letters of — the intelligent ones' . . ."

⁶⁴ Corman's letter apparently does not survive. However, Williams's

letter to Corman (2 August 1951), from which Corman has quoted to Olson, is preserved at the Humanities Research Center, University of Texas, and includes the following part of Williams's reaction to *Origin* 2:

> Creeley is on dangerous ground. He's very unformed. This makes him susceptible to influences. I'm curious to know what France will do to him. He can't ignore it. Will he fight it? I wonder. I'll bet he ends up by taking in England — and then what will happen? But if he comes back here unchanged, what good will it have done him to go abroad? I like him, I like him very much, he has an honest, enquiring mind; he puts down what he sees and seems listening internally to his own thinking. I'm interested to see what comes out of it. I wish him luck. It depends on his intelligence, what that finally comes to find. I wonder. He may turn out to be an important man.
>
> The intelligence is the crux of the matter in Olson's case also. What will he find? He's searching and he's making notes? He's got some good thoughts too, valuable thoughts[,] some of which I have already used but I'd like to see them a little more pulled together in firmer terms. I acknowledge that we're all searching, it's our present status in America. But we're the ones who've been destined to FIND.

[65] From *Webster's Collegiate Dictionary*, 5th ed., p. 288.

[66] Sydney Salt, *Christopher Columbus and Other Poems*, with an introduction by William Carlos Williams (Boston, 1937).

[67] *All Men Are Brothers (Shui Hu Chuan)*, trans. Pearl S. Buck, 2 vols. (New York, 1933). See also "Obit," *OLSON*, no. 2 (Fall 1974), p. 59, and "On Black Mountain," *Muthologos*, II, 78 and note on pp. 186-87 there.

[68] Emma Goldman (1869-1940) together with Alexander Berkman (1870-1936) published the anarchist magazine *Mother Earth*. The German revolutionaries Karl Liebknecht (1871-1919) and Rosa Luxembourg (1870-1919) were arrested after the Spartacist insurrection of January 1919 and murdered while being taken to prison.

[69] Dostoevsky habitually worked at such a pace, publishing his novels serially in the literary journals. Chapters of *Crime and Punishment*, e.g., began appearing in the monthly *Russki vestnik* (*Russian Herald*) in January 1866, and Dostoevsky raced throughout the year to furnish copy for each successive issue; *The Possessed*, *A Raw Youth*, and *The*

Brothers Karamazov likewise. See, e.g., Avrahm Yarmolinsky, *Dostoevsky: His Life and Art* (New York, 1934) – a volume that Olson owned.

[70] *Essence: Monatsschrift für originalgraphik und dichtung,* published in Zurich from 1950 to 1951.

[71] Creeley's story "The Unsuccessful Husband"; see I. 48-49 and note I. 43, and II. 155 and note II. 125. For "A Sort of a Song," see V. 128-33.

[72] From William Carlos Williams's "Perpetuum Mobile: The City" (*Complete Collected Poems,* p. 243; *Selected Poems,* p. 89).

[73] From Hart Crane's "The Bees of Paradise," "The Mermen," "The Bees of Paradise" again, and "Island Quarry," pp. 128, 118, 129, and 117, respectively, in his *Collected Poems,* ed. Waldo Frank.

[74] *In the American Grain,* p. 220, in the chapter on Edgar Allan Poe.

[75] Paul Klee, *On Modern Art,* p. 45: "He is perhaps unintentionally, a philosopher, and if he does not, with the optimists, hold this world to be the best of all possible worlds, nor to be so bad that it is unfit to serve as a model, yet he says: 'In its present shape it is not the only possible world.' Thus he surveys with penetrating eye the finished forms which nature places before him." Quoted in Creeley's 15 November 1950 letter to Corman, *Origin,* no. 2 (Summer 1951), p. 74.

[76] From Eliot's "The Hollow Men": "Eyes I dare not meet in dreams / In death's dream kingdom" (*Collected Poems 1909-1935,* New York, 1936, p. 101).

[77] From Crane's "A Name for All" (*Collected Poems,* p. 120).

[78] Ezra Pound, quoting A. E. Housman, in "Mr Housman at Little Bethel," *Polite Essays,* p. 24.

[79] Creeley may be alluding to *Merchant of Venice,* V.i.1ff.: "In such a night as this, / When the sweet wind did gently kiss the trees . . . in such a night . . ."

[80] Larry Hatt, who had studied at the Art Institute of Chicago, credited in *Apollonius of Tyana* as its designer. See also Olson's 12 August 1951 letter to Cid Corman (Glover, "Letters for Origin," p. 110).

[81] "Deuxième Sonate" by French composer-conductor Pierre Boulez (b. 1925), composed in 1948, was played the previous evening at Black Mountain by pianist David Tudor as part of a recital of contemporary music that also included work by Schoenberg, Wolpe, Feldman, Woronoff, Wolff, Cage, and Webern. See *Muthologos*, I, 119, and note on p. 127 there, and *Muthologos*, II, 92; also Olson's 4 October 1951 letter. The "Deuxième Sonate" can be heard, performed by Maurizio Pollini, on his Deutsche Grammophon recording, DG 2530803, produced in 1978.

[82] Edwin Parker (Cy) Twombly (1897-1974), father of the painter, pitched in seven games for the Chicago White Sox in 1921.

[83] From Hart Crane's "Lachrymae Christi" (*Collected Poems*, p. 84): ". . . where a sill / Sluices its one unyielding smile."

[84] See *Theory of Harmony* by Arnold Schoenberg (1874-1951), trans. Robert D. W. Adams (New York, 1948), p. viii: "But they do know that all depends on one thing: on seeking! I hope that my pupils will be seekers! For they will learn that we seek, only to seek further; that finding which to be sure is the goal, may easily put an end to striving."

[85] Cf. Pound, Canto 80 (*Pisan Cantos*, p. 72): "To communicate and then stop, that is the / law of discourse" (also Canto 79, p. 64: "in / discourse / what matters is / to get it across e poi basta").

[86] William Carlos Williams, *A Dream of Love: A Play in Three Acts and Eight Scenes* (New York, 1948).

[87] I.e., "TJ," how Dahlberg's letter to Williams incorporated in Book I of *Paterson* (New York, [1951], p. 40) is signed in early editions of the poem (see also note III. 66).

[88] See *A Dream of Love*, pp. 102-03: "The Greeks. Here's one of the most famous lines from their most famous poem: KAI SAY GAYRON TOW PREEN MEN HAKOIOMEN HOLBION EENAI. Sounds like a horse coughing, doesn't it? Achilles said that to Priam. Or does it, after all, remind you of Hiawatha? . . . TOW PREEN MEN HAKOIOMEN HOLBION EENAI. *They say, old man, that you were a tough guy too in your time.*"

The reference to the song "Dixie" in Olson's previous paragraph also comes from that same scene in Williams's play (p. 104).

[89] See the lines in "La Préface" (*Archaeologist of Morning*, p. [43]):

> Birth in the house is the One of Sticks, cunnus in the crotch.
> Draw it thus: (   ) 1910 (
> It is not obscure. We are the new born, and there are no flowers.
> Document means there are no flowers
> > and no parenthesis.

[90] Williams begins his *In the American Grain* with an account of the early Norse explorer, Eric the Red.

[91] Apparently Herodotus's account of Herakles and the Hylaean monster, half viper, half woman (Herodotus, IV. 9; Cary trans., New York, 1878, p. 420).

[92] See Olson's letter to Louis Martz, 8 August 1951 (VII. 68), and note 47. Mount Lycaon in Arcadia was where Lycaon, son of Pelasgus, sacrificed a child to Zeus and was turned into a wolf.

[93] "Cavalcanti," in *Make It New*, pp. 345-407.

[94] Cf. "As a hand addresses itself to the care of plants / and a sense of proportion, the house / is put to the earth" — Olson's "Move Over" (*Archaeologist of Morning*, p. [71]).

[95] In "Date Line" (*Make It New*, p. 19).

[96] Pound writes in "Henry James and Remy De Gourmont," *Make It New*, p. 288n.: "Most good prose arises, perhaps, from an instinct of negation; is the detailed, convincing analysis of something detestable; of something which one wants to eliminate."

[97] Source uncertain. Creeley wrote Jacob Leed, ca. September 1950 (letter, University of Connecticut Library): "I remember reading this summer, in a little booklet of Pound's Italian writings . . . not a damn idea after openers in ULYSSES, or something. Joyce is end. Ender. This as Ez put it, in the CULTURE: dead end, purge, the end of that period, etc." Pound writes in "James Joyce: to his memory" (originally in *"If This Be Treason . . . ,"* Siena, 1948): "Even Ulysses can be considered the first trilogy of live books, that is the series Ulysses, cummings' EIMI and Lewis' Apes of God. This is a healthier way of reading Ulysses than that of considering it the END of double decked stories, however much it be truly the tomb and muniment of a rotten era portrayed with the pen of a master" (reprinted in Forrest Read, *Pound/Joyce: The Letters*

of Ezra Pound to James Joyce, with Pound's Essays on Joyce, New York, 1967, p. 272). And although Pound found *Ulysses* "monumental" (i.e., a monument to the past, in Brancusi's terms) and a "retrospect" rather than a "pro-spect" (*Guide to Kulchur*, p. 96), no more specific reference to the limits of *Ulysses* is to be found in the public record, at least as assembled in Read's *Pound/Joyce*, nor in Pound's letters to Creeley (*Agenda*, 4, no. 2, 1965, pp. 11-21; letter from Timothy Murray, Manuscripts Curator, Washington University Libraries, 5 June 1985).

[98] A collection of stories by William Carlos Williams (Norfolk, Conn., 1938).

[99] See Creeley's 14 August 1951 letter (VII. 98) and note VII. 73. The poem is also quoted by Williams in *A Dream of Love*, pp. 18-20.

[100] From Canto 79 (*Pisan Cantos*, p. 62).

[101] Olson's "ABCs (3—for Rimbaud)" (*Archaeologist of Morning*, p. [52]): "Or shall it be rain, / on a tent   or grass   or birds / on a wire (5, count 'em, now 3 / on two—or does it come to 1 / on 1?"—alluding to Pound's Canto 79 (*Pisan Cantos*, pp. 63-65).

[102] See Olson's 8 August 1951 letter to Louis Martz (VII. 63) and note 55. Creeley quotes from Pound's Canto 78 (*Pisan Cantos*, p. 107).

[103] Latin, "the grove wants an altar"—occurs in Cantos 74, 78, and 97 (*Pisan Cantos*, pp. 24, 59, and 70). No source is given in Carroll F. Terrell's *Companion to the Cantos*, vol. 2 (Berkeley, 1984).

[104] See IV. 141 and note IV. 68.

[105] See "Projective Verse" (*Human Universe*, pp. 52-53): ". . . one statement (first pounded into my head by Edward Dahlberg): ONE PERCEPTION MUST IMMEDIATELY AND DIRECTLY LEAD TO A FURTHER PERCEPTION. It means exactly what it says, is a matter of, at *all* points . . . to get on with it, keep moving, keep in, speed, the nerves, their speed, the perceptions, theirs, the acts, the split second acts, the whole business, keep it moving as fast as you can, citizen. And if you also set up as a poet, USE USE USE the process at all points, in any given poem always, always one perception must must must MOVE, INSTANTER, ON ANOTHER!"

[106] Pound writes, e.g., in "Letters to a Young Poet [Iris Barry] from Ezra Pound," *Poetry*, 76 (September 1950), p. 349, of "concision, or style, or saying what you mean in the fewest and clearest words." (Creeley wrote Larry Eigner, September 1950, that Corman had sent him a copy of the magazine.) Pound would later make the dictum even more succinct (while thanking the "discovery" of Basil Bunting): "dichten = CONDENSARE" (*ABC of Reading*, pp. 36 and 92).

[107] Pound had written to Creeley in 1950: " 'Poetry: lofty thoughts expressed in beeeyewteeeful an' FLOWERY language' / B. o' D'L [O'Donnel?], Dublin 1888 . . ." (*Agenda*, 4, no. 2, October-November 1965, p. 19). Creeley also relayed the quotation to Larry Eigner, "Saturday" December 1950 (letter in Literary Archives, University of Connecticut Library): "sd Pound: Poetry: beautiful thoughts expressed in flowery language / Dublin, 1888."

[108] Harold Monro (1879-1932), proprietor of The Poetry Bookshop in London and publisher of *Poetry Review*, which in 1912 printed poems and reviews by Pound. Subject of a eulogy by Pound, collected in his *Polite Essays*, pp. 3-16.

[109] Olson's *Letter for Melville 1951* (Black Mountain, N.C., 1951).

[110] (B. 1923). He would design the cover for *Origin*, no. 5 (Spring 1952), and also provide the frontispiece drawing of Creeley for *Le Fou* in 1952. His retellings of African folktales, with illustrations, would be published in the 1970s, and he would serve as artist-in-residence at Dartmouth College.

[111] Joseph Blumenthal (b. 1897), director of the Spiral Press in New York. See, e.g., the Pierpont Morgan Library's exhibition catalogue, *The Spiral Press Through Four Decades*, with a commentary by Blumenthal (New York, 1966); or Blumenthal's *Typographic Years: A Printer's Journey Through a Half Century 1925-1975* (New York, 1982). See also Glover, "Letters for Origin," pp. 114-15, 119, and 126.

[112] See VI. 163 and note VI. 171.

[113] Olson's poem "La Chute," sent to Richard Wirtz Emerson for the proposed Golden Goose chapbook, appeared (along with Creeley's "A Note on the Objective") in the first issue of *Goad* (Summer 1951) — a

mimeographed magazine edited in Columbus, Ohio by Horace Schwartz with "help and advice" from Emerson.

[114] Rainer M. Gerhardt's translation of Olson's "The Praises," in *Fragmente*, no. 1 (1951), pp. 12-17.

[115] *African Folktales & Sculpture*, ed. Paul Radin with Elinore Marvel, Bollingen Series XXXII (New York, 1952). Bryan's drawings were not finally used; instead, photographs of African sculpture selected by James Johnson Sweeney appeared.

[116] French novelist Jean Giono (1895-1970), author of *Pour Saluer Melville* (Paris, 1943) and translator (with Lucien Jacques and Joan Smith) of *Moby-Dick* (Paris, 1948).

[117] See I. 71-72.

[118] William Gordon, owner of the Littleton, N.H. house (see Creeley's 25 August 1951 letter — VII. 124). Creeley also writes Jacob Leed, 6 September 1951 (Literary Archives, University of Connecticut Library): "Bill Gordon is fucking us, but good, on the house; a mess, altogether, but continue to hope there is, or can be, some simple way out."

[119] Ezra Pound, in *Patria Mia* (Chicago, 1950), p. 47.

[120] Published eventually in *Origin*, no. 6 (Summer 1952), pp. 80-86, along with the fable "Early History" in three parts, similar to the African tales in Frobenius and Fox's *African Genesis*.

[121] A letter from John Kasper, 15 September 1951, together with a carbon copy of a September 8 letter by him to Eleanor Melville Metcalf, which reads like a crude imitation of Olson's "Letter for Melville." Kasper himself describes the letter as a "schoolboyish" effort, with such passages as: "Lady, just what the hell do you think it's all about, this business of literature? Have you understood the difference between that which *is living* and that which is institutionalized, more often than not, for the genuflections of some idiotic group? If you read Melville's work you're likely to find that this man, THIS MAN, did not stand for the labor day weekend, nor tittering middle aged women nor the various yatters of certain moleish professors . . ."

Olson notes on the bottom of the carbon for Creeley: "This burns

my arse   I put it in, for full gauge   Such a fucking cheap rewrite   And
g.d. IGNORANT." Creeley returns the letter with the following notes
pencilled on the back, continuing the discussion in his September 27-29
letter:

> thought — to come to :
> \ strokes on a gong
>   infinitely silent, and
>   distant.

narrative:
"I"   impression on the depth of any
       one perception
"he"   emphasis is on the *passage* between any *two*
       perceptions, that quickness
man *is* the above "passage" in the 2nd
instance. There he is, *variant.*

But the 1st — is the plunge.
one has no *alternative.*

The Grace — most *quick* yet instance
            of the 2nd category.
            [*Added:*] or Party, [*illegible*]
Blue   — of the 1st; that
            potential.

In his letter to Olson, Kasper also offers his congratulations for the
"baby Olse on the way," "since a man shd replace himself, and since
I know what it means to you, that babys are life, and that that (life)
is more interesting to you etc." — which Creeley responds to in his
September 25th letter.

[122] *Vou*, no. 35 (August 1951), containing notes by Creeley concerning the short story, in a Japanese translation by Katue Kitasono, pp.
27-28 (see also note VI. 194).

[123] *Botteghe Oscure*, published from 1949 to 1960 by the American-
born Marguerite Caetani from the street of that name in Rome.

[124] Phrase from Pound's Cantos 47 and 49 (*Pisan Cantos*, pp. 43 and 66); originally from Confucius, *Analects*, IX, 30. Quoted by Olson in "Apollonius of Tyana" (*The Fiery Hunt*, p. 61).

[125] Not present with letter.

[126] Paul Klee, *On Modern Art*, p. 31: "While the artist is still exerting all his efforts to group the formal elements purely and logically so that each in its place is right and none clashes with the other, a layman, watching from behind, pronounces the devastating words, 'But that isn't a bit like uncle.' The artist, if his nerve is disciplined, thinks to himself, 'To hell with uncle! I must get on with my building.' "

[127] Freud's *Leonardo Da Vinci: A Study in Psychosexuality* (see note VI. 21).

[128] Ernest Fenollosa, *The Chinese Written Character as a Medium for Poetry* — an offset reprint of the 1936 London edition, bound together with the 1949 Calcutta reprint of Confucius, *The Unwobbling Pivot & The Great Digest*, published in 1951 by the Square $ Series of Kasper and Horton, and apparently distributed by the Cleaners Press on Pound's behalf (see notes I. 3 and 23).

[129] Walter Allen, "Writers in Society," *New Statesman & Nation*, 16 December 1950, pp. 630 and 632 — a review of Wyndham Lewis's *Rude Assignment*.

[130] Fenollosa, *The Chinese Written Character*, p. 9.

[131] Confucius's *Unwobbling Pivot & The Great Digest*, trans. Ezra Pound ([Norfolk, Conn.], 1947), and *Confucian Analects*, also translated by Pound, in the Spring 1950 issue of *Hudson Review* (separately published, New York, [1951]).

[132] From Pound's prefatory note to the *Unwobbling Pivot*, explaining the Confucian metaphysic.

[133] Source unknown (beyond Heraclitus).

[134] Robert Hunter West, *The Invisible World: A Study of Pneumatology in Elizabethan Drama* (Athens, Ga., 1939), and Francis W. Galpin, *The Music of the Sumerians and Their Immediate Successors*

the Babylonians & Assyrians (Cambridge, 1937).

[135] Max Dehn (1878-1952), mathematician teaching at Black Mountain. Duberman, *Black Mountain*, p. 224, reports that he "read Greek as easily as English."

[136] See V. 117 and note V. 113.

[137] Mentioned here for the first time in the correspondence are Jane Ellen Harrison (1850-1928), English classical scholar, whose *Prolegomena to the Study of Greek Religion* (Cambridge, 1903) and *Themis: A Study of the Social Origins of Greek Religion*, 2nd ed. (Cambridge, 1927) were important books for Olson, much read, marked, and referred to in his writings; Gaston Maspero (1846-1916), French Egyptologist, whose *Popular Stories of Ancient Egypt* (1882) is cited in Bérard, *Did Homer Live?*; Henri Frankfort (1897-1954), author of *Kingship and the Gods: A Study of Ancient Near Eastern Religion* (Chicago, 1948) and *The Birth of Civilization in the Near East* (Bloomington, Ind., 1951); and the English archeologist, Charles Leonard Woolley (1880-1960), whose writings include the popular *Digging Up the Past* (Harmondsworth, 1950; first published, 1930). The other scholars — Victor Bérard, L. A. Waddell, Samuel Noah Kramer, and Edith Porada, have been cited earlier.

[138]J. A. K. Thomson, *The Art of the Logos* (London, 1935); also, *Theatre of the Greeks, Containing . . . A Great Body of Information Relative to the Rise, Progress, and Exhibition of the Drama; together with an Account of Dramatic Writers from Thespis to Meander . . .* (Cambridge, 1825), a copy of which is in Olson's library.

[139] See II. 80 and note II. 45, and note I. 131. The German anthropologist Leo Frobenius (1873-1938) is mentioned throughout Olson's earlier letters.

[140] Henry A. Murray (b. 1893), Melville scholar and director of the Harvard Psychological Clinic — "the doctor, whom I love," of "Letter for Melville" (*Archaeologist of Morning*, p. [36]) — and oil industrialist Jean de Menil and his wife Dominique, of Houston, friends of Jean Riboud. Olson requests Corman to send them a copy of *Origin* 1 (Glover, "Letters for Origin," p. 58); they would be patrons of the original Jargon volumes of *The Maximus Poems*.

[141] The poem was written from materials called to Olson's attention by Frances Boldereff.

[142] "Con-gen" as in "congenital," or, as Olson writes elsewhere, his "own kin and / concentration" (*The Maximus Poems*, p. 32). *Katabasis* (from Greek *kata* "down") is the return or withdrawal of troops after an invasion, the opposite of *anabasis* (as in the title of Xenophon's narrative or Perse's poem), an advance.

[143] See "Apollonius of Tyana" (*The Fiery Hunt*, p. 74): "St. Augustine said of his experience of recognition, 'It was a conflagration of myself.' " From Augustine's *Contra Academicos*, V, a passage quoted as epigraph to a poem by Olson's acquaintance Harvey Breit, "The Visitation," in *Montevallo Review*, 1, no. 2 (Summer 1951), p. 22 (following Olson's narrative "Stocking Cap" in the issue): "It is past belief, Romanianus, past belief, and past what ever you believe of me, nay to myself it is past belief, what a conflagration of myself they lighted . . ."

[144] The opening lines of Shakespeare's sonnet 129 (see also Olson's 11 November 1951 letter to come).

[145] A character in *Moby-Dick*, minister of the Whaleman's Chapel in New Bedford, famous for his sermons. The one in Chapter IX of *Moby-Dick* concludes with many "delights": "But oh! shipmates! on the starboard hand of every woe, there is a sure delight; and higher the top of that delight, than the bottom of the woe is deep. . . . Delight is to him — a far, far upward, and inward delight," etc.

[146] Alexander Gardner (1821-1882), Scottish-born photographer. Olson writes in an unpublished "*Memo* to a publisher," 17 July 1950, concerning him: "an expert in the wet-plate process whom [Matthew] Brady had brought over in the '50's," while noting that "3 quarters of the scenes of the Army of the Potomac were made by him." Gardner published a two-volume photographic *Sketch Book of the War* (Washington, 1865-66), a collection of one hundred photographs (actual prints, not reproductions).

Two of the other three Confederate photographers referred to can be identified as A. D. Lytle of Baton Rouge and George F. Cook of Charleston, S.C. (unless it is S. R. Siebert of the same place), although in notes concerning Civil War photographers among his papers, Olson mentions an "Edwards" as being a photographer from New Orleans. See *The Photographic History of the Civil War in Ten Volumes*, published by The Review of Reviews (New York, 1912), p. 42 (where it is mentioned that "three-fourths of the scenes with the Army of the Potomac were made by Gardner"), and Robert Taft, *Photography and the American Scene: A Social History, 1839-1889* (New York, 1938), p. 231. Neither work mentions a St. Louis photographer.

[147] *The Rebellion Record: A Diary of American Events, with Documents, Narratives, Illustrative Incidents, Poetry, Etc.*, ed. Frank Moore, 11 vols. with supplement (New York, 1861-68).

[148] Olson makes the distinction as learned from Thomson, *The Art of the Logos*, pp. 17 ff., again and again in his writings. See e.g. "The Law" below (VII. 237), also *The Maximus Poems*, pp. 104-05: "*Muthos* / is false. *Logos* / isn't — was facts. Thus / Thucydides // I would be an historian as Herodotus was . . ." Other examples, with relevant passages from Thomson, are quoted in Butterick, *Guide to The Maximus Poems*, pp. 145-47. The distinction presented by Thomson is not only the basis of Olson's understanding of history, but also, in part, his sense of myth.

[149] Italian "shops." But see also note 123 above.

[150] Ben Shahn illustrated articles for magazines such as *Harper's* in March and August 1948, and December 1950, and for *Scientific American* in April 1950.

[151] Pound writes in a first version of Canto 1 (*Poetry*, 10, June 1917, p. 113):

> . . . say I take your whole bag
> of tricks
> Let in your quirks and tweeks, and say the
> thing's an art-form,
> . . . and that the modern world
> Needs such a rag-bag to stuff all its thought in.

See also "GrandPa GoodBye," *Charles Olson & Ezra Pound*, p. 98.

[152] Presumably, Creeley's 8 January 1951 letter (IV. 104 ff.) and not one, now lost, concerning his unpublished poem "The Hawk" (see notes V. 72 and VI. 47).

[153] Creeley's poem "Love" beginning, "The thing comes / of

itself . . . ," *Origin*, no. 2 (Summer 1951), p. 68 (*Collected Poems*, p. 19); not the "Love" beginning, "Not enough . . . ," which would be published in *Origin*, no. 3 (Fall 1951), p. 167 (*Collected Poems*, p. 26).

[154] Arthur Rimbaud, *A Season in Hell*, trans. Louise Varese (Norfolk, Conn., 1945), pp. 6-7. The quotations that follow are from pp. 56-57 there. (Creeley reports to Olson remembering that Olson had quoted a couplet from Rimbaud's "Délires" in "The Kingfishers.")

Varese's remarks concerning her translation, quoted by Creeley further below, come in her introductory note, p. vi.

[155] See especially Lawrence's "Foreword" to his *Fantasia of the Unconscious* (London, 1923), pp. [54]-[55]:

> . . . to my mind there is a great field of science which is as yet quite closed to us. I refer to the science which proceeds in terms of life and is established on data of living experience and of sure intuition. Call it subjective science if you like. . . .
>
> I honestly think that the great pagan world of which Egypt and Greece were the last living terms, the great pagan world which preceded our own era, once had a vast and perhaps perfect science of its own, a science in terms of life. In our era this science crumbled into magic and charlatanry. But even wisdom crumbles.
>
> I believe that this great science previous to ours and quite different in constitution and nature from our science once was universal, established all over the then existing globe. I believe it was esoteric, invested in a large priesthood. Just as mathematics and mechanics and physics are defined and expounded in the same way in the universities of China or Bolivia or London or Moscow today, so, it seems to me, in the great world previous to ours a great science and cosmology were taught esoterically in all countries of the globe, Asia, Polynesia, America, Atlantis, and Europe. . . .

See also Olson's 27 July 1950 letter (II. 84).

[156] Adams's date for man's leaving the "mechanical" phase of history and entering the "ethereal" phase, when thought would be brought "to the limit of its possibilities," according to his "phase" theory of history as presented in *The Degradation of the Democratic Dogma* (New York, 1920), p. 308.

[157] The dropping of the atomic bomb on Hiroshima and Nagasaki.

[158] See, e.g., Norbert Wiener, *Cybernetics; or, Control and Communication in the Animal and the Machine* (New York, 1948), pp. 11 ff. Also, Natasha Goldowski, "High Speed Computing Machines," *Black Mountain College Review*, 1, no. 1 (June 1951), [6]-[13].

[159] See Frederick Jackson Turner's essay, "The Significance of the Frontier in American History" (in his *The Frontier in American History*, New York, 1920, pp. 1-38), which begins by quoting the bulletin of the Superintendent of the Census for 1890 on the disappearance of the frontier as a factor in the settlement of the country.

[160] See Olson's 8 August 1951 letter to Louis Martz and note VII. 58.

[161] Cf., e.g., "Human Universe," *Human Universe*, pp. 4-5.

[162] See Creeley's 29 September 1951 letter above (VII. 203).

[163] Novalis writes in a surviving fragment: "Alle Methode ist Rhythmus: hat man den Rhythmus der Welt weg, so hat man auch die Welt weg. Jeder Mensch hat seinen individuellen Rhythmus. – Die Algeber ist die Poesie. Rhythmischer Sinn ist Genie." (*Fragmente*, ed. Ernst Kamnitzer, Dresden, 1929, p. 584). He also writes in another fragment (*ibid.*, p. 199): "In allen Handwerken und Künsten, allen Maschinen, den organischen Körpern, unsren täglichen Verrichtungen, überall: Rhythmus, Metrum, Taktschlag, Melodie. Alles, was wir mit einer gewissen Fertigkeit tun, machen mir unvermerkt rhythmisch. Rhythmus findet sich überall, schleicht sich überall ein. Aller Mechanism ist metrisch, rhythmisch. . . ."
See also "Human Universe" (*Human Universe*, p. 10) – "the man said, he who possesses rhythm possesses the universe" – also "Against Wisdom As Such" (*Human Universe*, p. 71). Olson also wrote Corman, 10 June 1951 (Glover, "Letters for Origin," p. 92): "he who has rhythm has the universe," and again to Robin Blaser, 13 May 1958 (photocopy courtesy Blaser): "And surely we are used to giving rhythm what Novalis gave it: he who controls it controls the universe, he sd!"

[164] See Galpin, *The Music of the Sumerians*, pp. 2 ff., especially p. 4.

[165] Located behind Olson's boyhood home in Worcester, Mass. See "ABCs" (*Archaeologist of Morning*, p. [50]), also *The Maximus Poems*, p. 498.

[166] I.e., the red-headed Ezra Pound.

[167] Archibald M. Willard's familiar "Spirit of '76," painted in 1876 for the hundredth anniversary of the Revolution, in which fife player and drummer are predominant. That the old English pipe and tabor were popularly called the "wittle" and "dub" is known to Olson from Galpin, *The Music of the Sumerians*, p. 6.

[168] The entertainer Jimmy Durante (1893-1980) and jazz trumpeter and singer Louis "Satchmo" Armstrong (1900-1971).

Index of Persons Named in the Letters

Index of Works by Charles Olson and Robert Creeley Cited in the Text

Printed January 1987 in Santa Barbara & Ann Arbor
for the Black Sparrow Press by Graham Mackintosh
& Edwards Brothers Inc. Design by Barbara Martin.
This edition is published in paper wrappers; there
are 500 hardcover trade copies; 200 hardcover copies
have been numbered & signed by Robert Creeley; &
26 lettered copies have been handbound in boards
by Earle Gray & signed by George Butterick &
Robert Creeley.

GEORGE F. BUTTERICK studied with both Charles Olson and Robert Creeley at the State University of New York at Buffalo, where he received his Ph.D. in 1970. He is Curator of the Literary Archives at the University of Connecticut, and lives with his family in the nearby city of Willimantic. He recently completed his edition of Charles Olson's *Collected Poems* (outside of the *Maximus* series) and is presently at work on Olson's *Collected Prose* as well as a biography of the poet. His essays and reviews have appeared widely in journals, including most recently *American Poetry*, *Conjunctions*, *Credences*, *Exquisite Corpse*, *Sagetrieb*, and *Sulfur*. He is also the author of four books of poetry.